RUNNING
FROM THE
DEVIL

MARKOSIA

a memoir of a boy possessed

steve kissing
+ friends

steve kissing - writer
charles santino - scripter
jim jiminez - artist
lauren hayes - cover design
santosh kumar rath - colorist for pages 1-10
marlon ilagan - colorist for pages 11-132
zach matheny - letterer for pages 1-100
kathryn renta - letterer for pages 101-132

runningfromthedevil.com

for **markosia enterprises** ltd
harry markos - publisher & managing partner
gm jordan - special projects co-ordinator
annika eade - media manager
andy briggs - creative consultant
meiron jones - marketing director
ian sharman - editor in chief

 Published by Markosia Enterprises, PO BOX 3477, Barnet, Hertfordshire, EN5 9HN. FIRST PRINTING, April 2018.
Harry Markos, Director.

ISBN 978-1-911243-77-9

www.markosia.com

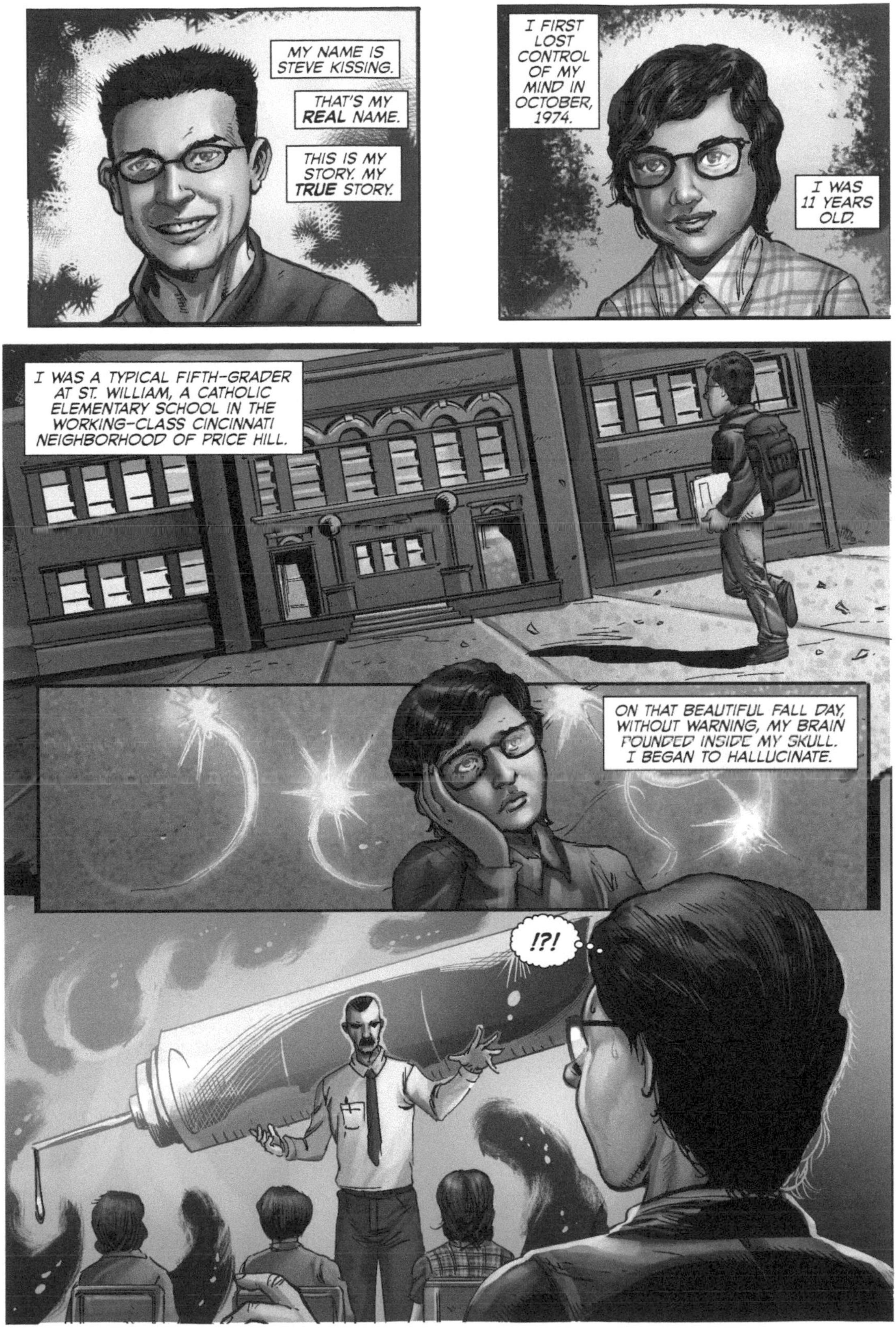
MY NAME IS STEVE KISSING.
THAT'S MY **REAL** NAME.
THIS IS MY STORY. MY **TRUE** STORY.
I FIRST LOST CONTROL OF MY MIND IN OCTOBER, 1974.
I WAS 11 YEARS OLD.
I WAS A TYPICAL FIFTH-GRADER AT ST. WILLIAM, A CATHOLIC ELEMENTARY SCHOOL IN THE WORKING-CLASS CINCINNATI NEIGHBORHOOD OF PRICE HILL.
ON THAT BEAUTIFUL FALL DAY, WITHOUT WARNING, MY BRAIN POUNDED INSIDE MY SKULL. I BEGAN TO HALLUCINATE.
!?!

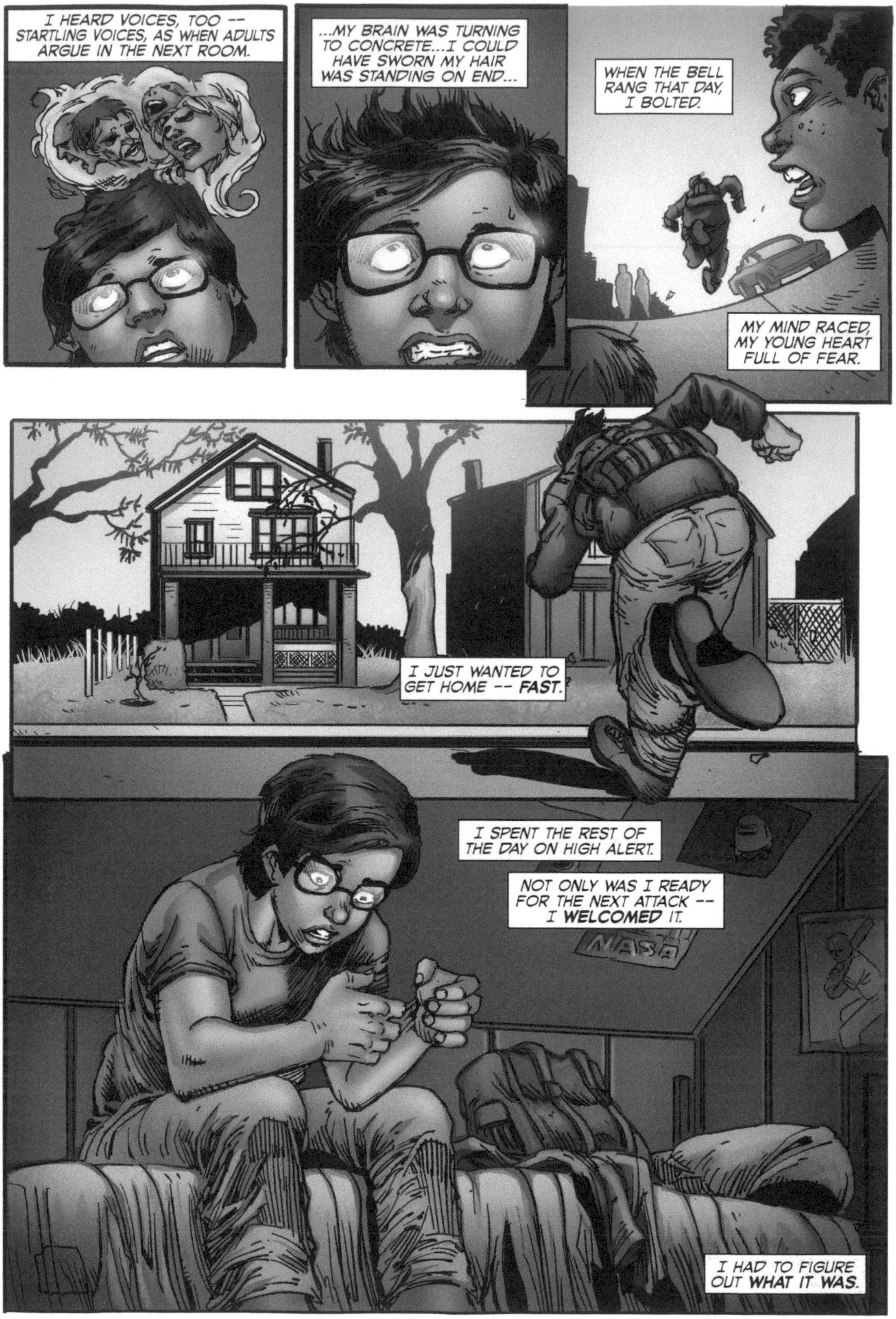
I HEARD VOICES, TOO -- STARTLING VOICES, AS WHEN ADULTS ARGUE IN THE NEXT ROOM.
...MY BRAIN WAS TURNING TO CONCRETE...I COULD HAVE SWORN MY HAIR WAS STANDING ON END...
WHEN THE BELL RANG THAT DAY, I BOLTED.
MY MIND RACED, MY YOUNG HEART FULL OF FEAR.
I JUST WANTED TO GET HOME -- **FAST**.
I SPENT THE REST OF THE DAY ON HIGH ALERT.
NOT ONLY WAS I READY FOR THE NEXT ATTACK -- I **WELCOMED** IT.
NASA
I HAD TO FIGURE OUT **WHAT IT WAS**.

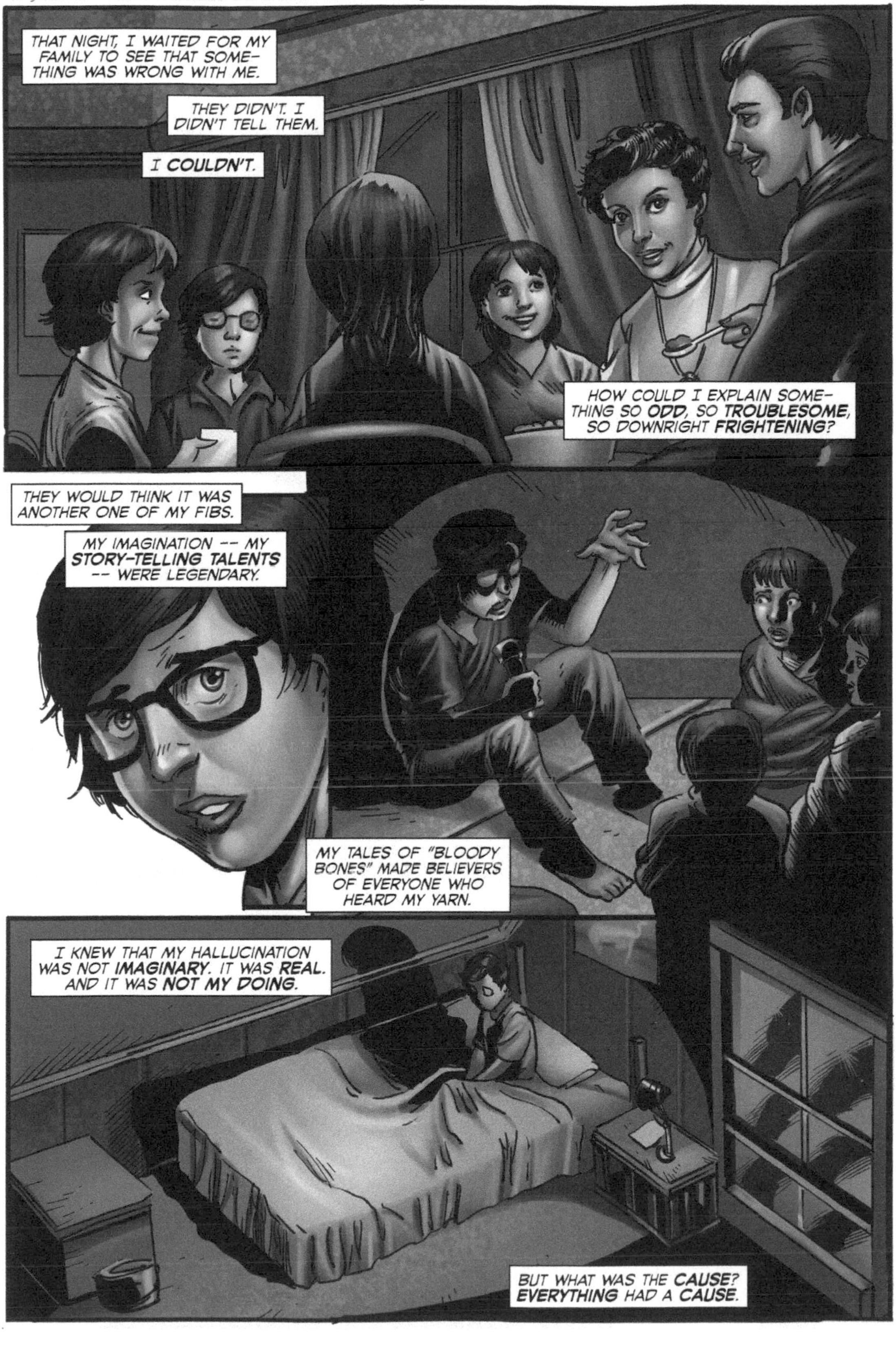
THAT NIGHT, I WAITED FOR MY FAMILY TO SEE THAT SOMETHING WAS WRONG WITH ME.
THEY DIDN'T. I DIDN'T TELL THEM.
I **COULDN'T**.
HOW COULD I EXPLAIN SOMETHING SO **ODD**, SO **TROUBLESOME**, SO DOWNRIGHT **FRIGHTENING**?
THEY WOULD THINK IT WAS ANOTHER ONE OF MY FIBS.
MY IMAGINATION -- MY **STORY-TELLING TALENTS** -- WERE LEGENDARY.
MY TALES OF "BLOODY BONES" MADE BELIEVERS OF EVERYONE WHO HEARD MY YARN.
I KNEW THAT MY HALLUCINATION WAS NOT **IMAGINARY**. IT WAS **REAL**. AND IT WAS **NOT MY DOING**.
BUT WHAT WAS THE **CAUSE**? **EVERYTHING** HAD A **CAUSE**.

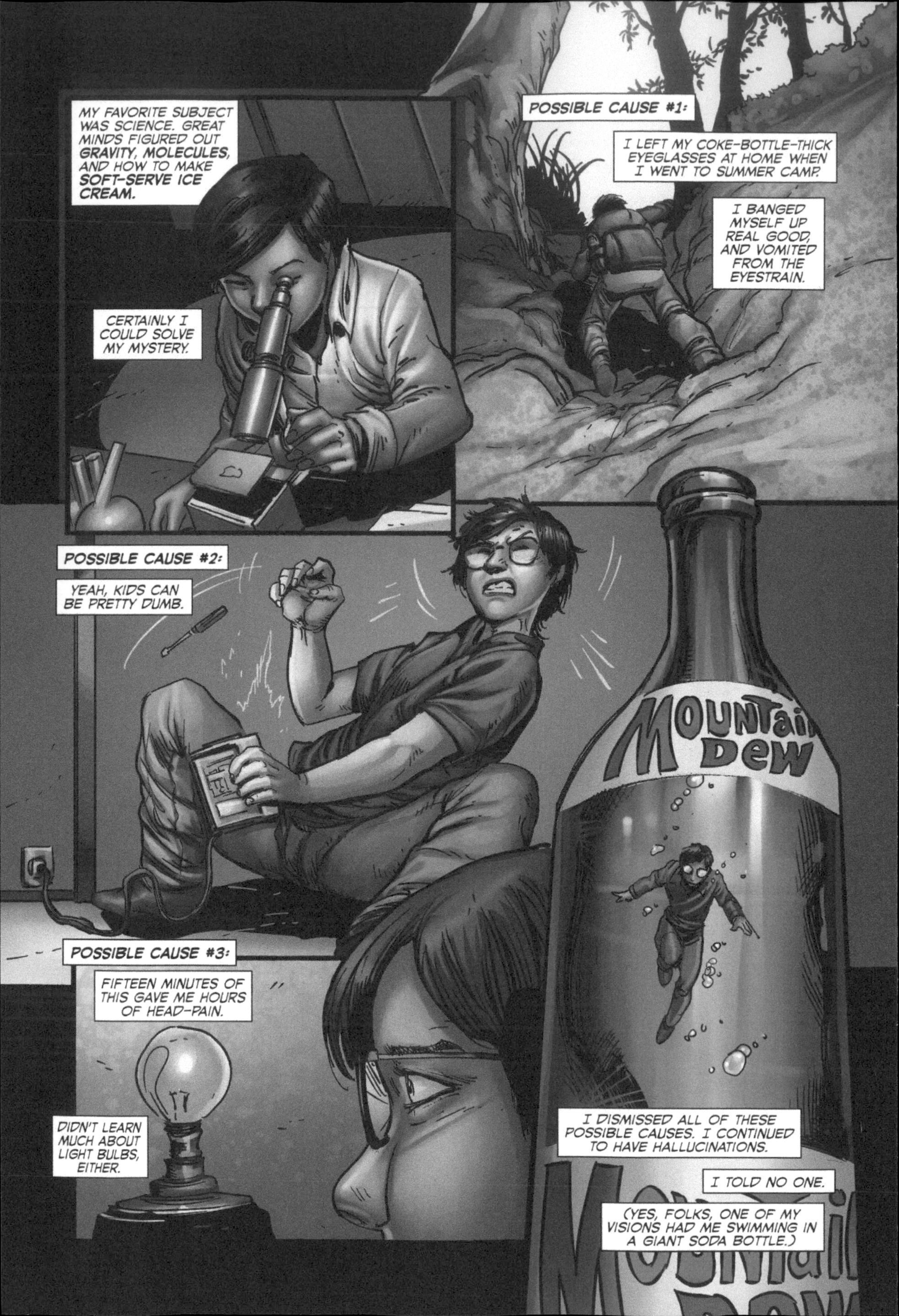
MY FAVORITE SUBJECT WAS SCIENCE. GREAT MINDS FIGURED OUT GRAVITY, MOLECULES, AND HOW TO MAKE SOFT-SERVE ICE CREAM.
CERTAINLY I COULD SOLVE MY MYSTERY.
POSSIBLE CAUSE #1:
I LEFT MY COKE-BOTTLE-THICK EYEGLASSES AT HOME WHEN I WENT TO SUMMER CAMP.
I BANGED MYSELF UP REAL GOOD, AND VOMITED FROM THE EYESTRAIN.
POSSIBLE CAUSE #2:
YEAH, KIDS CAN BE PRETTY DUMB.
POSSIBLE CAUSE #3:
FIFTEEN MINUTES OF THIS GAVE ME HOURS OF HEAD-PAIN.
DIDN'T LEARN MUCH ABOUT LIGHT BULBS, EITHER.
MOUNTAIN DEW
I DISMISSED ALL OF THESE POSSIBLE CAUSES. I CONTINUED TO HAVE HALLUCINATIONS.
I TOLD NO ONE.
(YES, FOLKS, ONE OF MY VISIONS HAD ME SWIMMING IN A GIANT SODA BOTTLE.)

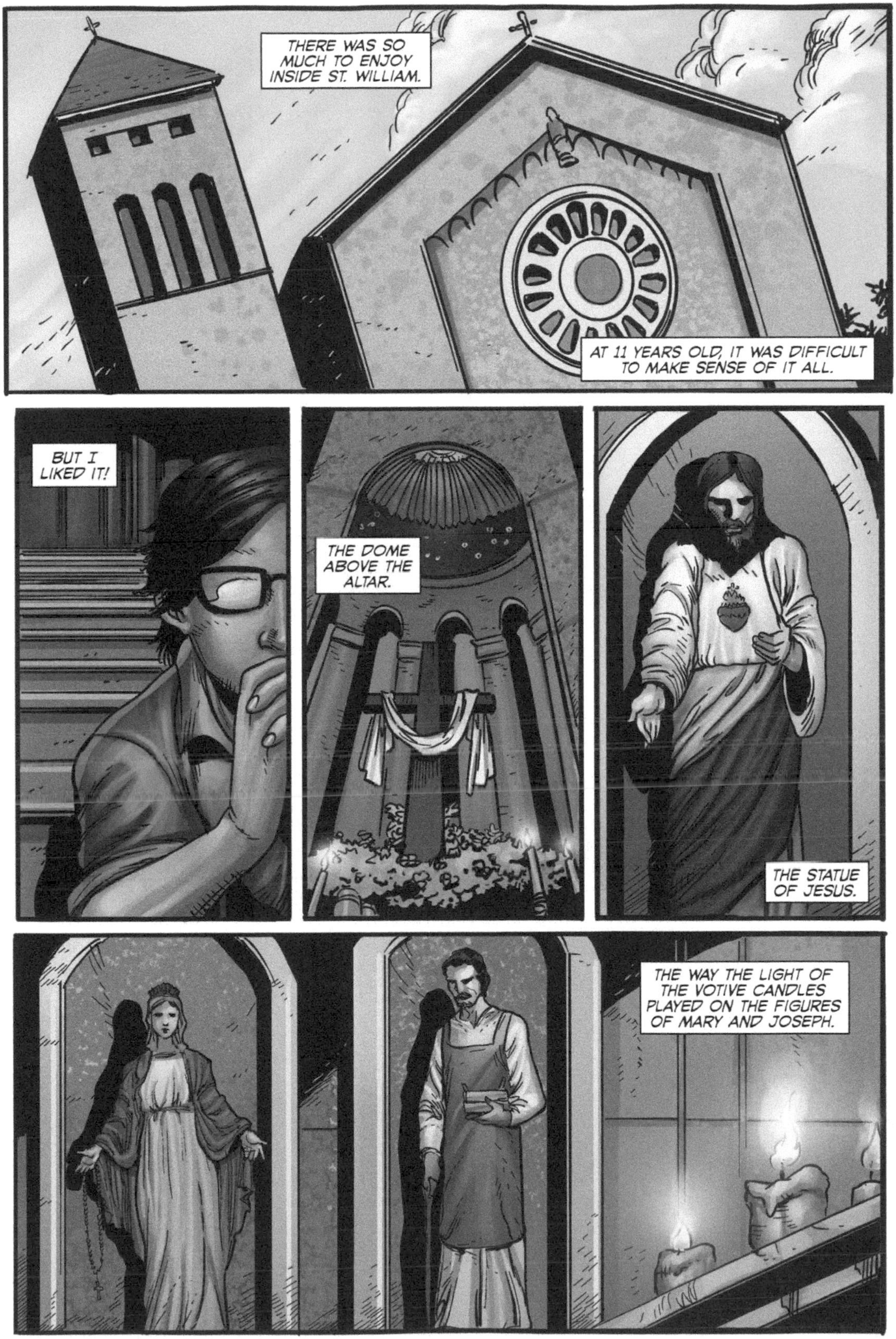
THERE WAS SO MUCH TO ENJOY INSIDE ST. WILLIAM.
AT 11 YEARS OLD, IT WAS DIFFICULT TO MAKE SENSE OF IT ALL.
BUT I LIKED IT!
THE DOME ABOVE THE ALTAR.
THE STATUE OF JESUS.
THE WAY THE LIGHT OF THE VOTIVE CANDLES PLAYED ON THE FIGURES OF MARY AND JOSEPH.

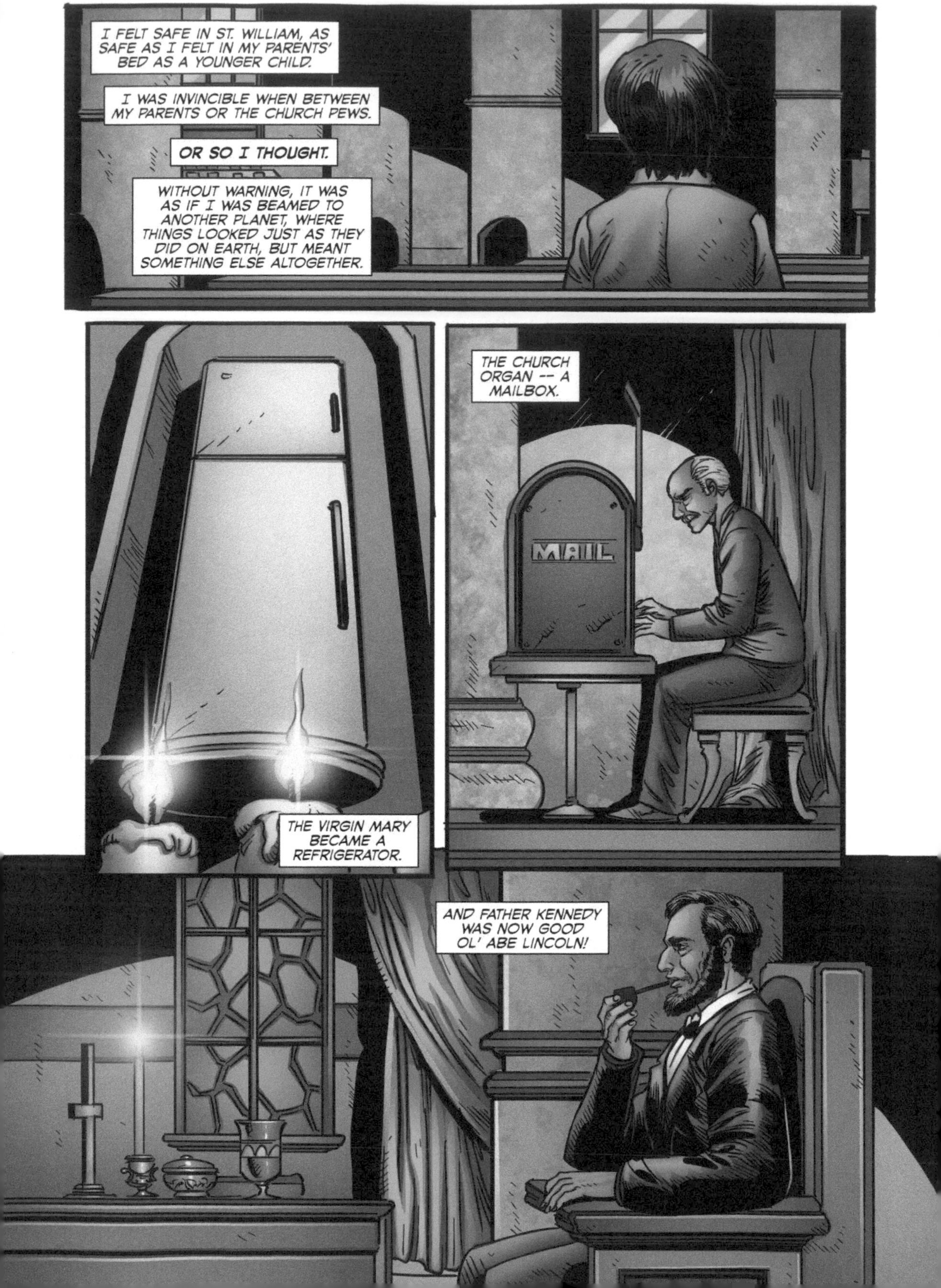
I FELT SAFE IN ST. WILLIAM, AS SAFE AS I FELT IN MY PARENTS' BED AS A YOUNGER CHILD.
I WAS INVINCIBLE WHEN BETWEEN MY PARENTS OR THE CHURCH PEWS.
OR SO I THOUGHT.
WITHOUT WARNING, IT WAS AS IF I WAS BEAMED TO ANOTHER PLANET, WHERE THINGS LOOKED JUST AS THEY DID ON EARTH, BUT MEANT SOMETHING ELSE ALTOGETHER.
THE VIRGIN MARY BECAME A REFRIGERATOR.
THE CHURCH ORGAN -- A MAILBOX.
MAIL
AND FATHER KENNEDY WAS NOW GOOD OL' ABE LINCOLN!

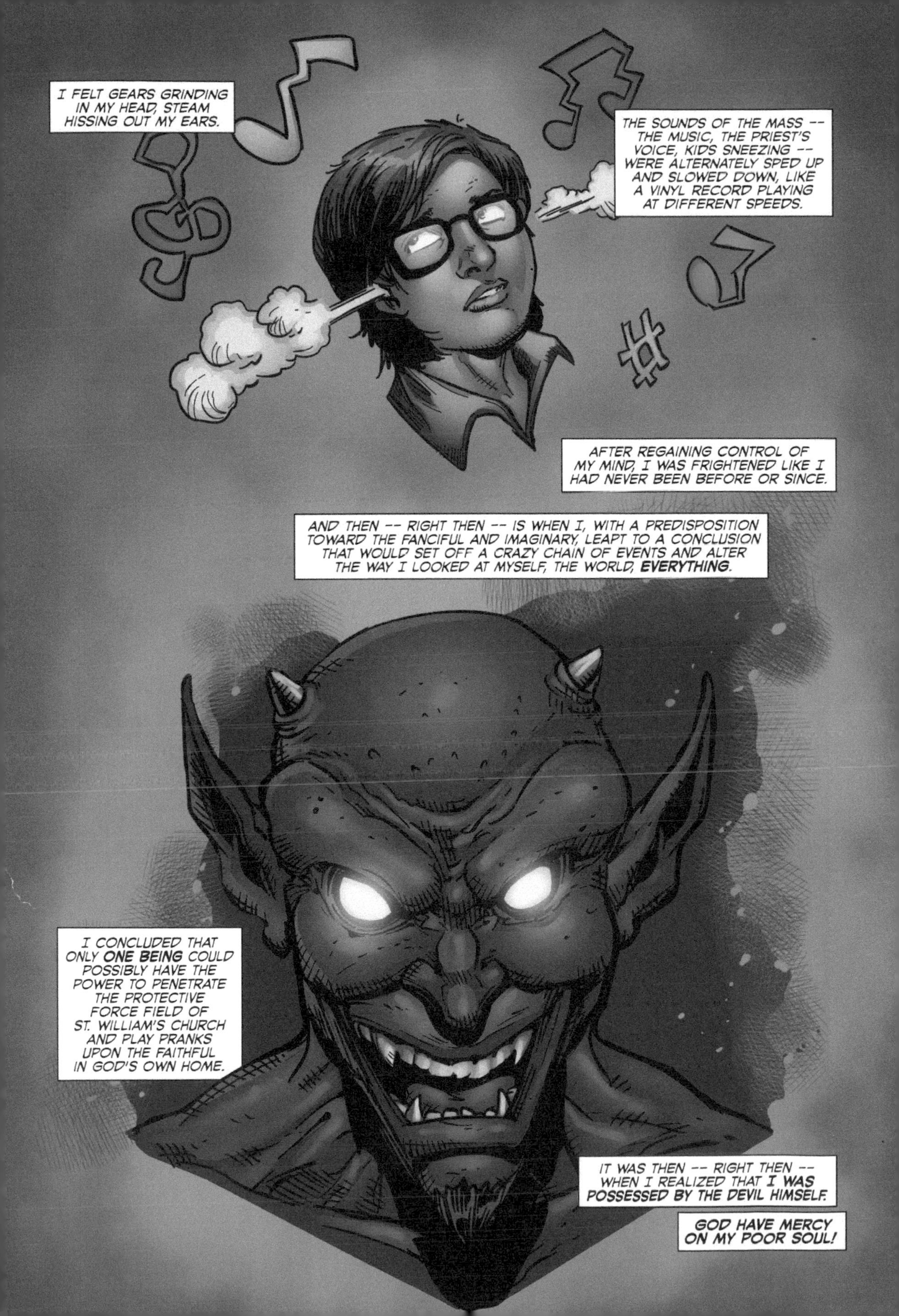
I FELT GEARS GRINDING IN MY HEAD, STEAM HISSING OUT MY EARS.
THE SOUNDS OF THE MASS -- THE MUSIC, THE PRIEST'S VOICE, KIDS SNEEZING -- WERE ALTERNATELY SPED UP AND SLOWED DOWN, LIKE A VINYL RECORD PLAYING AT DIFFERENT SPEEDS.
AFTER REGAINING CONTROL OF MY MIND, I WAS FRIGHTENED LIKE I HAD NEVER BEEN BEFORE OR SINCE.
AND THEN -- RIGHT THEN -- IS WHEN I, WITH A PREDISPOSITION TOWARD THE FANCIFUL AND IMAGINARY, LEAPT TO A CONCLUSION THAT WOULD SET OFF A CRAZY CHAIN OF EVENTS AND ALTER THE WAY I LOOKED AT MYSELF, THE WORLD, **EVERYTHING**.
I CONCLUDED THAT ONLY **ONE BEING** COULD POSSIBLY HAVE THE POWER TO PENETRATE THE PROTECTIVE FORCE FIELD OF ST. WILLIAM'S CHURCH AND PLAY PRANKS UPON THE FAITHFUL IN GOD'S OWN HOME.
IT WAS THEN -- RIGHT THEN -- WHEN I REALIZED THAT **I WAS POSSESSED BY THE DEVIL HIMSELF**.
GOD HAVE MERCY ON MY POOR SOUL!

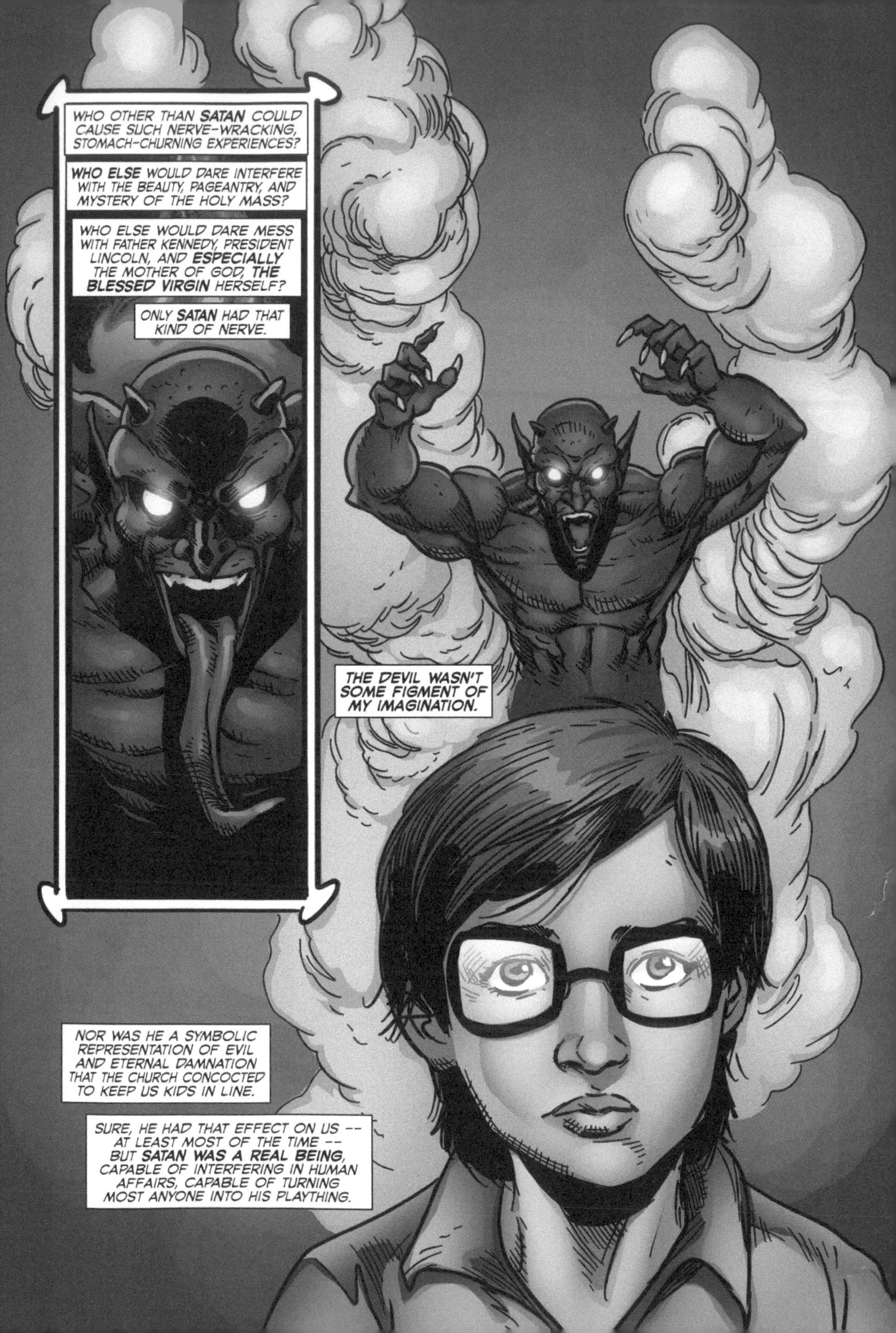
WHO OTHER THAN SATAN COULD CAUSE SUCH NERVE-WRACKING, STOMACH-CHURNING EXPERIENCES?
WHO ELSE WOULD DARE INTERFERE WITH THE BEAUTY, PAGEANTRY, AND MYSTERY OF THE HOLY MASS?
WHO ELSE WOULD DARE MESS WITH FATHER KENNEDY, PRESIDENT LINCOLN, AND ESPECIALLY THE MOTHER OF GOD, THE BLESSED VIRGIN HERSELF?
ONLY SATAN HAD THAT KIND OF NERVE.
THE DEVIL WASN'T SOME FIGMENT OF MY IMAGINATION.
NOR WAS HE A SYMBOLIC REPRESENTATION OF EVIL AND ETERNAL DAMNATION THAT THE CHURCH CONCOCTED TO KEEP US KIDS IN LINE.
SURE, HE HAD THAT EFFECT ON US -- AT LEAST MOST OF THE TIME -- BUT SATAN WAS A REAL BEING, CAPABLE OF INTERFERING IN HUMAN AFFAIRS, CAPABLE OF TURNING MOST ANYONE INTO HIS PLAYTHING.

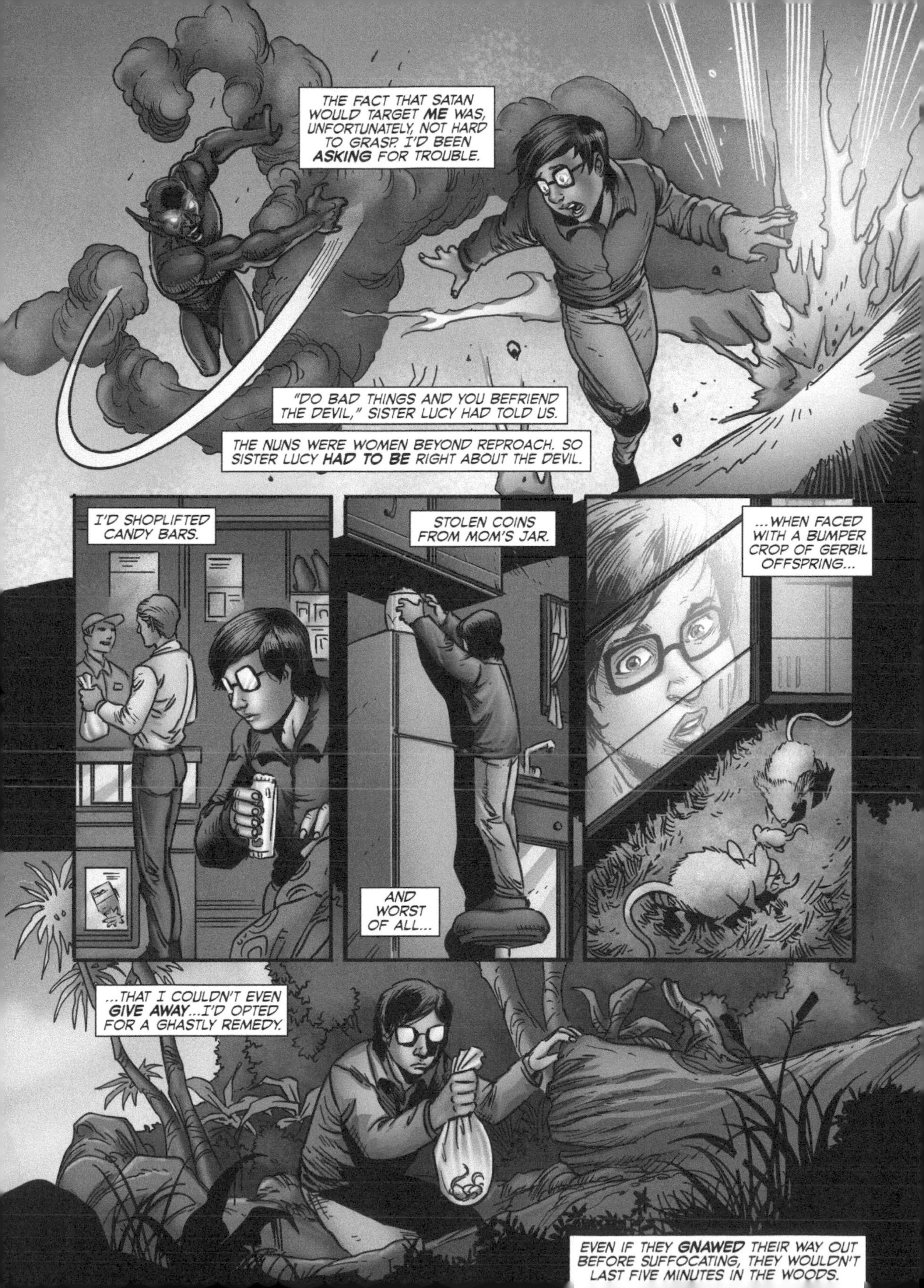
THE FACT THAT SATAN WOULD TARGET **ME** WAS, UNFORTUNATELY, NOT HARD TO GRASP. I'D BEEN **ASKING** FOR TROUBLE.
"DO BAD THINGS AND YOU BEFRIEND THE DEVIL," SISTER LUCY HAD TOLD US.
THE NUNS WERE WOMEN BEYOND REPROACH. SO SISTER LUCY **HAD TO BE** RIGHT ABOUT THE DEVIL.
I'D SHOPLIFTED CANDY BARS.
STOLEN COINS FROM MOM'S JAR.
AND WORST OF ALL...
...WHEN FACED WITH A BUMPER CROP OF GERBIL OFFSPRING...
...THAT I COULDN'T EVEN **GIVE AWAY**...I'D OPTED FOR A GHASTLY REMEDY.
EVEN IF THEY **GNAWED** THEIR WAY OUT BEFORE SUFFOCATING, THEY WOULDN'T LAST FIVE MINUTES IN THE WOODS.

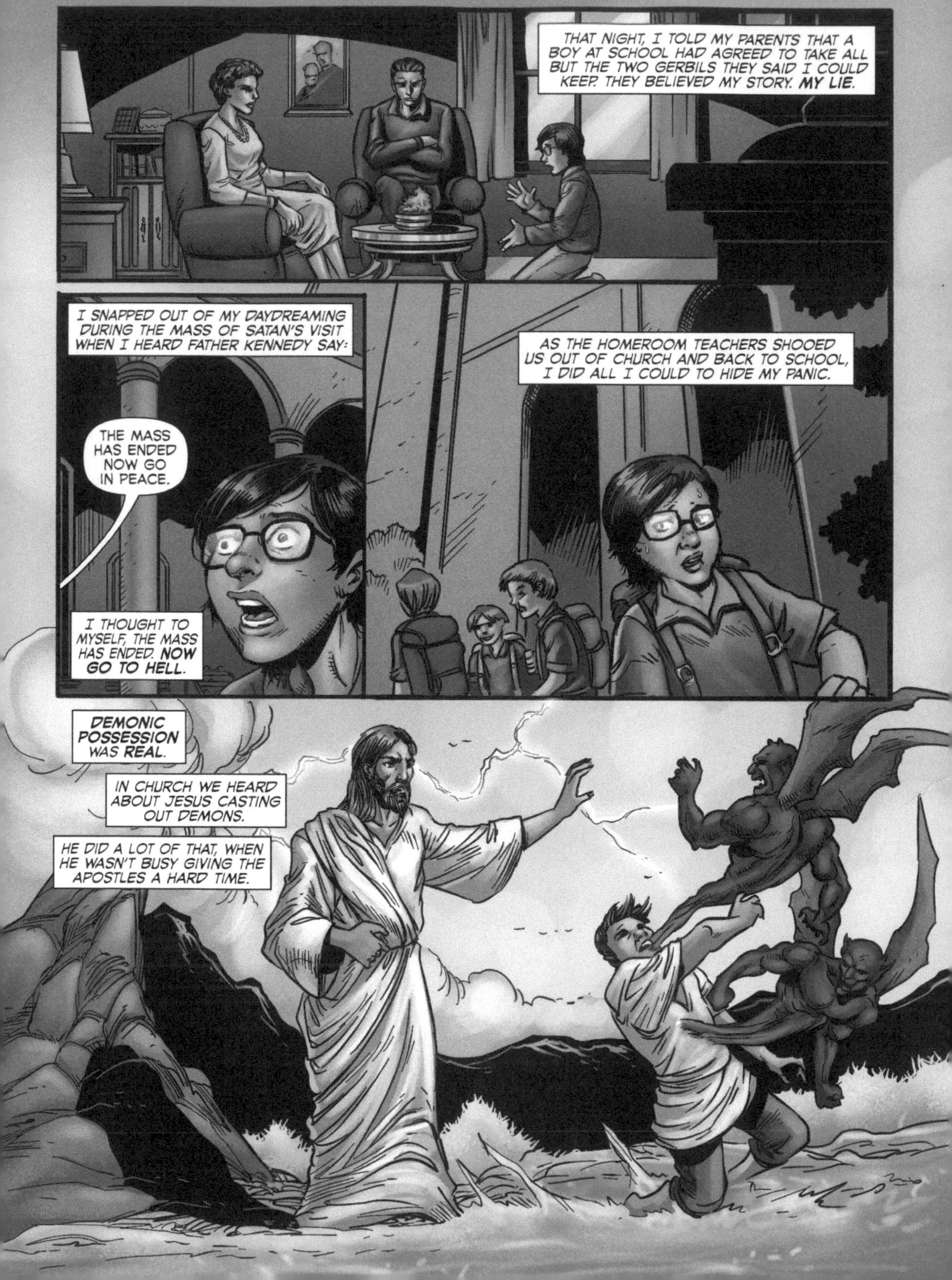
THAT NIGHT, I TOLD MY PARENTS THAT A BOY AT SCHOOL HAD AGREED TO TAKE ALL BUT THE TWO GERBILS THEY SAID I COULD KEEP. THEY BELIEVED MY STORY. **MY LIE.**
I SNAPPED OUT OF MY DAYDREAMING DURING THE MASS OF SATAN'S VISIT WHEN I HEARD FATHER KENNEDY SAY:
THE MASS HAS ENDED NOW GO IN PEACE.
I THOUGHT TO MYSELF, THE MASS HAS ENDED. **NOW GO TO HELL.**
AS THE HOMEROOM TEACHERS SHOOED US OUT OF CHURCH AND BACK TO SCHOOL, I DID ALL I COULD TO HIDE MY PANIC.
DEMONIC POSSESSION WAS **REAL.**
IN CHURCH WE HEARD ABOUT JESUS CASTING OUT DEMONS.
HE DID A LOT OF THAT, WHEN HE WASN'T BUSY GIVING THE APOSTLES A HARD TIME.

BUT THE MOST CONVINCING EVIDENCE OF SATAN'S EXISTENCE WAS THE WILDLY POPULAR MOVIE, **THE EXORCIST**, WHICH HAD MADE ITS DEBUT THE YEAR BEFORE.

IT WAS BASED ON A **TRUE STORY**, WE WERE TOLD. ALTHOUGH I HADN'T SEEN THE R-RATED FLICK, I HEARD ALL THE DETAILS.

LEVITATION. SPINNING HEADS. GREEN PUKE.

NOTHING COULD BE THE SAME NOW. THAT DAY DIVIDED MY LIFE IN TWO PARTS: **BD** AND **AD**.

BEFORE DEVIL...

AFTER DEVIL...

I HAD NOWHERE TO TURN. MY BELOVED CHURCH WAS NO LONGER A SANCTUARY.

I NEEDED TIME TO FIGURE THIS ONE OUT. AND LIKE THE GREAT SCIENTISTS, I WOULD HAVE TO GO IT ALONE.

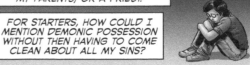

I COULDN'T APPROACH A TEACHER, MY PARENTS, OR A PRIEST.

FOR STARTERS, HOW COULD I MENTION DEMONIC POSSESSION WITHOUT THEN HAVING TO COME CLEAN ABOUT ALL MY SINS?

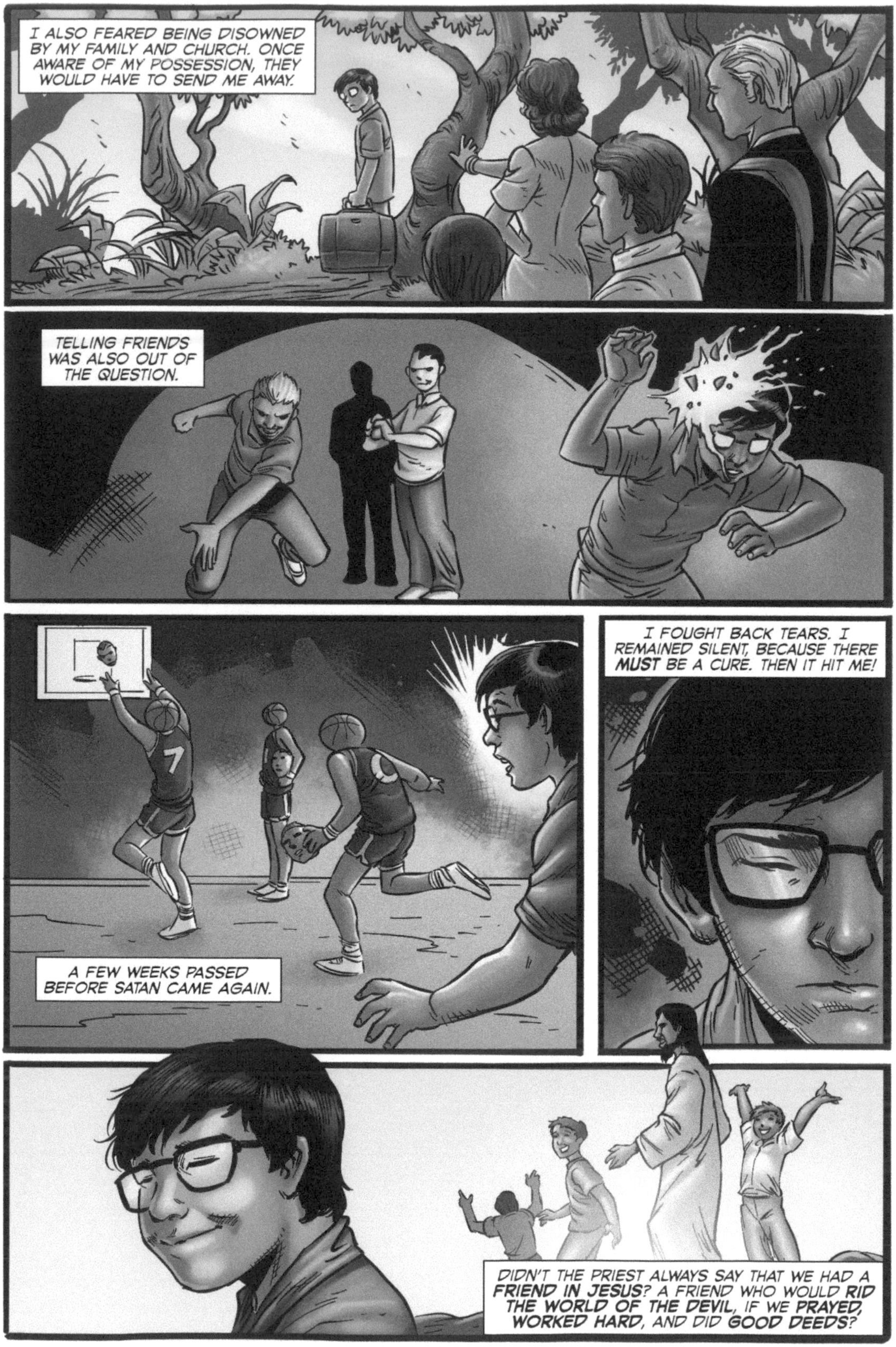
I ALSO FEARED BEING DISOWNED BY MY FAMILY AND CHURCH. ONCE AWARE OF MY POSSESSION, THEY WOULD HAVE TO SEND ME AWAY.
TELLING FRIENDS WAS ALSO OUT OF THE QUESTION.
A FEW WEEKS PASSED BEFORE SATAN CAME AGAIN.
7
I FOUGHT BACK TEARS. I REMAINED SILENT, BECAUSE THERE MUST BE A CURE. THEN IT HIT ME!
DIDN'T THE PRIEST ALWAYS SAY THAT WE HAD A FRIEND IN JESUS? A FRIEND WHO WOULD RID THE WORLD OF THE DEVIL, IF WE PRAYED, WORKED HARD, AND DID GOOD DEEDS?

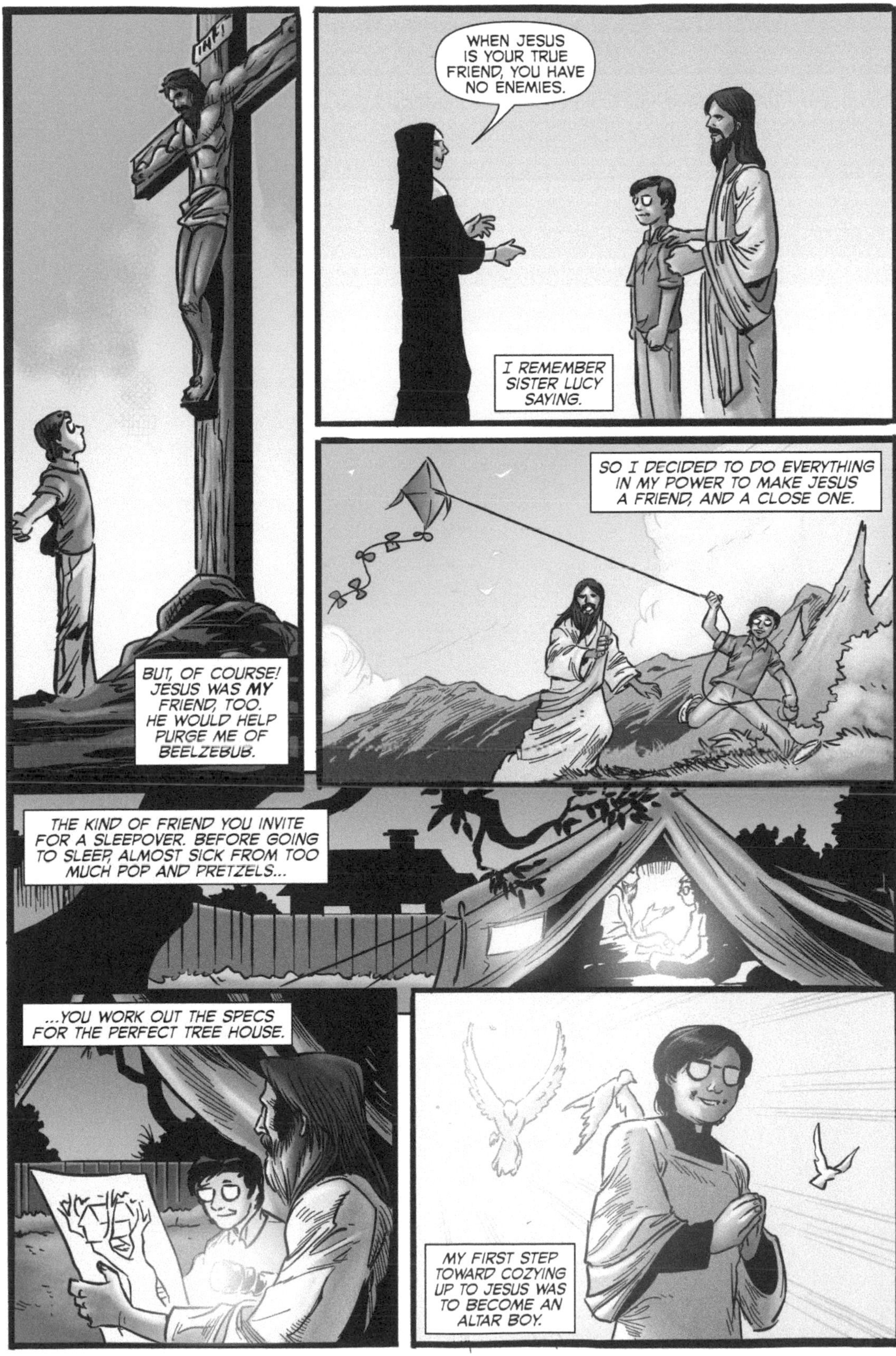
BUT, OF COURSE! JESUS WAS MY FRIEND, TOO. HE WOULD HELP PURGE ME OF BEELZEBUB.
WHEN JESUS IS YOUR TRUE FRIEND, YOU HAVE NO ENEMIES.
I REMEMBER SISTER LUCY SAYING.
SO I DECIDED TO DO EVERYTHING IN MY POWER TO MAKE JESUS A FRIEND, AND A CLOSE ONE.
THE KIND OF FRIEND YOU INVITE FOR A SLEEPOVER. BEFORE GOING TO SLEEP, ALMOST SICK FROM TOO MUCH POP AND PRETZELS...
...YOU WORK OUT THE SPECS FOR THE PERFECT TREE HOUSE.
MY FIRST STEP TOWARD COZYING UP TO JESUS WAS TO BECOME AN ALTAR BOY.

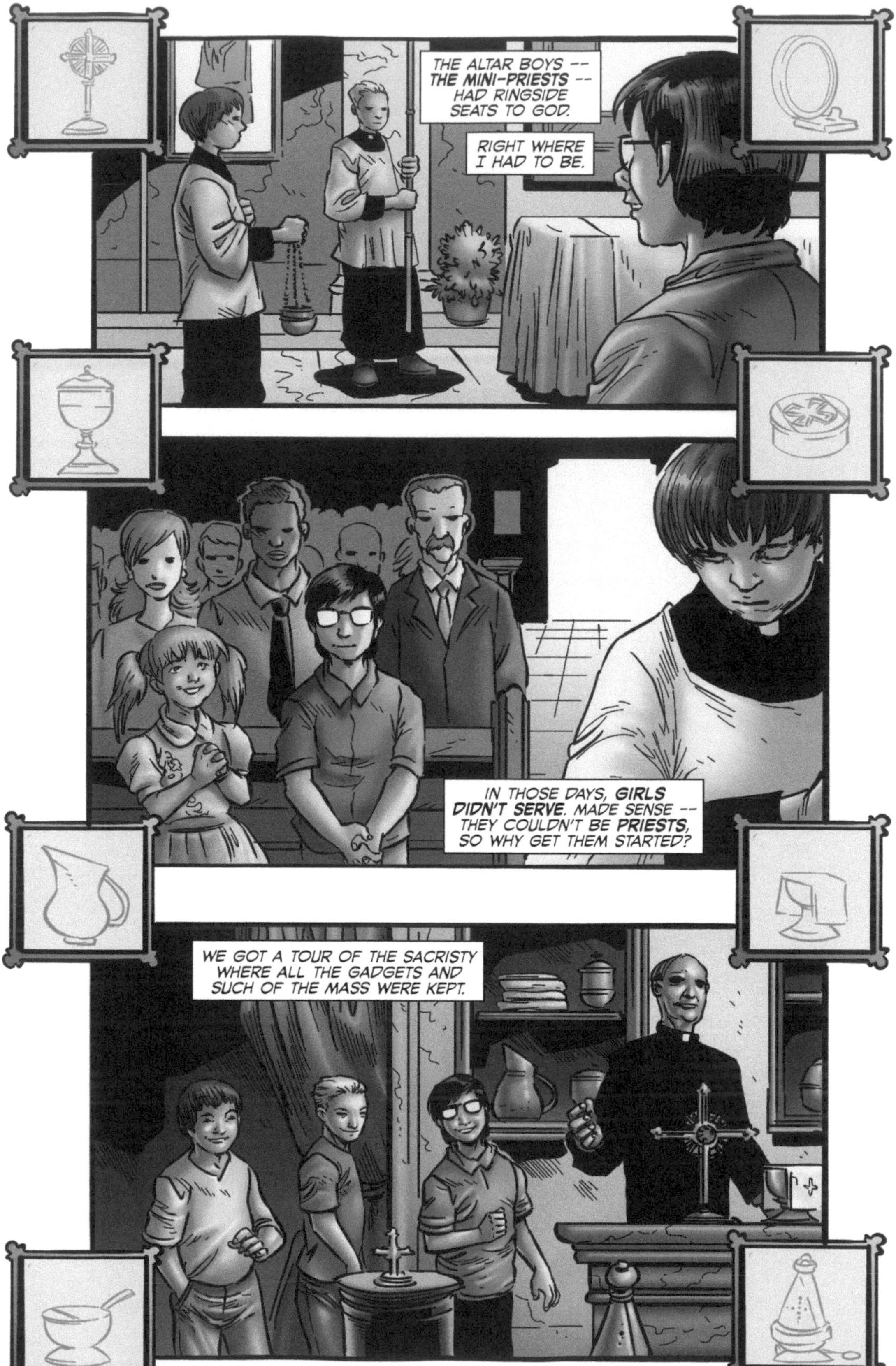
THE ALTAR BOYS -- **THE MINI-PRIESTS** -- HAD RINGSIDE SEATS TO GOD.
RIGHT WHERE I HAD TO BE.
IN THOSE DAYS, **GIRLS DIDN'T SERVE**. MADE SENSE -- THEY COULDN'T BE **PRIESTS**, SO WHY GET THEM STARTED?
WE GOT A TOUR OF THE SACRISTY WHERE ALL THE GADGETS AND SUCH OF THE MASS WERE KEPT.

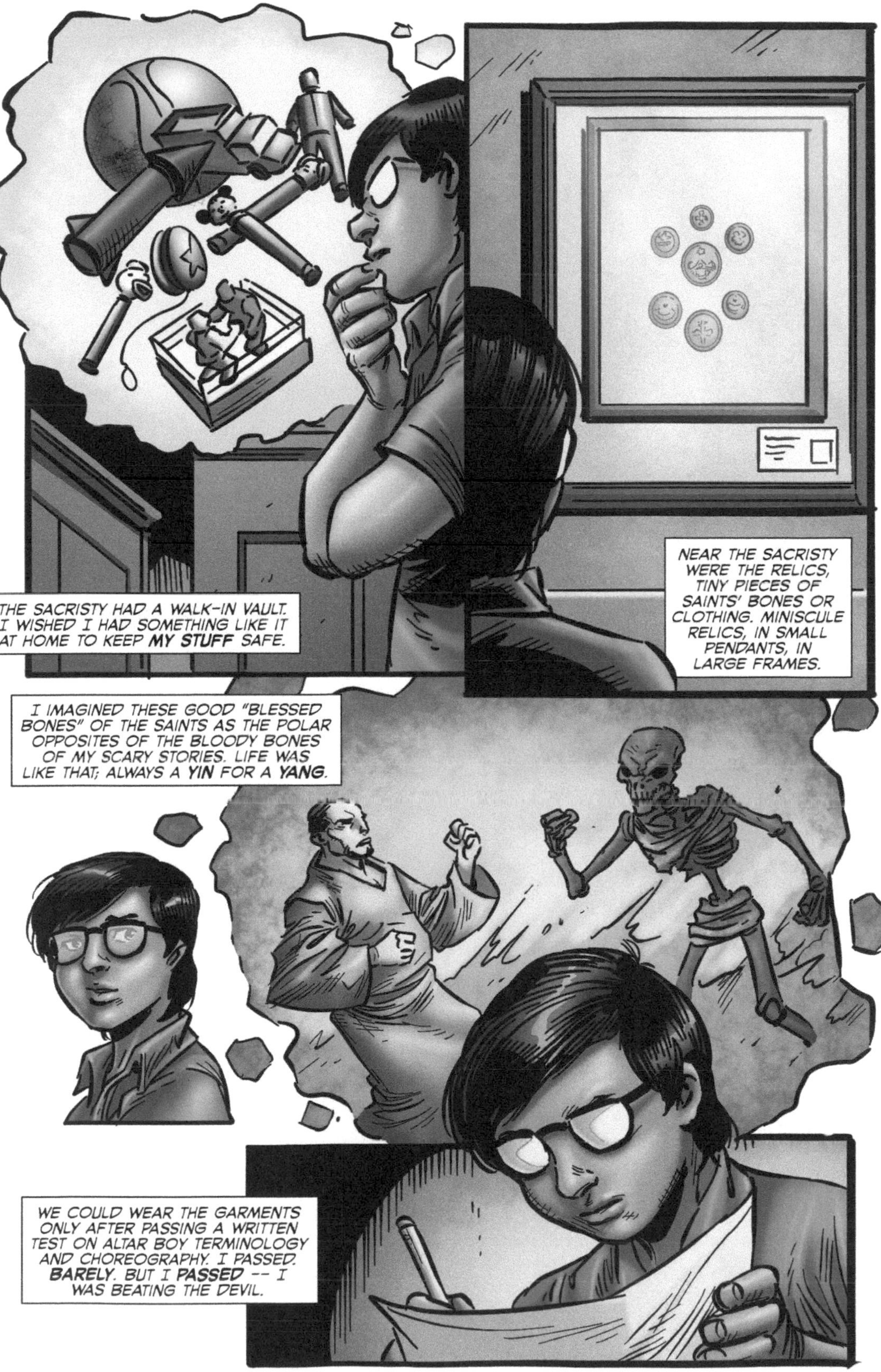
THE SACRISTY HAD A WALK-IN VAULT. I WISHED I HAD SOMETHING LIKE IT AT HOME TO KEEP **MY STUFF** SAFE.
NEAR THE SACRISTY WERE THE RELICS, TINY PIECES OF SAINTS' BONES OR CLOTHING. MINISCULE RELICS, IN SMALL PENDANTS, IN LARGE FRAMES.
I IMAGINED THESE GOOD "BLESSED BONES" OF THE SAINTS AS THE POLAR OPPOSITES OF THE BLOODY BONES OF MY SCARY STORIES. LIFE WAS LIKE THAT; ALWAYS A **YIN** FOR A **YANG**.
WE COULD WEAR THE GARMENTS ONLY AFTER PASSING A WRITTEN TEST ON ALTAR BOY TERMINOLOGY AND CHOREOGRAPHY. I PASSED. **BARELY**. BUT I **PASSED** -- I WAS BEATING THE DEVIL.

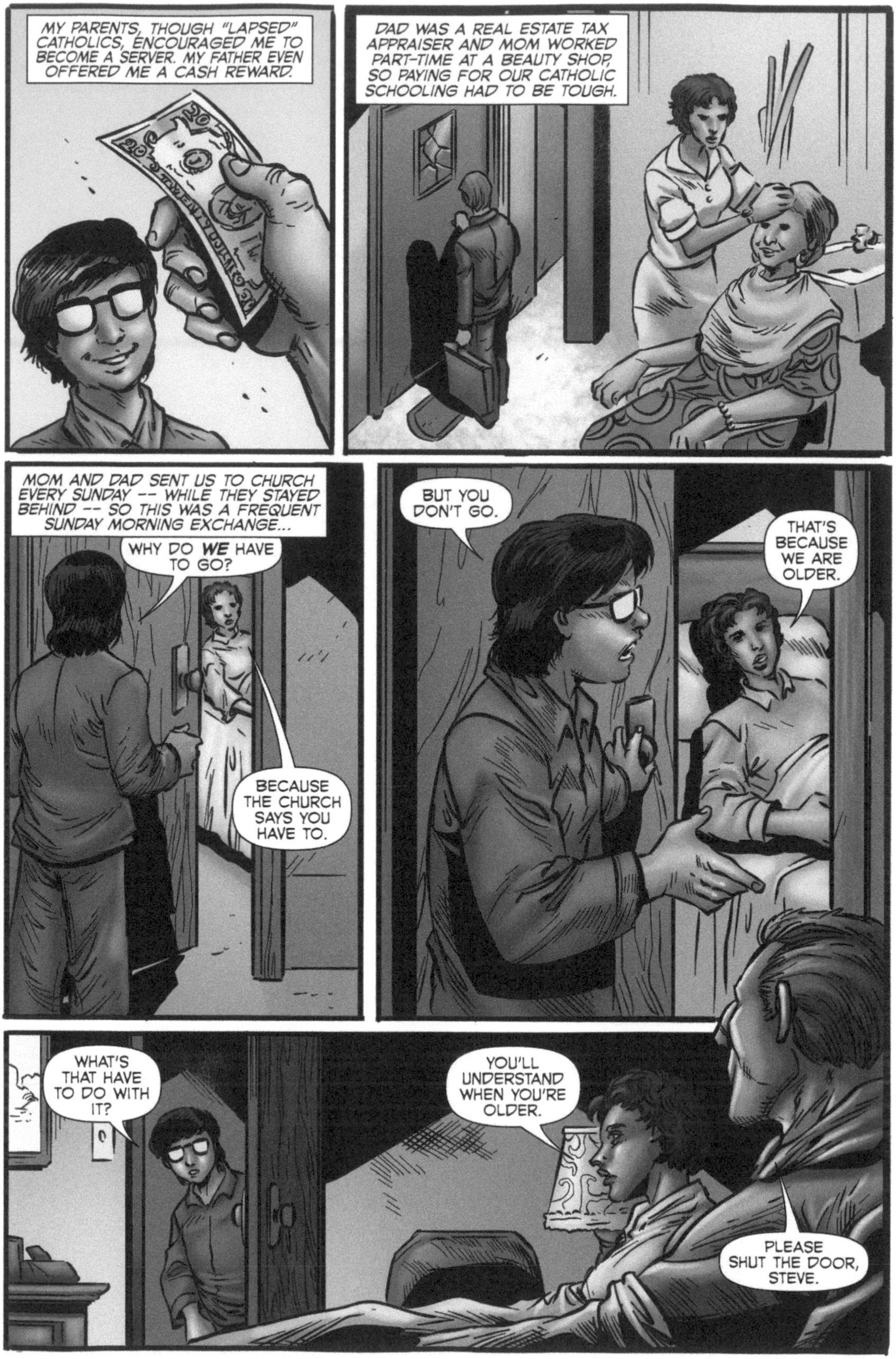

MY PARENTS, THOUGH "LAPSED" CATHOLICS, ENCOURAGED ME TO BECOME A SERVER. MY FATHER EVEN OFFERED ME A CASH REWARD.
DAD WAS A REAL ESTATE TAX APPRAISER AND MOM WORKED PART-TIME AT A BEAUTY SHOP, SO PAYING FOR OUR CATHOLIC SCHOOLING HAD TO BE TOUGH.
MOM AND DAD SENT US TO CHURCH EVERY SUNDAY -- WHILE THEY STAYED BEHIND -- SO THIS WAS A FREQUENT SUNDAY MORNING EXCHANGE...
WHY DO **WE** HAVE TO GO?
BECAUSE THE CHURCH SAYS YOU HAVE TO.
BUT YOU DON'T GO.
THAT'S BECAUSE WE ARE OLDER.
WHAT'S THAT HAVE TO DO WITH IT?
YOU'LL UNDERSTAND WHEN YOU'RE OLDER.
PLEASE SHUT THE DOOR, STEVE.

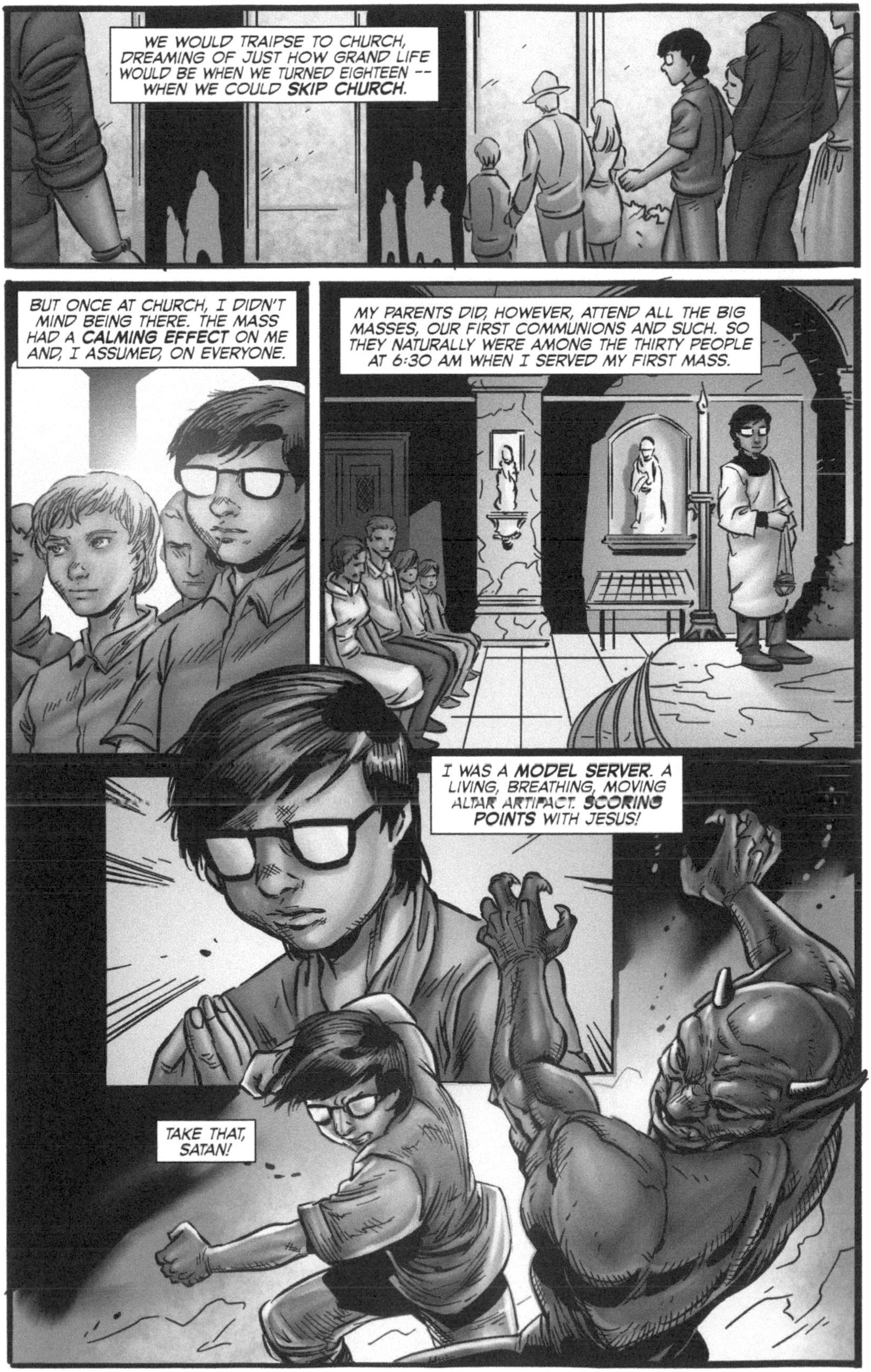
WE WOULD TRAIPSE TO CHURCH, DREAMING OF JUST HOW GRAND LIFE WOULD BE WHEN WE TURNED EIGHTEEN -- WHEN WE COULD SKIP CHURCH.
BUT ONCE AT CHURCH, I DIDN'T MIND BEING THERE. THE MASS HAD A CALMING EFFECT ON ME AND, I ASSUMED, ON EVERYONE.
MY PARENTS DID, HOWEVER, ATTEND ALL THE BIG MASSES, OUR FIRST COMMUNIONS AND SUCH. SO THEY NATURALLY WERE AMONG THE THIRTY PEOPLE AT 6:30 AM WHEN I SERVED MY FIRST MASS.
I WAS A MODEL SERVER. A LIVING, BREATHING, MOVING ALTAR ARTIFACT. SCORING POINTS WITH JESUS!
TAKE THAT, SATAN!

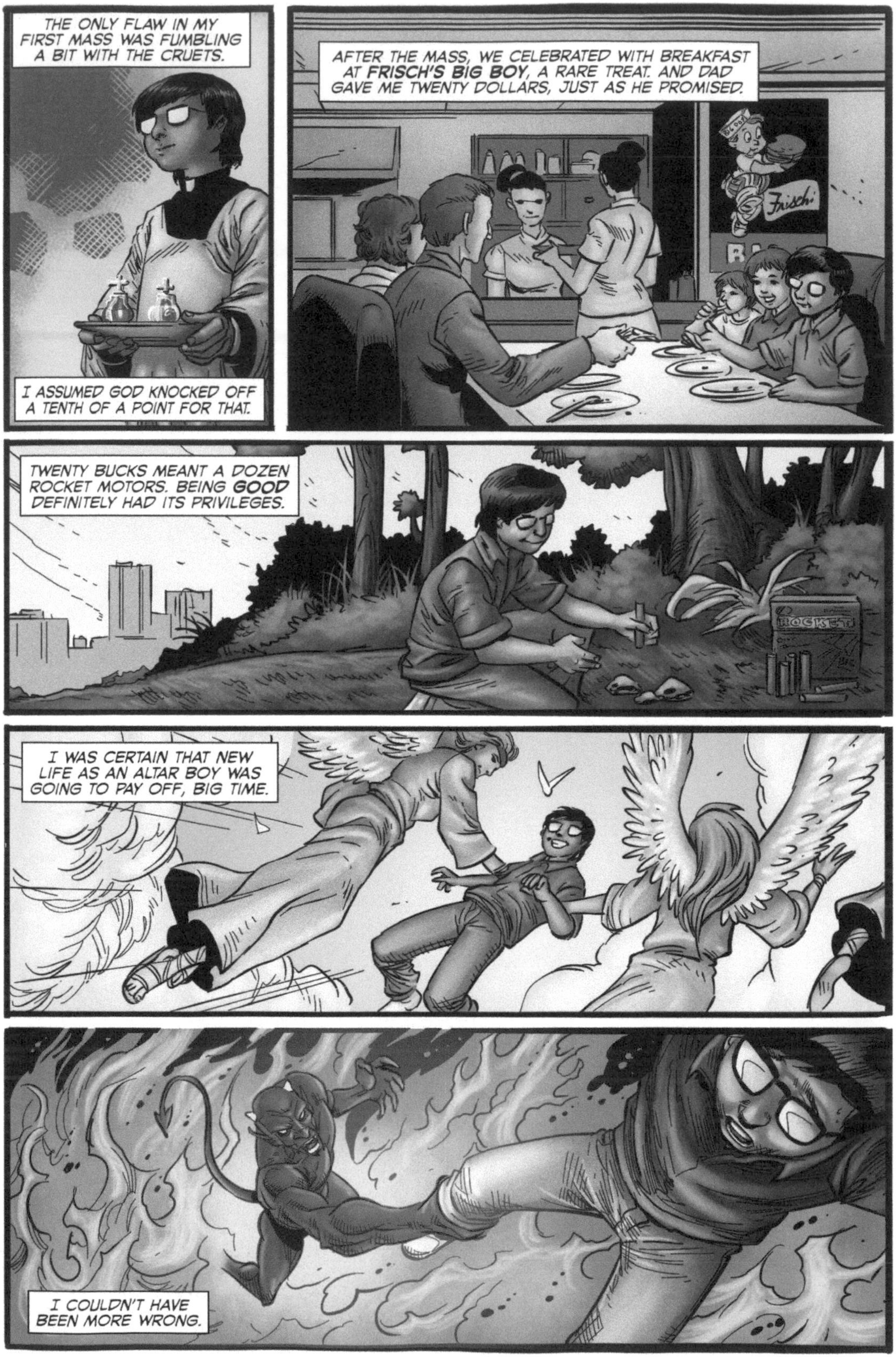
THE ONLY FLAW IN MY FIRST MASS WAS FUMBLING A BIT WITH THE CRUETS.
I ASSUMED GOD KNOCKED OFF A TENTH OF A POINT FOR THAT.
AFTER THE MASS, WE CELEBRATED WITH BREAKFAST AT FRISCH'S BIG BOY, A RARE TREAT. AND DAD GAVE ME TWENTY DOLLARS, JUST AS HE PROMISED.
Frisch's
TWENTY BUCKS MEANT A DOZEN ROCKET MOTORS. BEING GOOD DEFINITELY HAD ITS PRIVILEGES.
ROCKETS
I WAS CERTAIN THAT NEW LIFE AS AN ALTAR BOY WAS GOING TO PAY OFF, BIG TIME.
I COULDN'T HAVE BEEN MORE WRONG.

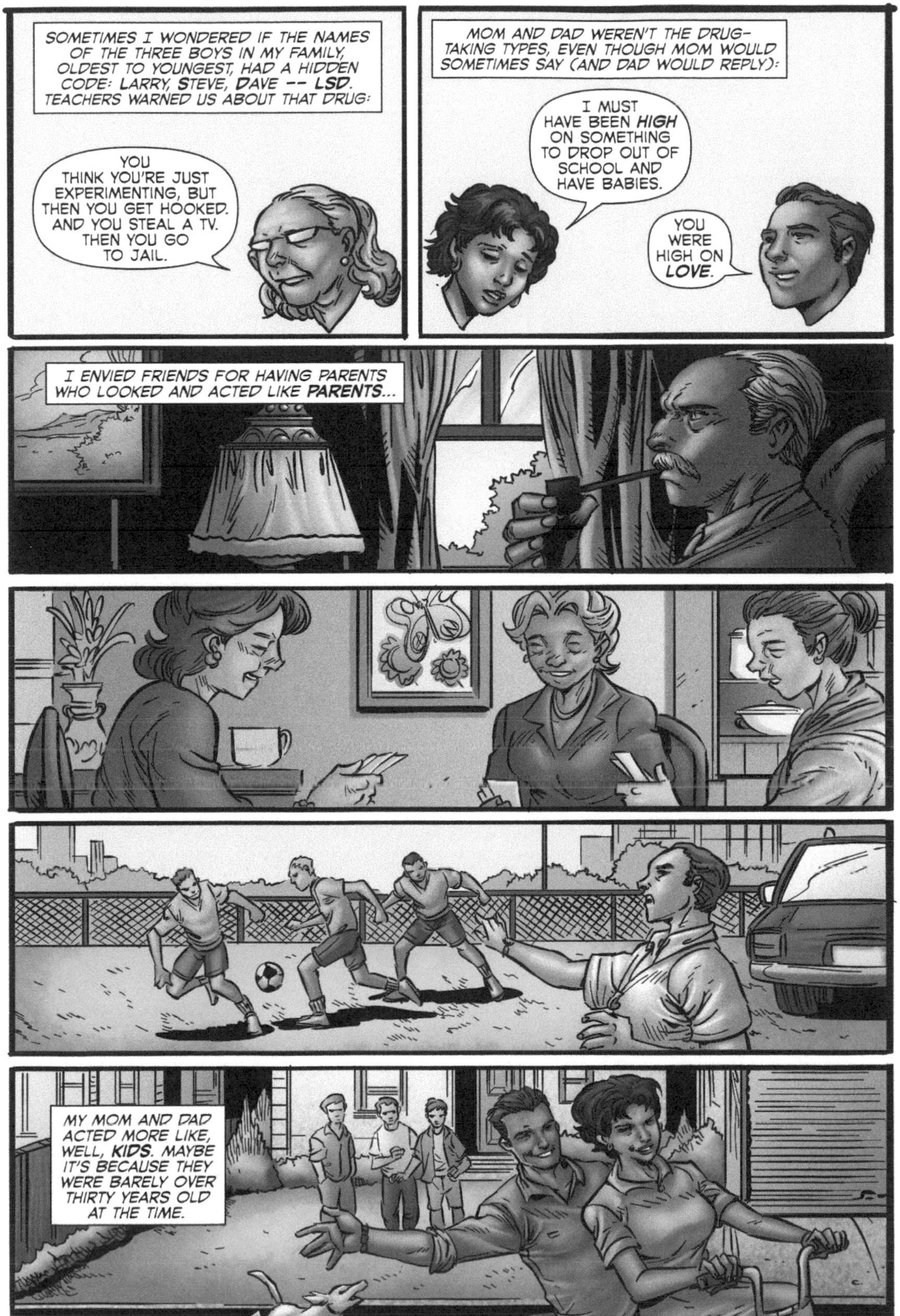
SOMETIMES I WONDERED IF THE NAMES OF THE THREE BOYS IN MY FAMILY, OLDEST TO YOUNGEST, HAD A HIDDEN CODE: LARRY, STEVE, DAVE -- LSD. TEACHERS WARNED US ABOUT THAT DRUG:
YOU THINK YOU'RE JUST EXPERIMENTING, BUT THEN YOU GET HOOKED. AND YOU STEAL A TV. THEN YOU GO TO JAIL.
MOM AND DAD WEREN'T THE DRUG-TAKING TYPES, EVEN THOUGH MOM WOULD SOMETIMES SAY (AND DAD WOULD REPLY):
I MUST HAVE BEEN HIGH ON SOMETHING TO DROP OUT OF SCHOOL AND HAVE BABIES.
YOU WERE HIGH ON LOVE.
I ENVIED FRIENDS FOR HAVING PARENTS WHO LOOKED AND ACTED LIKE PARENTS...
MY MOM AND DAD ACTED MORE LIKE, WELL, KIDS. MAYBE IT'S BECAUSE THEY WERE BARELY OVER THIRTY YEARS OLD AT THE TIME.

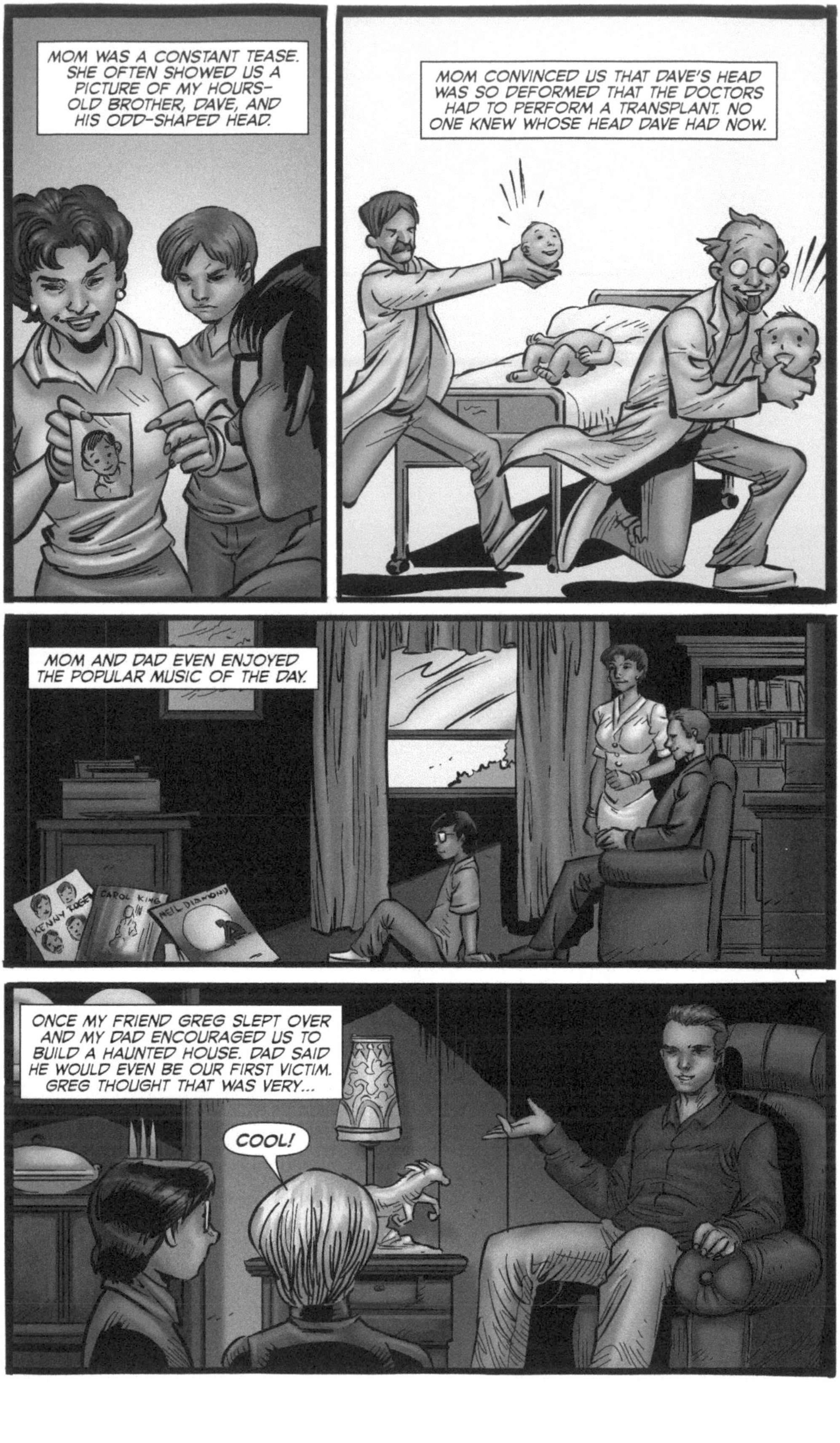
MOM WAS A CONSTANT TEASE. SHE OFTEN SHOWED US A PICTURE OF MY HOURS-OLD BROTHER, DAVE, AND HIS ODD-SHAPED HEAD.
MOM CONVINCED US THAT DAVE'S HEAD WAS SO DEFORMED THAT THE DOCTORS HAD TO PERFORM A TRANSPLANT. NO ONE KNEW WHOSE HEAD DAVE HAD NOW.
MOM AND DAD EVEN ENJOYED THE POPULAR MUSIC OF THE DAY.
KENNY
CAROL KING
NEIL DIAMOND
ONCE MY FRIEND GREG SLEPT OVER AND MY DAD ENCOURAGED US TO BUILD A HAUNTED HOUSE. DAD SAID HE WOULD EVEN BE OUR FIRST VICTIM. GREG THOUGHT THAT WAS VERY...
COOL!

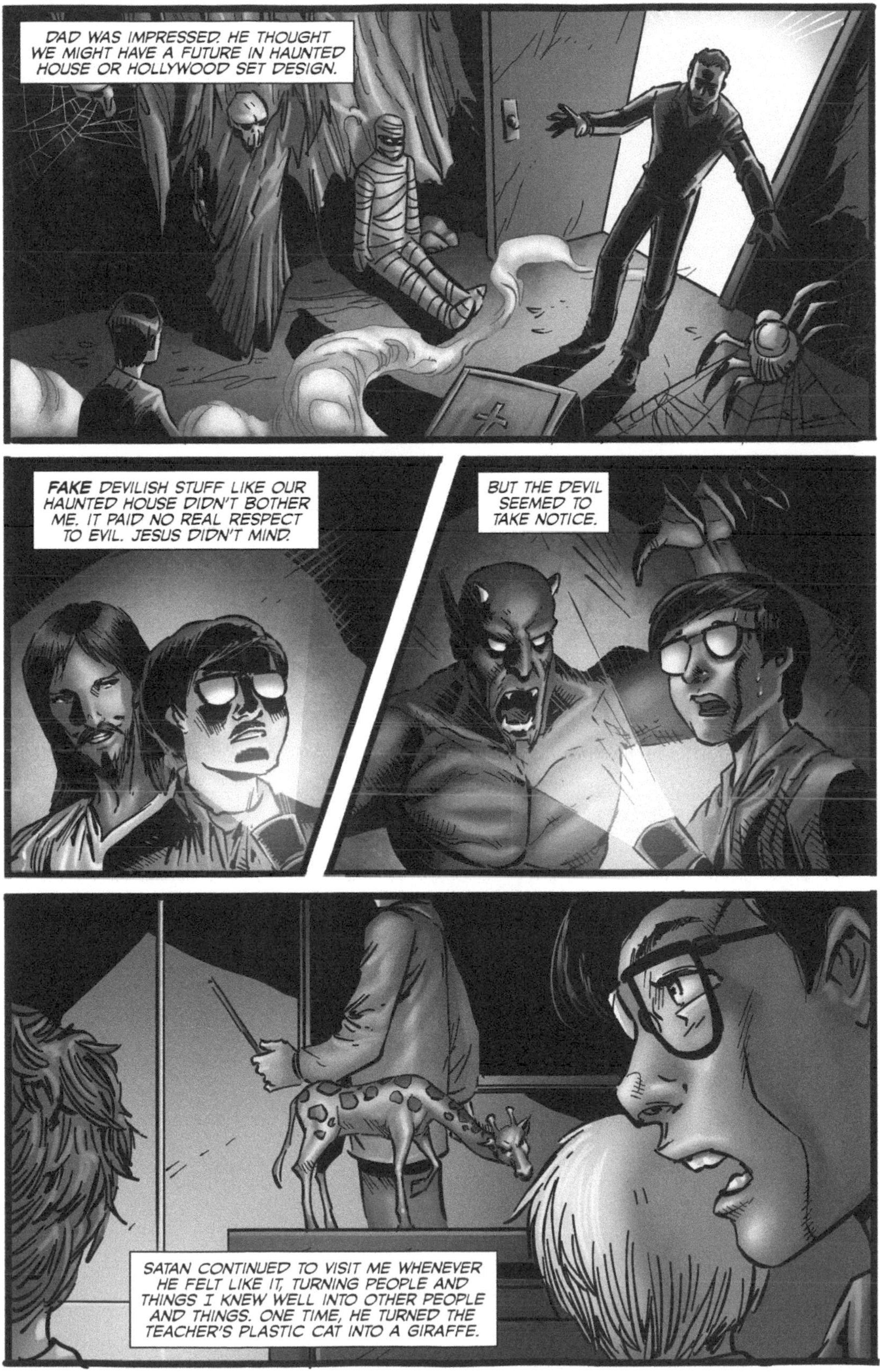
DAD WAS IMPRESSED. HE THOUGHT WE MIGHT HAVE A FUTURE IN HAUNTED HOUSE OR HOLLYWOOD SET DESIGN.
FAKE DEVILISH STUFF LIKE OUR HAUNTED HOUSE DIDN'T BOTHER ME. IT PAID NO REAL RESPECT TO EVIL. JESUS DIDN'T MIND.
BUT THE DEVIL SEEMED TO TAKE NOTICE.
SATAN CONTINUED TO VISIT ME WHENEVER HE FELT LIKE IT, TURNING PEOPLE AND THINGS I KNEW WELL INTO OTHER PEOPLE AND THINGS. ONE TIME, HE TURNED THE TEACHER'S PLASTIC CAT INTO A GIRAFFE.

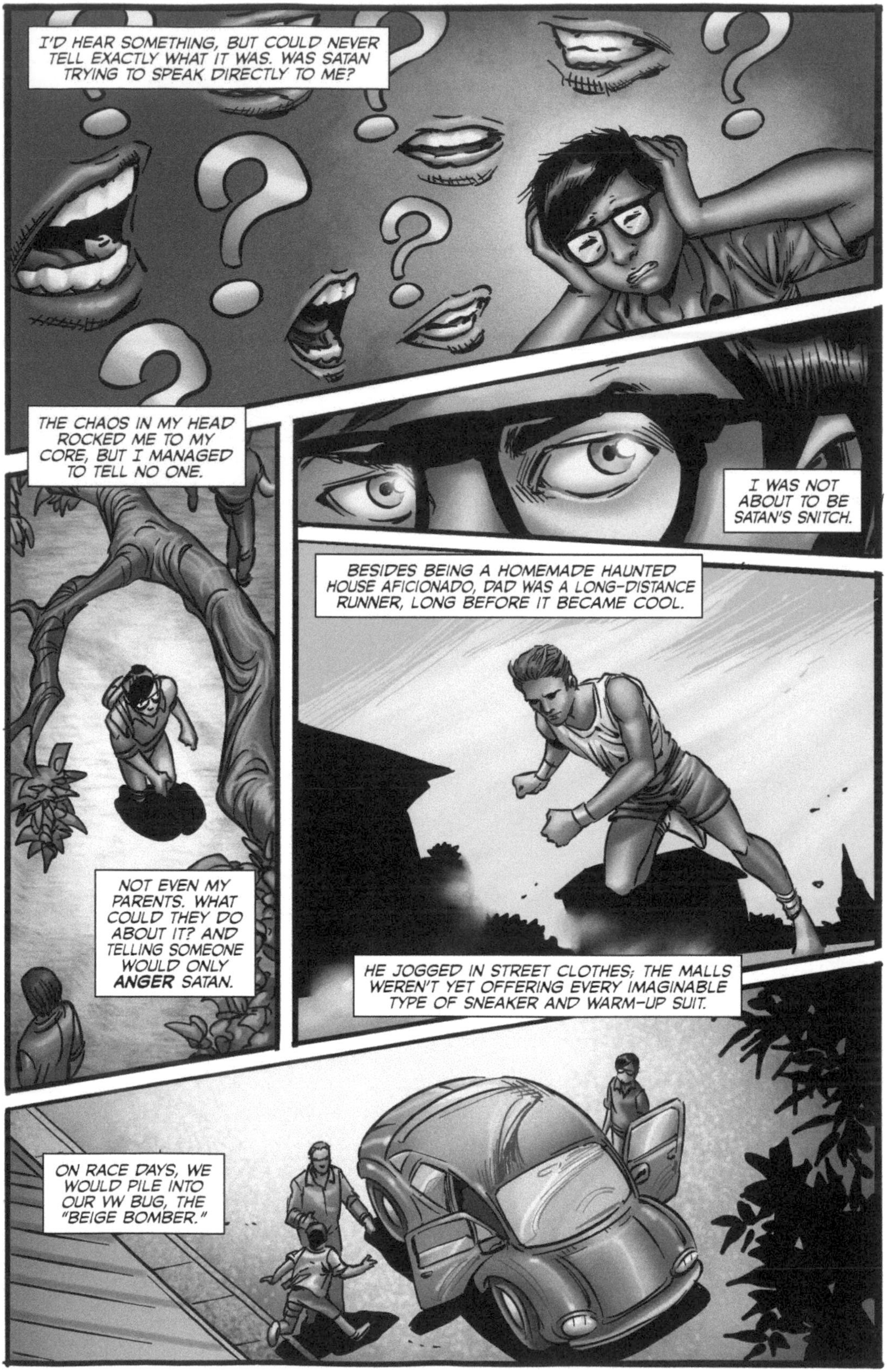
I'D HEAR SOMETHING, BUT COULD NEVER TELL EXACTLY WHAT IT WAS. WAS SATAN TRYING TO SPEAK DIRECTLY TO ME?
THE CHAOS IN MY HEAD ROCKED ME TO MY CORE, BUT I MANAGED TO TELL NO ONE.
NOT EVEN MY PARENTS. WHAT COULD THEY DO ABOUT IT? AND TELLING SOMEONE WOULD ONLY **ANGER** SATAN.
I WAS NOT ABOUT TO BE SATAN'S SNITCH.
BESIDES BEING A HOMEMADE HAUNTED HOUSE AFICIONADO, DAD WAS A LONG-DISTANCE RUNNER, LONG BEFORE IT BECAME COOL.
HE JOGGED IN STREET CLOTHES; THE MALLS WEREN'T YET OFFERING EVERY IMAGINABLE TYPE OF SNEAKER AND WARM-UP SUIT.
ON RACE DAYS, WE WOULD PILE INTO OUR VW BUG, THE "BEIGE BOMBER."

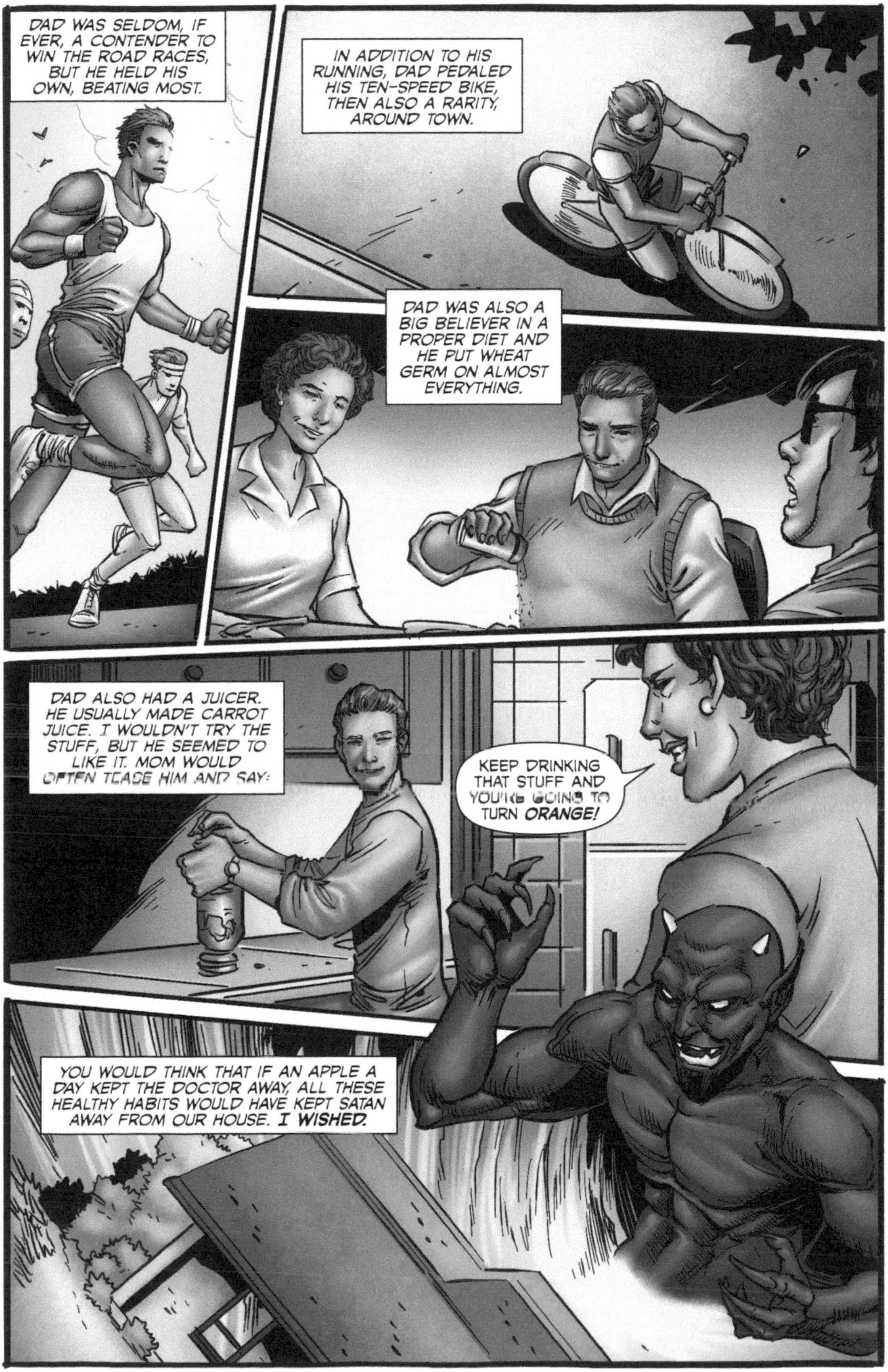

DAD WAS SELDOM, IF EVER, A CONTENDER TO WIN THE ROAD RACES, BUT HE HELD HIS OWN, BEATING MOST.
IN ADDITION TO HIS RUNNING, DAD PEDALED HIS TEN-SPEED BIKE, THEN ALSO A RARITY, AROUND TOWN.
DAD WAS ALSO A BIG BELIEVER IN A PROPER DIET AND HE PUT WHEAT GERM ON ALMOST EVERYTHING.
DAD ALSO HAD A JUICER. HE USUALLY MADE CARROT JUICE. I WOULDN'T TRY THE STUFF, BUT HE SEEMED TO LIKE IT. MOM WOULD OFTEN TEASE HIM AND SAY:
KEEP DRINKING THAT STUFF AND YOU'RE GOING TO TURN **ORANGE!**
YOU WOULD THINK THAT IF AN APPLE A DAY KEPT THE DOCTOR AWAY, ALL THESE HEALTHY HABITS WOULD HAVE KEPT SATAN AWAY FROM OUR HOUSE. **I WISHED.**

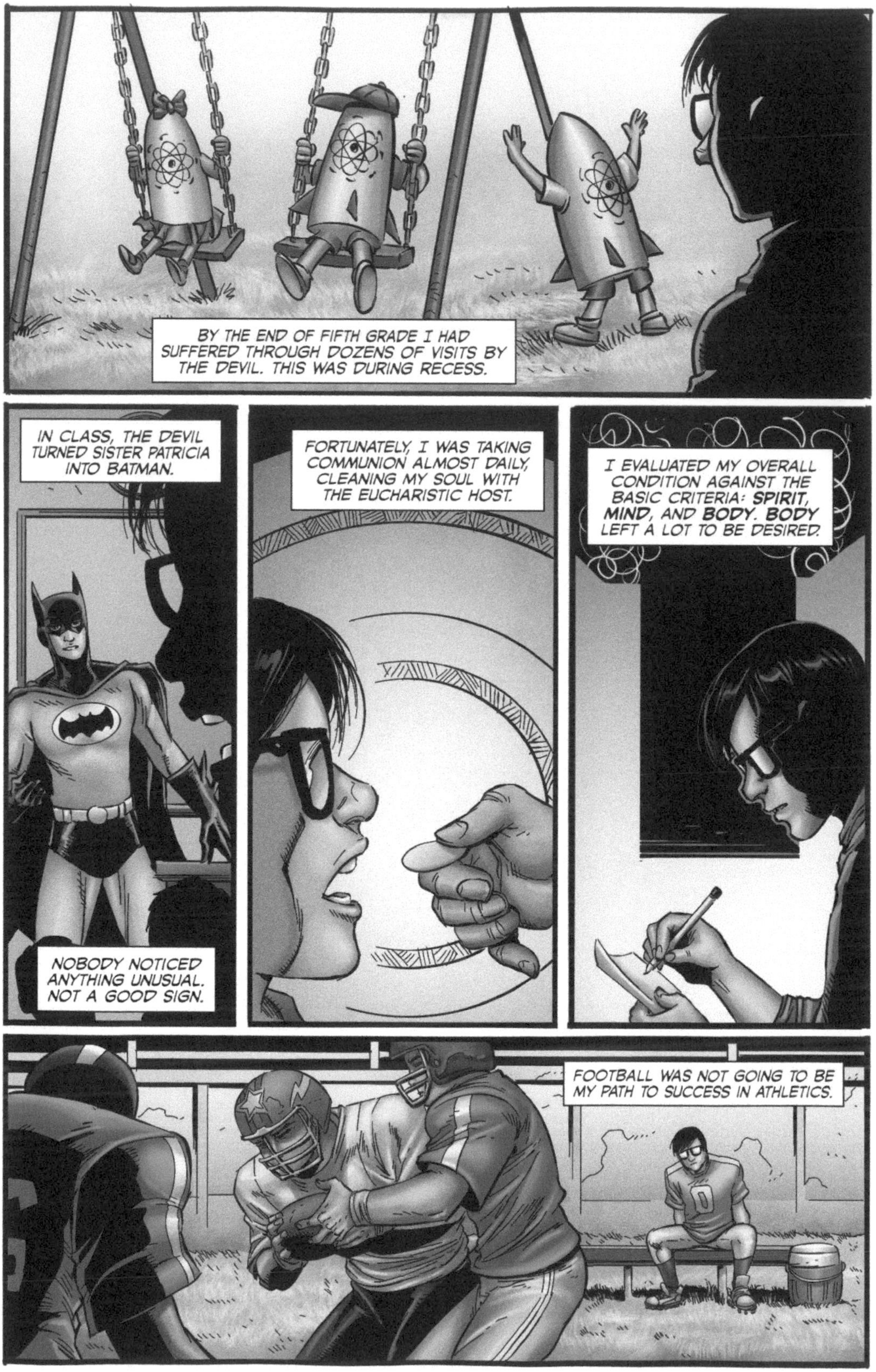
BY THE END OF FIFTH GRADE I HAD SUFFERED THROUGH DOZENS OF VISITS BY THE DEVIL. THIS WAS DURING RECESS.
IN CLASS, THE DEVIL TURNED SISTER PATRICIA INTO BATMAN.
NOBODY NOTICED ANYTHING UNUSUAL. NOT A GOOD SIGN.
FORTUNATELY, I WAS TAKING COMMUNION ALMOST DAILY, CLEANING MY SOUL WITH THE EUCHARISTIC HOST.
I EVALUATED MY OVERALL CONDITION AGAINST THE BASIC CRITERIA: **SPIRIT**, **MIND**, AND **BODY**. **BODY** LEFT A LOT TO BE DESIRED.
FOOTBALL WAS NOT GOING TO BE MY PATH TO SUCCESS IN ATHLETICS.

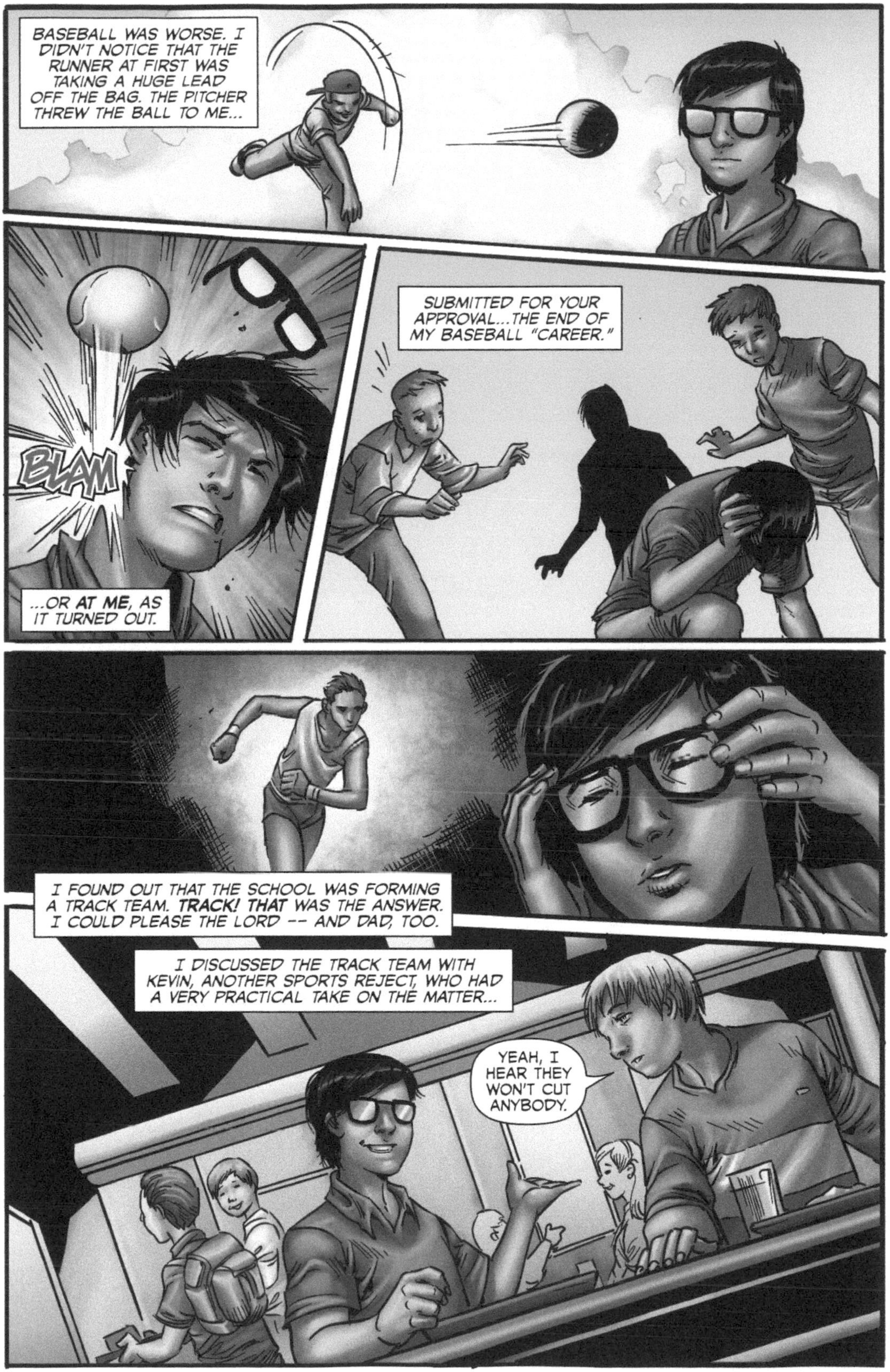
BASEBALL WAS WORSE. I DIDN'T NOTICE THAT THE RUNNER AT FIRST WAS TAKING A HUGE LEAD OFF THE BAG. THE PITCHER THREW THE BALL TO ME...
BLAM
...OR AT ME, AS IT TURNED OUT.
SUBMITTED FOR YOUR APPROVAL...THE END OF MY BASEBALL "CAREER."
I FOUND OUT THAT THE SCHOOL WAS FORMING A TRACK TEAM. TRACK! THAT WAS THE ANSWER. I COULD PLEASE THE LORD -- AND DAD, TOO.
I DISCUSSED THE TRACK TEAM WITH KEVIN, ANOTHER SPORTS REJECT, WHO HAD A VERY PRACTICAL TAKE ON THE MATTER...
YEAH, I HEAR THEY WON'T CUT ANYBODY.

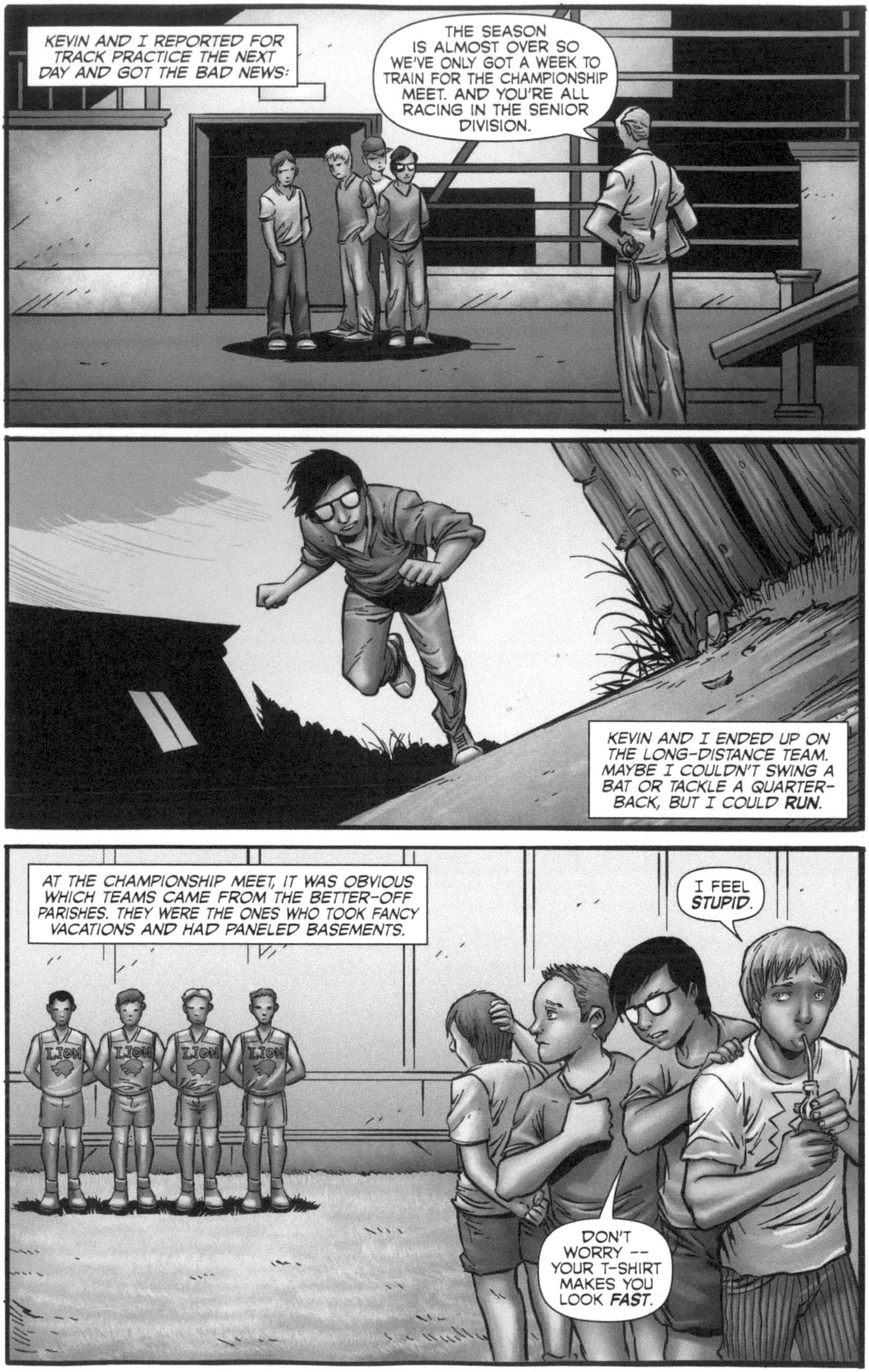
KEVIN AND I REPORTED FOR TRACK PRACTICE THE NEXT DAY AND GOT THE BAD NEWS:
THE SEASON IS ALMOST OVER SO WE'VE ONLY GOT A WEEK TO TRAIN FOR THE CHAMPIONSHIP MEET. AND YOU'RE ALL RACING IN THE SENIOR DIVISION.
KEVIN AND I ENDED UP ON THE LONG-DISTANCE TEAM. MAYBE I COULDN'T SWING A BAT OR TACKLE A QUARTER-BACK, BUT I COULD **RUN**.
AT THE CHAMPIONSHIP MEET, IT WAS OBVIOUS WHICH TEAMS CAME FROM THE BETTER-OFF PARISHES. THEY WERE THE ONES WHO TOOK FANCY VACATIONS AND HAD PANELED BASEMENTS.
I FEEL **STUPID**.
DON'T WORRY -- YOUR T-SHIRT MAKES YOU LOOK **FAST**.

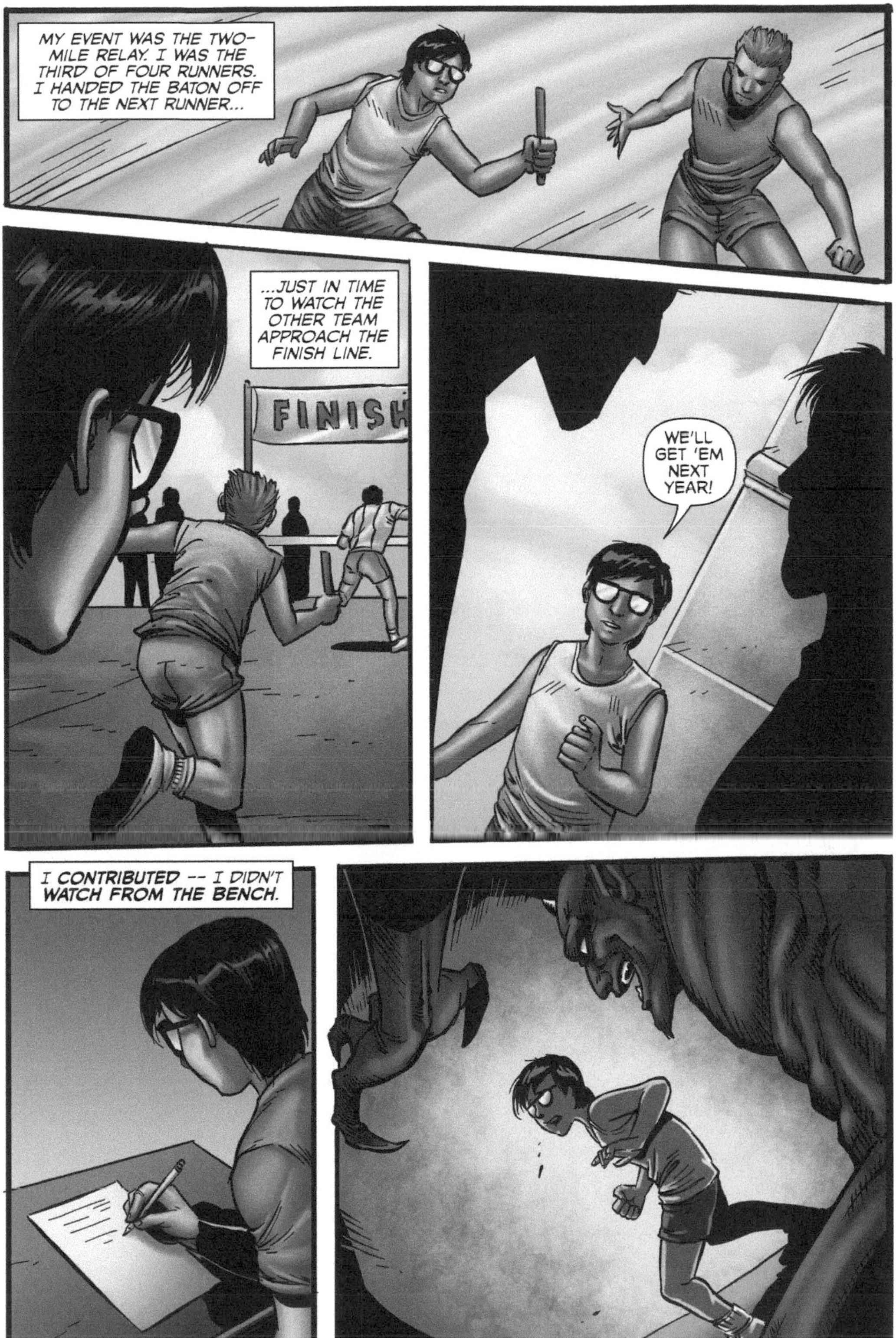
MY EVENT WAS THE TWO-MILE RELAY. I WAS THE THIRD OF FOUR RUNNERS. I HANDED THE BATON OFF TO THE NEXT RUNNER...
...JUST IN TIME TO WATCH THE OTHER TEAM APPROACH THE FINISH LINE.
FINISH
WE'LL GET 'EM NEXT YEAR!
I CONTRIBUTED -- I DIDN'T WATCH FROM THE BENCH.
I COMPETED -- I DIDN'T CRY. THAT NIGHT, I REVIEWED THE PAPER ON WHICH I EVALUATED MYSELF.
BUT DID I HAVE THE ENDURANCE TO STAY ON THE PATH OF GOODNESS FOR AS LONG AS I HAD TO? OR WOULD THE PRINCE OF DARKNESS CATCH ME?

THE DEVIL'S VISITS CONTINUED. ALWAYS UNANNOUNCED. ALWAYS SUDDEN. ALWAYS UPSETTING. I'D GOTTEN VERY GOOD AT MAKING EXCUSES WHEN PEOPLE TOLD ME: *"YOU SEEM DISTRACTED."*

JUST AS THERE WERE DEMONS, THERE WERE ANGELS, TOO, WHO BEAMED POWER INTO RELIGIOUS MEDALS. GUARDIAN ANGELS EVEN GRANTED WISHES.

I WAS A BELIEVER IN SUCH MAGIC AND MYSTERY. I'D EVEN USED ITS POWER TO AFFECT EVENTS IN BINGO PARLORS AND IN VIETNAM. I'LL EXPLAIN...

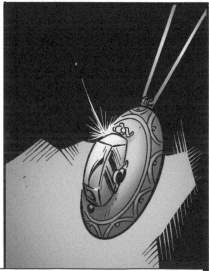

GRANDMA MARGE WAS AN ITALIAN GRANDMOTHER WHOSE COOKING WAS *OUTSTANDING.*

I'D TURNED THE BINGO WORLD UPSIDE DOWN WITH A *MAGIC, POLISHED ROCK,* ON A KEY CHAIN THAT I BOUGHT -- WITH STOLEN MONEY -- FOR GRANDMA MARGE.

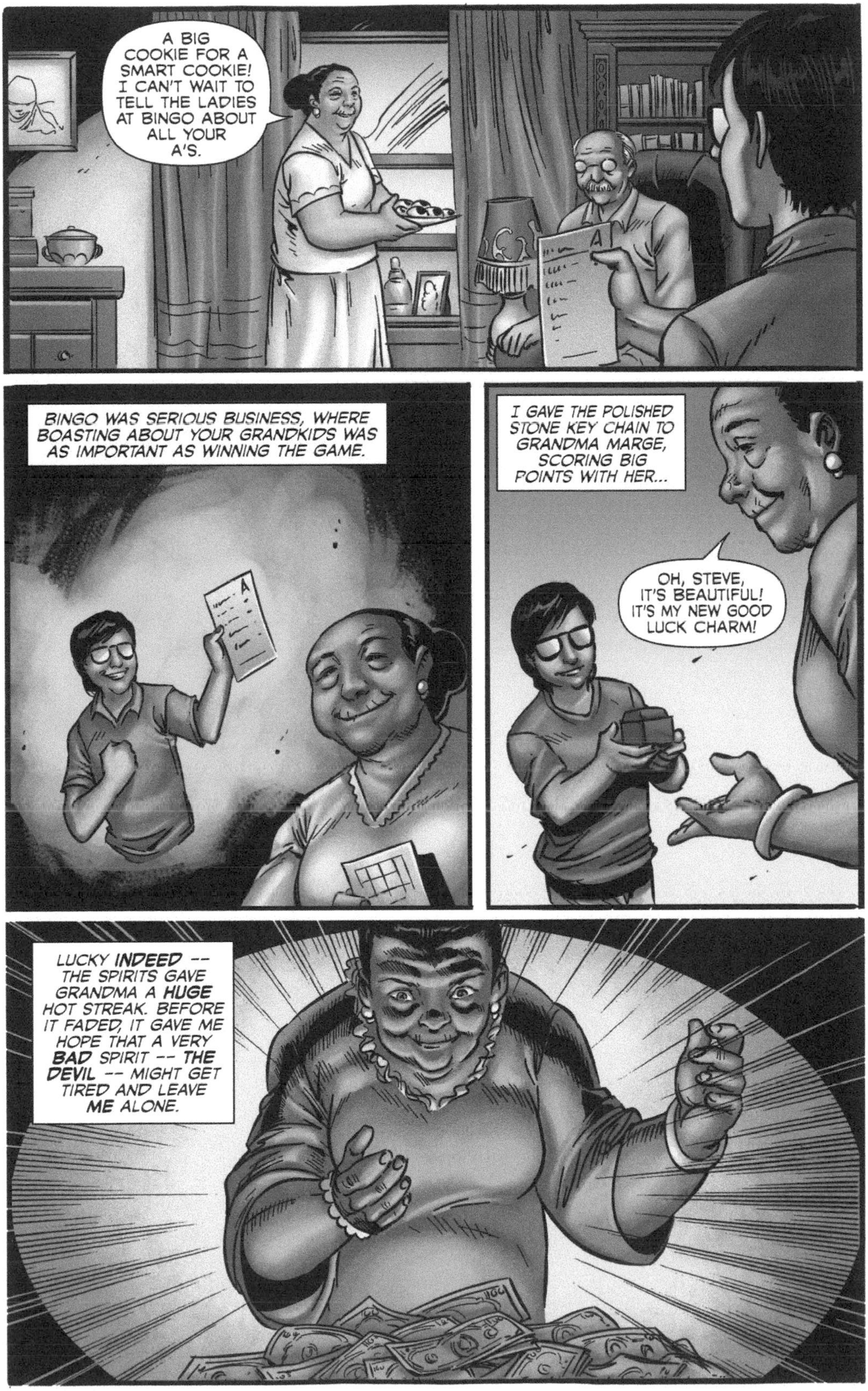
A BIG COOKIE FOR A SMART COOKIE! I CAN'T WAIT TO TELL THE LADIES AT BINGO ABOUT ALL YOUR A'S.
A
BINGO WAS SERIOUS BUSINESS, WHERE BOASTING ABOUT YOUR GRANDKIDS WAS AS IMPORTANT AS WINNING THE GAME.
A
I GAVE THE POLISHED STONE KEY CHAIN TO GRANDMA MARGE, SCORING BIG POINTS WITH HER...
OH, STEVE, IT'S BEAUTIFUL! IT'S MY NEW GOOD LUCK CHARM!
LUCKY INDEED -- THE SPIRITS GAVE GRANDMA A HUGE HOT STREAK. BEFORE IT FADED, IT GAVE ME HOPE THAT A VERY BAD SPIRIT -- THE DEVIL -- MIGHT GET TIRED AND LEAVE ME ALONE.

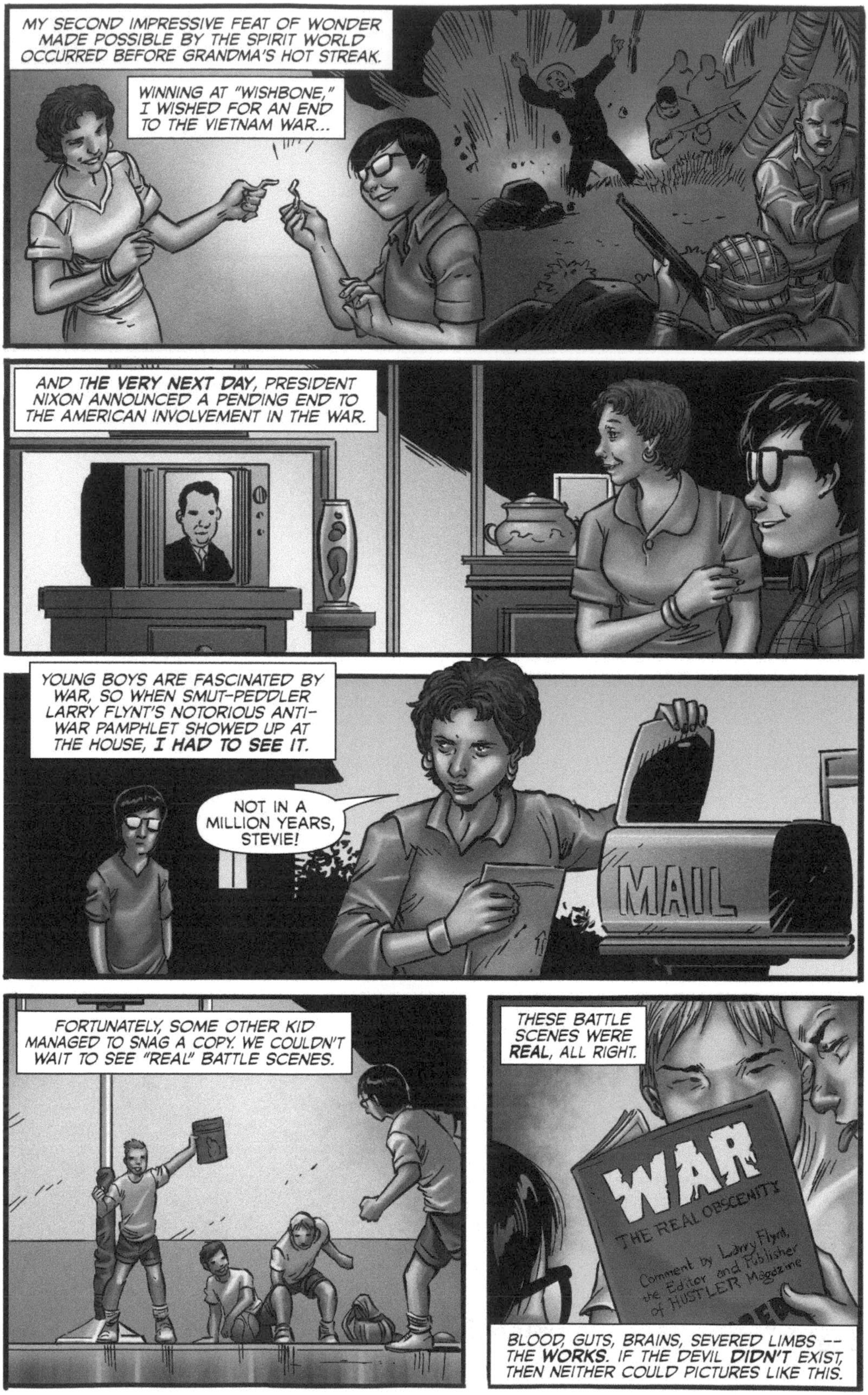
MY SECOND IMPRESSIVE FEAT OF WONDER MADE POSSIBLE BY THE SPIRIT WORLD OCCURRED BEFORE GRANDMA'S HOT STREAK.
WINNING AT "WISHBONE," I WISHED FOR AN END TO THE VIETNAM WAR...
AND THE **VERY NEXT DAY**, PRESIDENT NIXON ANNOUNCED A PENDING END TO THE AMERICAN INVOLVEMENT IN THE WAR.
YOUNG BOYS ARE FASCINATED BY WAR, SO WHEN SMUT-PEDDLER LARRY FLYNT'S NOTORIOUS ANTI-WAR PAMPHLET SHOWED UP AT THE HOUSE, **I HAD TO SEE IT**.
NOT IN A MILLION YEARS, STEVIE!
MAIL
FORTUNATELY, SOME OTHER KID MANAGED TO SNAG A COPY. WE COULDN'T WAIT TO SEE "REAL" BATTLE SCENES.
THESE BATTLE SCENES WERE **REAL**, ALL RIGHT.
WAR
THE REAL OBSCENITY
Comment by Larry Flynt, the Editor and Publisher of HUSTLER Magazine
BLOOD, GUTS, BRAINS, SEVERED LIMBS -- THE **WORKS**. IF THE DEVIL **DIDN'T** EXIST, THEN NEITHER COULD PICTURES LIKE THIS.

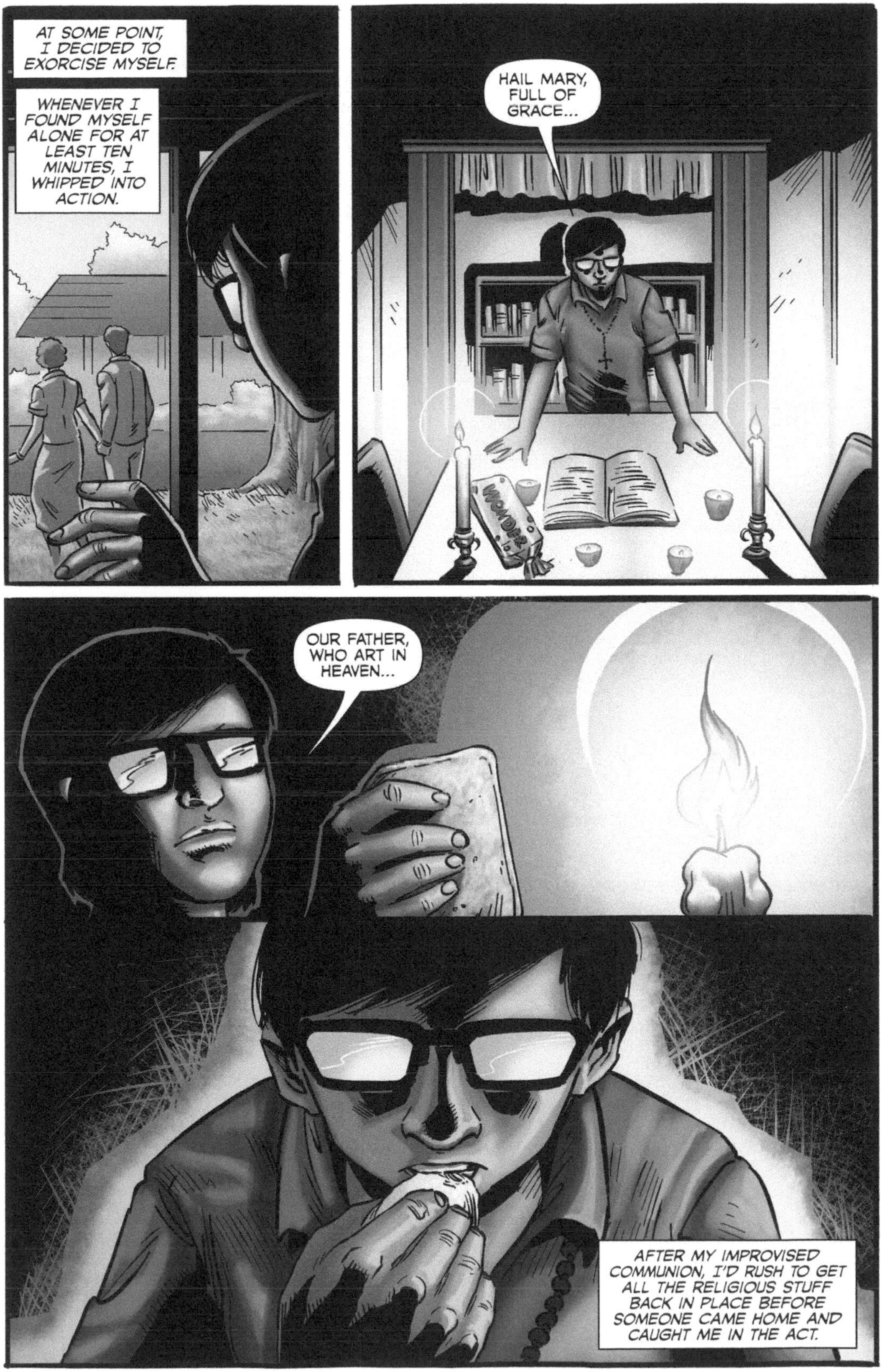
AT SOME POINT, I DECIDED TO EXORCISE MYSELF.
WHENEVER I FOUND MYSELF ALONE FOR AT LEAST TEN MINUTES, I WHIPPED INTO ACTION.
HAIL MARY, FULL OF GRACE...
WONDER
OUR FATHER, WHO ART IN HEAVEN...
AFTER MY IMPROVISED COMMUNION, I'D RUSH TO GET ALL THE RELIGIOUS STUFF BACK IN PLACE BEFORE SOMEONE CAME HOME AND CAUGHT ME IN THE ACT.

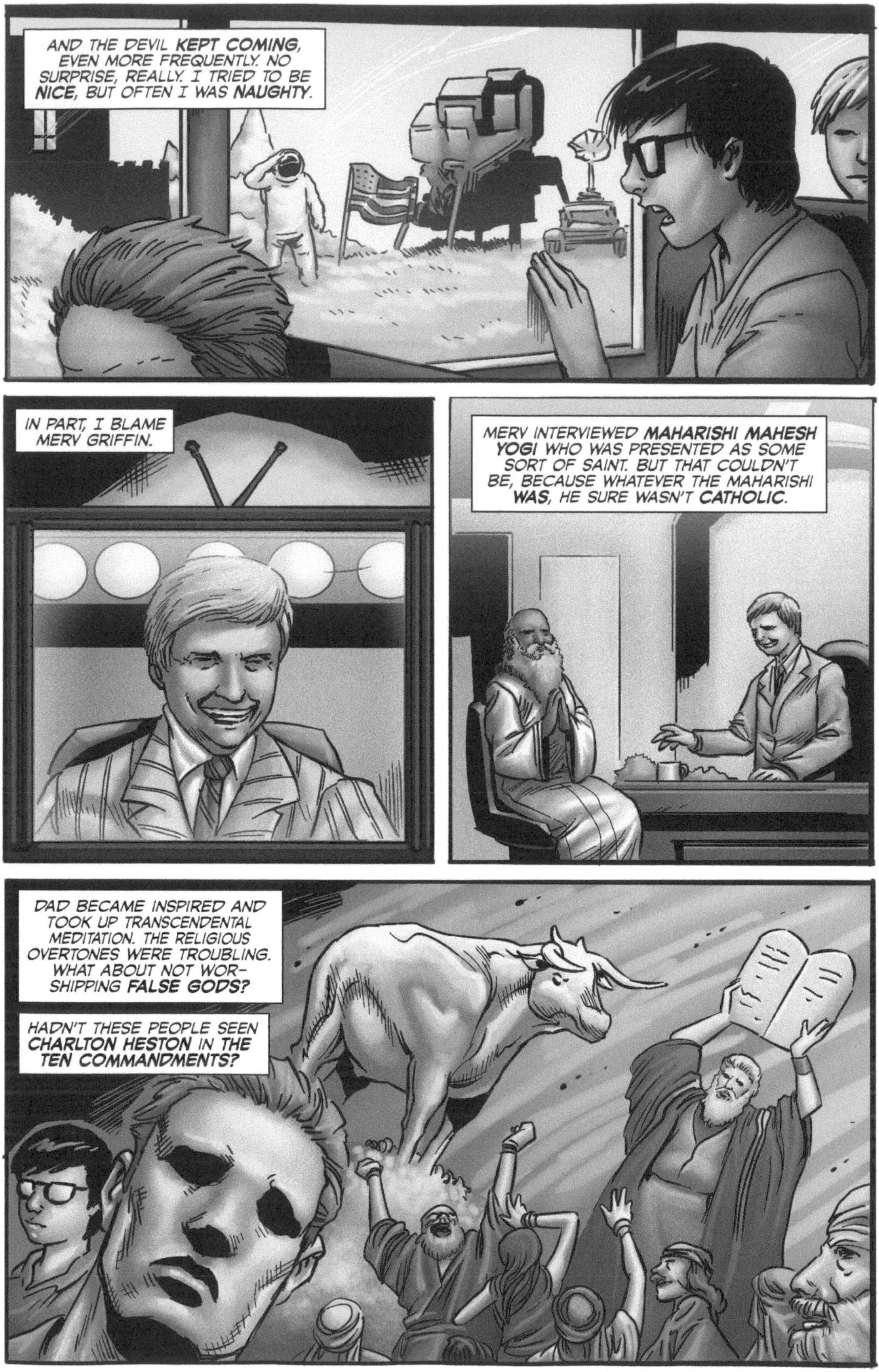
AND THE DEVIL KEPT COMING, EVEN MORE FREQUENTLY. NO SURPRISE, REALLY. I TRIED TO BE NICE, BUT OFTEN I WAS NAUGHTY.
IN PART, I BLAME MERV GRIFFIN.
MERV INTERVIEWED MAHARISHI MAHESH YOGI WHO WAS PRESENTED AS SOME SORT OF SAINT. BUT THAT COULDN'T BE, BECAUSE WHATEVER THE MAHARISHI WAS, HE SURE WASN'T CATHOLIC.
DAD BECAME INSPIRED AND TOOK UP TRANSCENDENTAL MEDITATION. THE RELIGIOUS OVERTONES WERE TROUBLING. WHAT ABOUT NOT WOR-SHIPPING FALSE GODS?
HADN'T THESE PEOPLE SEEN CHARLTON HESTON IN THE TEN COMMANDMENTS?

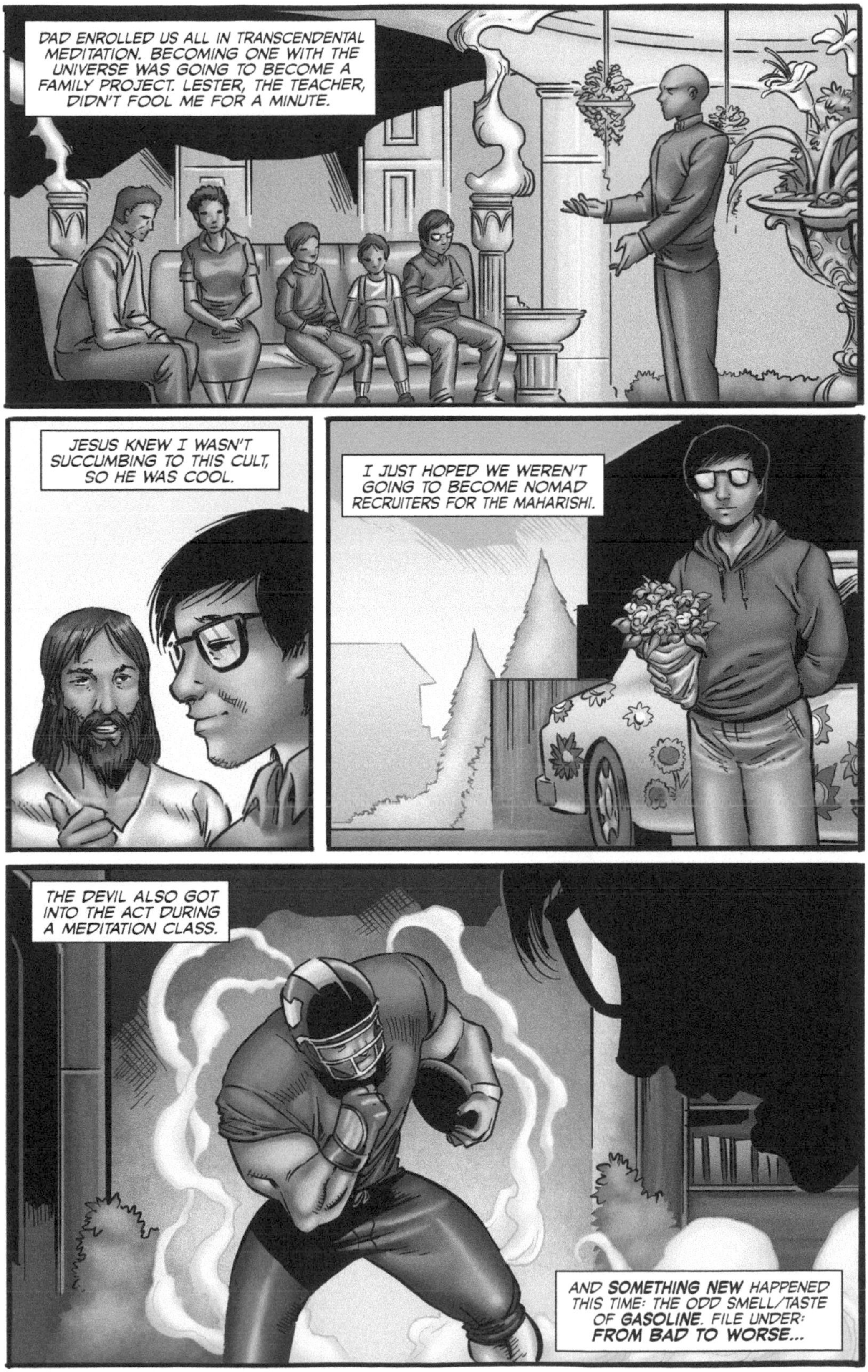
DAD ENROLLED US ALL IN TRANSCENDENTAL MEDITATION. BECOMING ONE WITH THE UNIVERSE WAS GOING TO BECOME A FAMILY PROJECT. LESTER, THE TEACHER, DIDN'T FOOL ME FOR A MINUTE.
JESUS KNEW I WASN'T SUCCUMBING TO THIS CULT, SO HE WAS COOL.
I JUST HOPED WE WEREN'T GOING TO BECOME NOMAD RECRUITERS FOR THE MAHARISHI.
THE DEVIL ALSO GOT INTO THE ACT DURING A MEDITATION CLASS.
AND **SOMETHING NEW** HAPPENED THIS TIME: THE ODD SMELL/TASTE OF **GASOLINE**. FILE UNDER: **FROM BAD TO WORSE...**

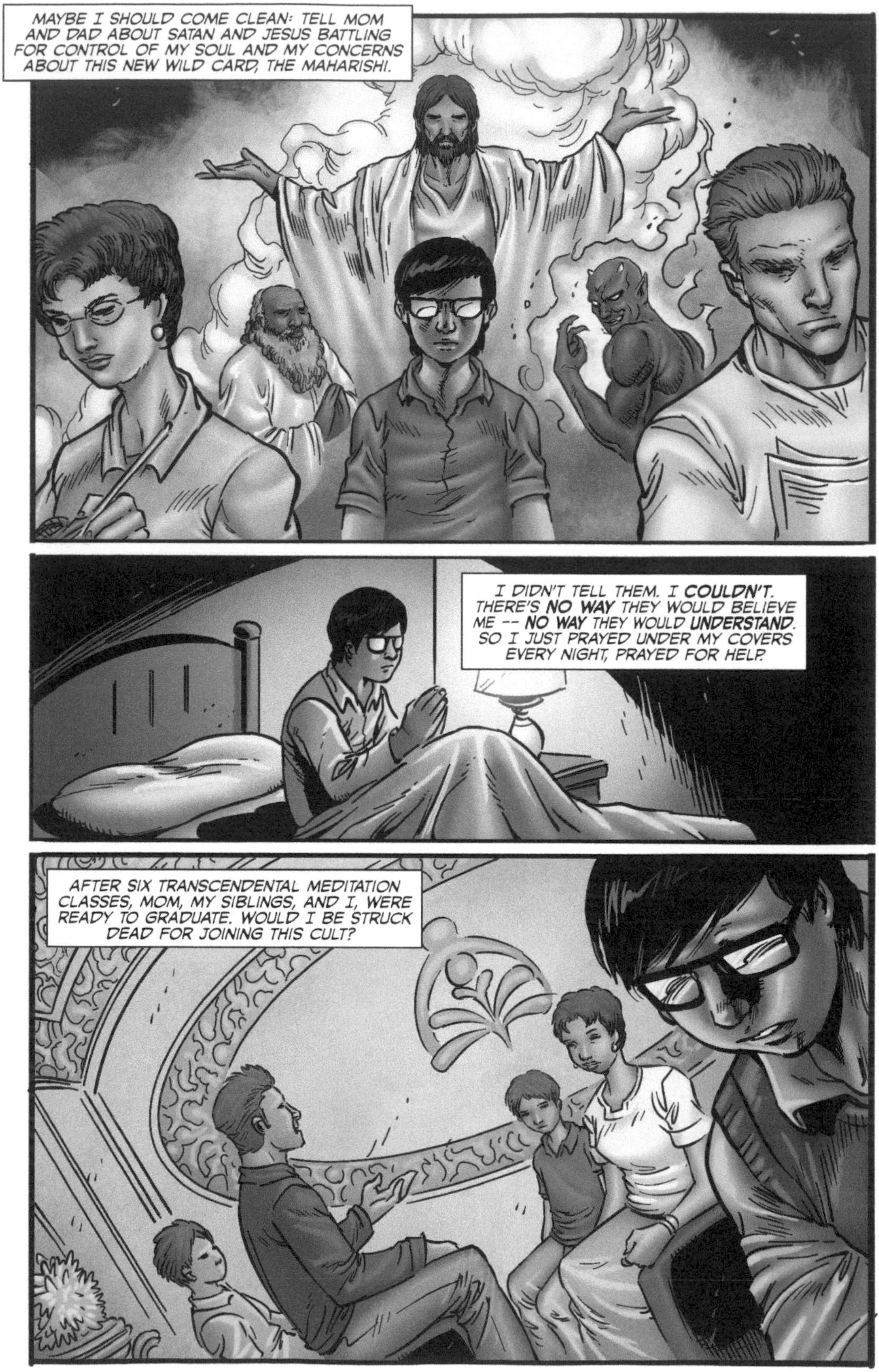
MAYBE I SHOULD COME CLEAN: TELL MOM AND DAD ABOUT SATAN AND JESUS BATTLING FOR CONTROL OF MY SOUL AND MY CONCERNS ABOUT THIS NEW WILD CARD, THE MAHARISHI.
I DIDN'T TELL THEM. I **COULDN'T**. THERE'S **NO WAY** THEY WOULD BELIEVE ME -- **NO WAY** THEY WOULD **UNDERSTAND**. SO I JUST PRAYED UNDER MY COVERS EVERY NIGHT, PRAYED FOR HELP.
AFTER SIX TRANSCENDENTAL MEDITATION CLASSES, MOM, MY SIBLINGS, AND I, WERE READY TO GRADUATE. WOULD I BE STRUCK DEAD FOR JOINING THIS CULT?

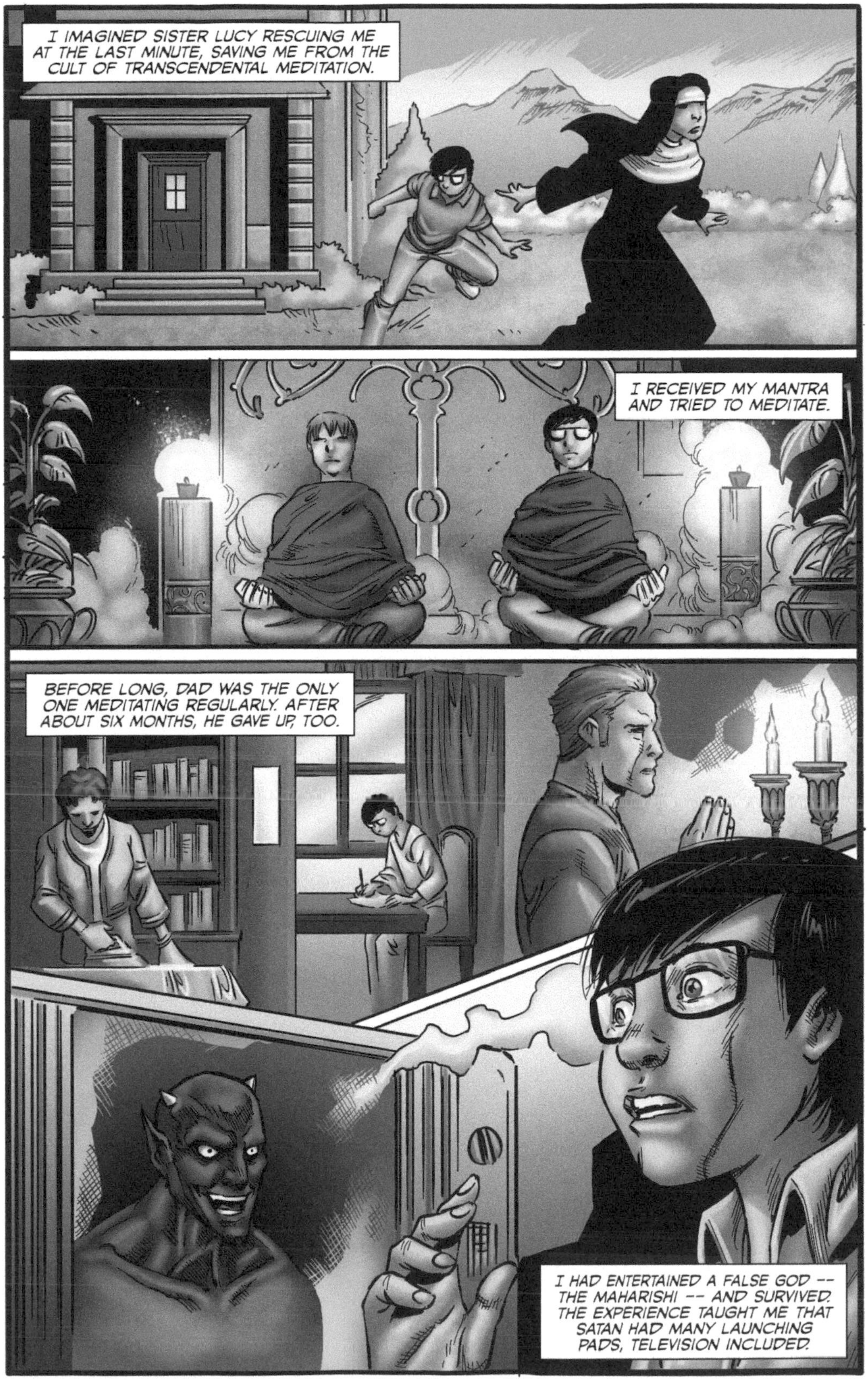
I IMAGINED SISTER LUCY RESCUING ME AT THE LAST MINUTE, SAVING ME FROM THE CULT OF TRANSCENDENTAL MEDITATION.
I RECEIVED MY MANTRA AND TRIED TO MEDITATE.
BEFORE LONG, DAD WAS THE ONLY ONE MEDITATING REGULARLY. AFTER ABOUT SIX MONTHS, HE GAVE UP, TOO.
I HAD ENTERTAINED A FALSE GOD -- THE MAHARISHI -- AND SURVIVED. THE EXPERIENCE TAUGHT ME THAT SATAN HAD MANY LAUNCHING PADS, TELEVISION INCLUDED.

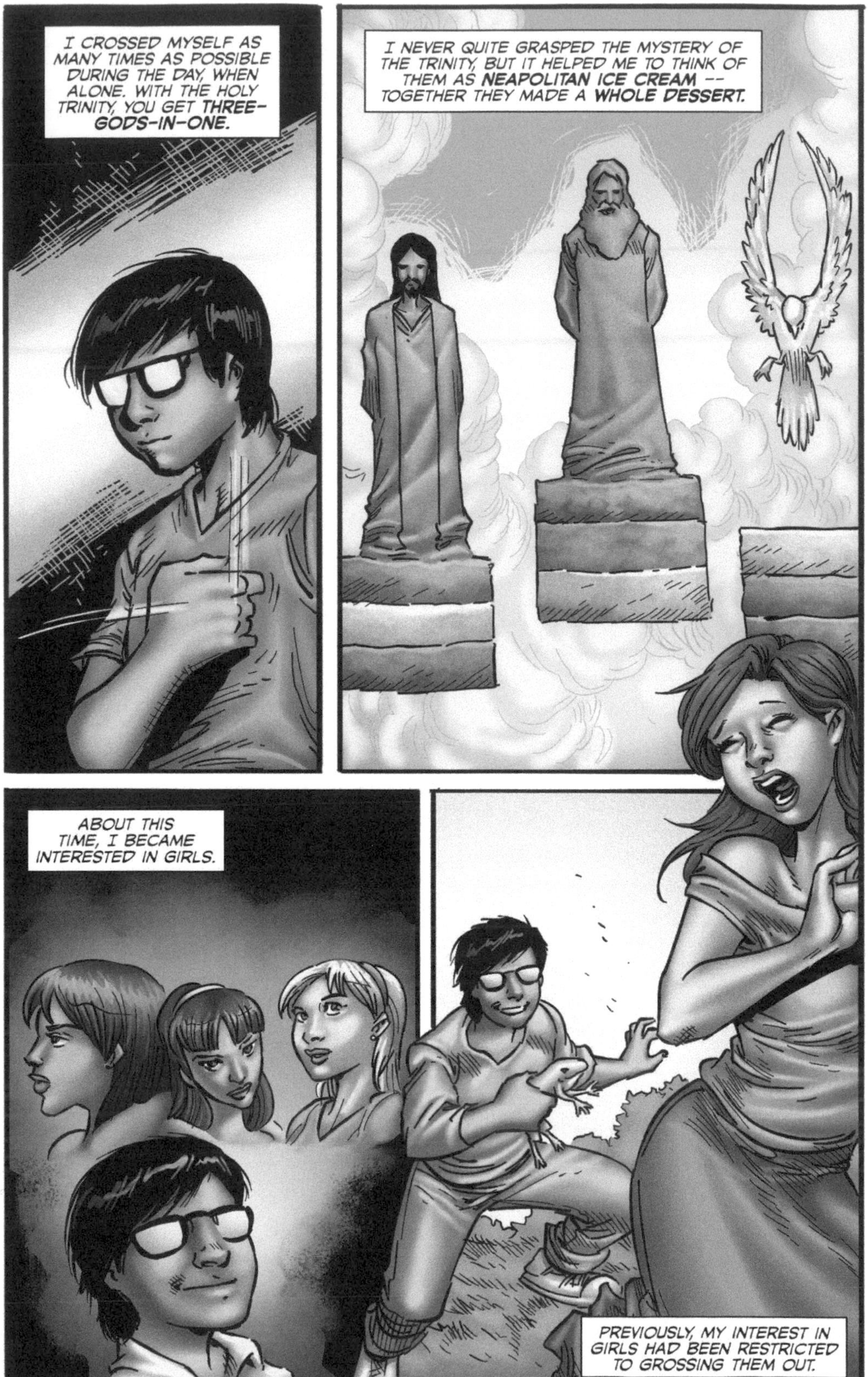

I CROSSED MYSELF AS MANY TIMES AS POSSIBLE DURING THE DAY, WHEN ALONE. WITH THE HOLY TRINITY, YOU GET **THREE-GODS-IN-ONE.**
I NEVER QUITE GRASPED THE MYSTERY OF THE TRINITY, BUT IT HELPED ME TO THINK OF THEM AS **NEAPOLITAN ICE CREAM** -- TOGETHER THEY MADE A **WHOLE DESSERT.**
ABOUT THIS TIME, I BECAME INTERESTED IN GIRLS.
PREVIOUSLY, MY INTEREST IN GIRLS HAD BEEN RESTRICTED TO GROSSING THEM OUT.

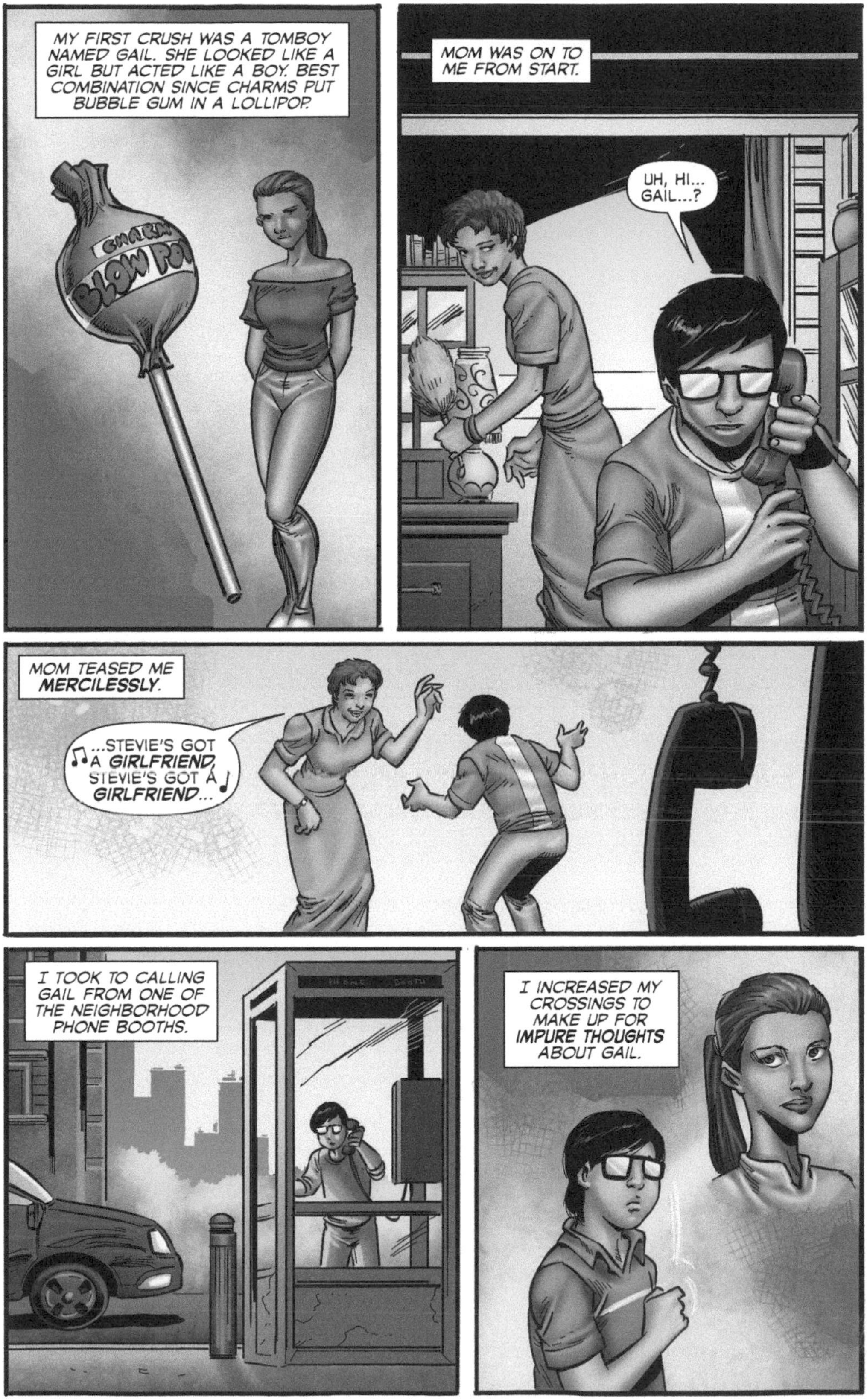

MY FIRST CRUSH WAS A TOMBOY NAMED GAIL. SHE LOOKED LIKE A GIRL BUT ACTED LIKE A BOY. BEST COMBINATION SINCE CHARMS PUT BUBBLE GUM IN A LOLLIPOP.
MOM WAS ON TO ME FROM START.
UH, HI... GAIL...?
MOM TEASED ME **MERCILESSLY**.
♫ ...STEVIE'S GOT A **GIRLFRIEND**, STEVIE'S GOT A **GIRLFRIEND**... ♩
I TOOK TO CALLING GAIL FROM ONE OF THE NEIGHBORHOOD PHONE BOOTHS.
I INCREASED MY CROSSINGS TO MAKE UP FOR **IMPURE THOUGHTS** ABOUT GAIL.

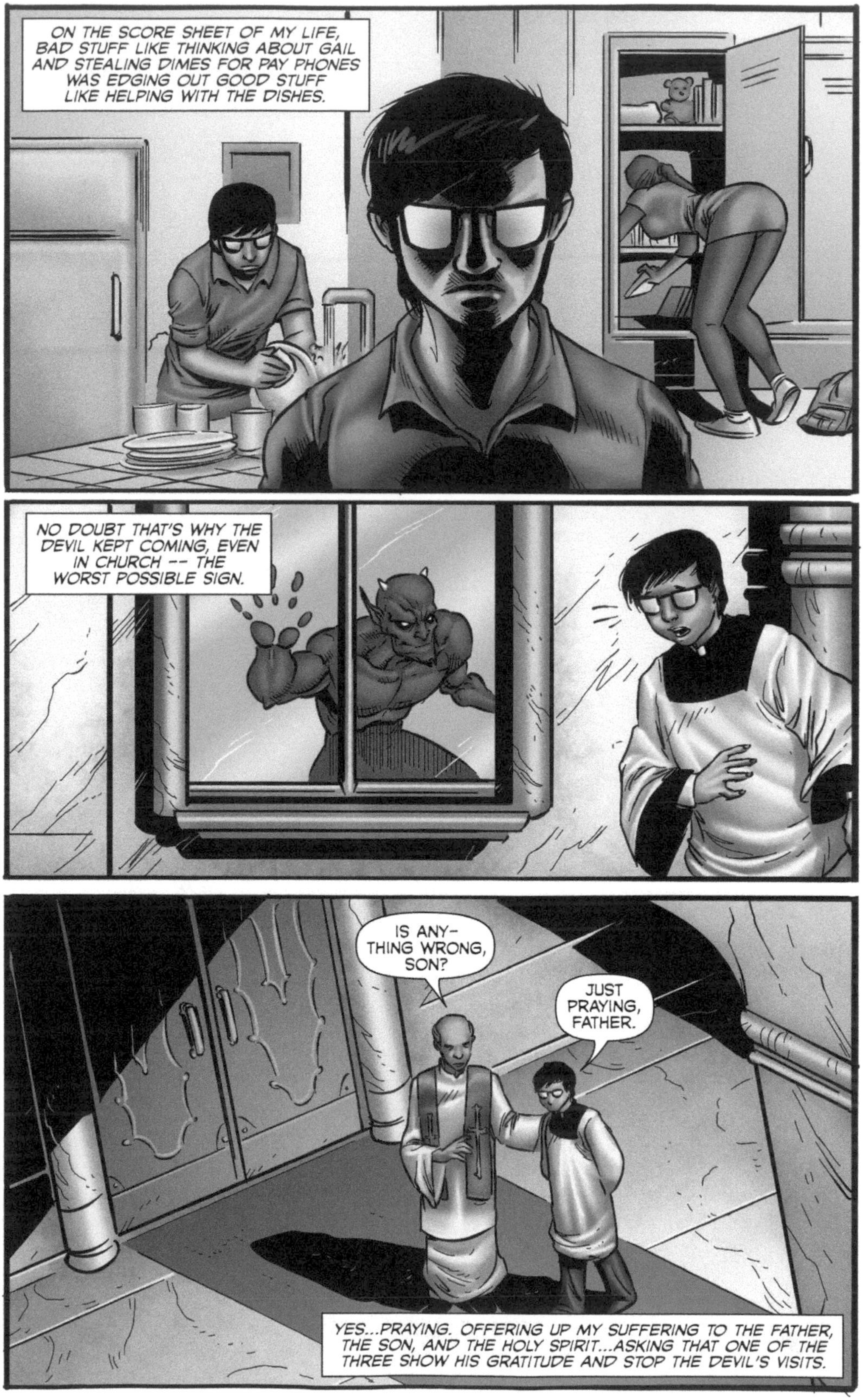
ON THE SCORE SHEET OF MY LIFE, BAD STUFF LIKE THINKING ABOUT GAIL AND STEALING DIMES FOR PAY PHONES WAS EDGING OUT GOOD STUFF LIKE HELPING WITH THE DISHES.
NO DOUBT THAT'S WHY THE DEVIL KEPT COMING, EVEN IN CHURCH -- THE WORST POSSIBLE SIGN.
IS ANY-THING WRONG, SON?
JUST PRAYING, FATHER.
YES...PRAYING. OFFERING UP MY SUFFERING TO THE FATHER, THE SON, AND THE HOLY SPIRIT...ASKING THAT ONE OF THE THREE SHOW HIS GRATITUDE AND STOP THE DEVIL'S VISITS.

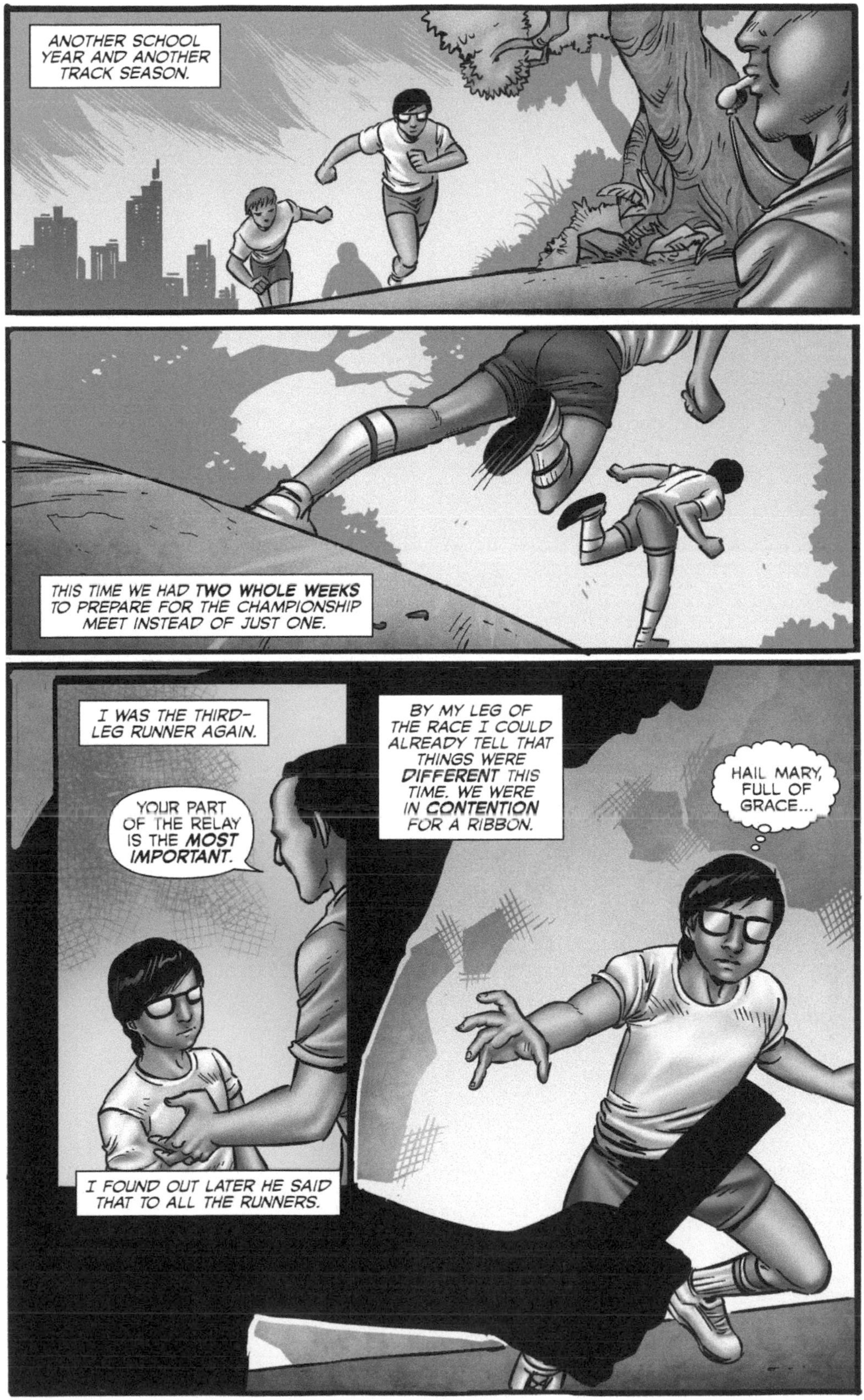
ANOTHER SCHOOL YEAR AND ANOTHER TRACK SEASON.
THIS TIME WE HAD **TWO WHOLE WEEKS** TO PREPARE FOR THE CHAMPIONSHIP MEET INSTEAD OF JUST ONE.
I WAS THE THIRD-LEG RUNNER AGAIN.
YOUR PART OF THE RELAY IS THE ***MOST IMPORTANT***.
I FOUND OUT LATER HE SAID THAT TO ALL THE RUNNERS.
BY MY LEG OF THE RACE I COULD ALREADY TELL THAT THINGS WERE ***DIFFERENT*** THIS TIME. WE WERE IN **CONTENTION** FOR A RIBBON.
HAIL MARY, FULL OF GRACE...

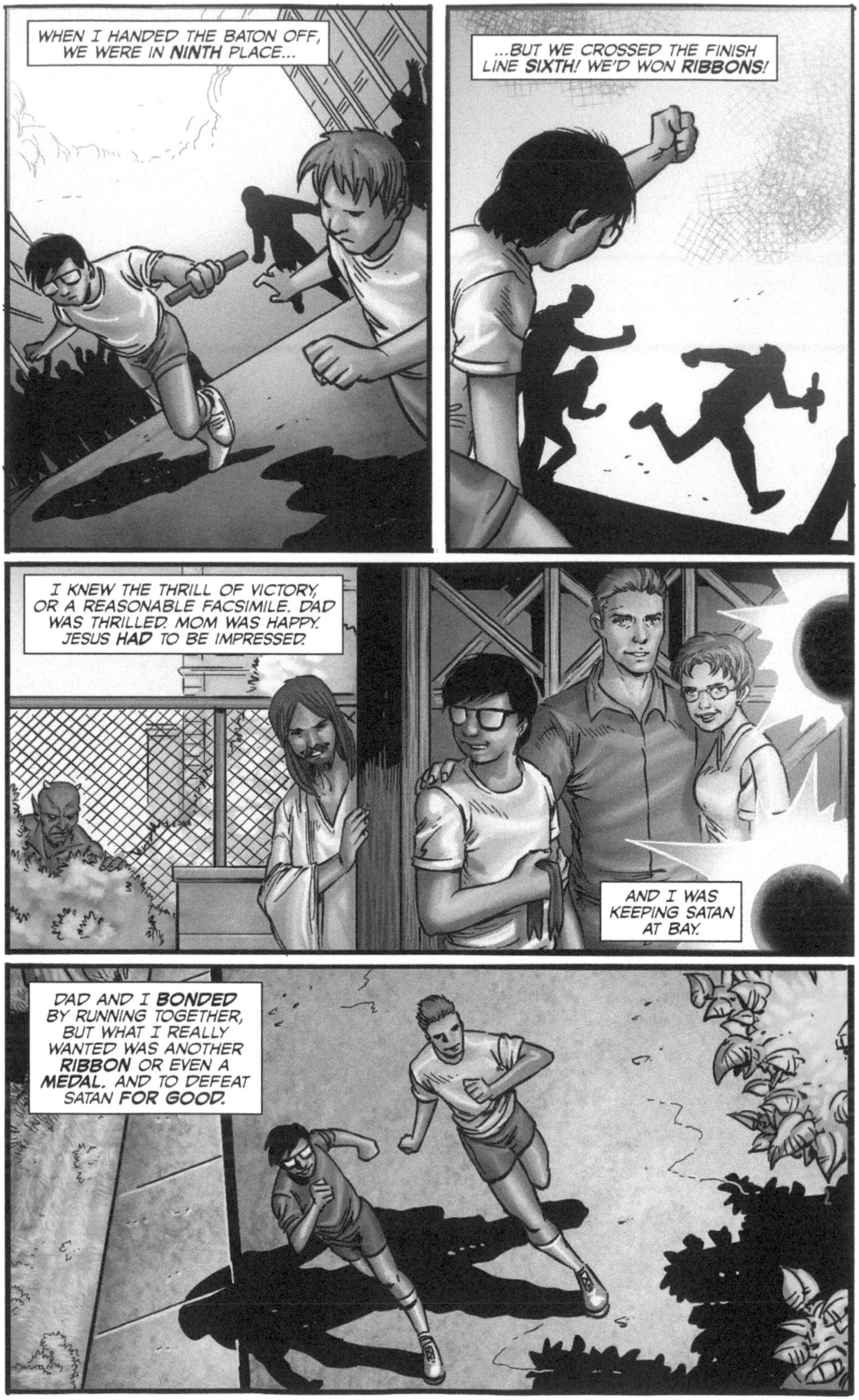
WHEN I HANDED THE BATON OFF, WE WERE IN NINTH PLACE...
...BUT WE CROSSED THE FINISH LINE SIXTH! WE'D WON RIBBONS!
I KNEW THE THRILL OF VICTORY, OR A REASONABLE FACSIMILE. DAD WAS THRILLED. MOM WAS HAPPY. JESUS HAD TO BE IMPRESSED.
AND I WAS KEEPING SATAN AT BAY.
DAD AND I BONDED BY RUNNING TOGETHER, BUT WHAT I REALLY WANTED WAS ANOTHER RIBBON OR EVEN A MEDAL. AND TO DEFEAT SATAN FOR GOOD.

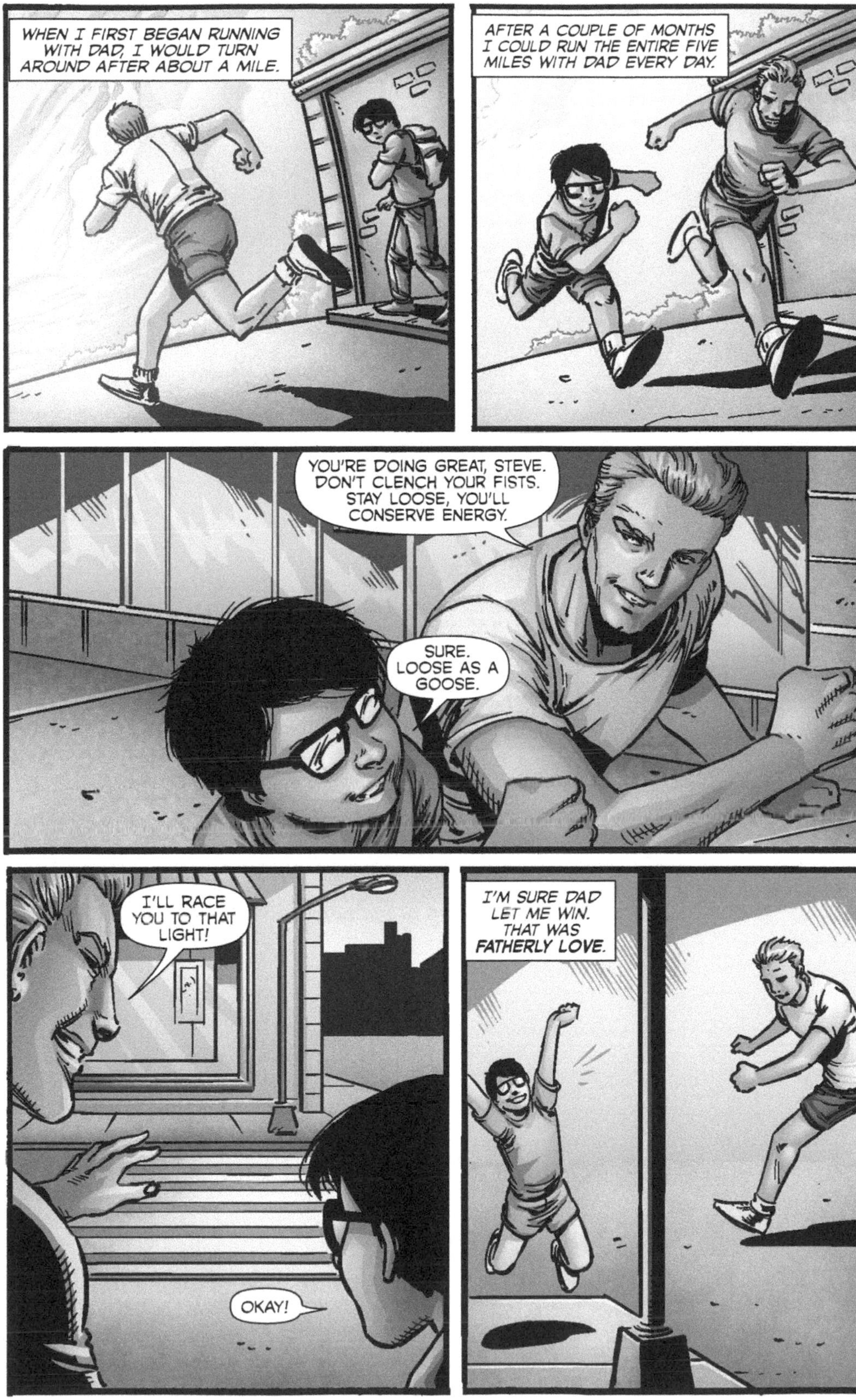
WHEN I FIRST BEGAN RUNNING WITH DAD, I WOULD TURN AROUND AFTER ABOUT A MILE.
AFTER A COUPLE OF MONTHS I COULD RUN THE ENTIRE FIVE MILES WITH DAD EVERY DAY.
YOU'RE DOING GREAT, STEVE. DON'T CLENCH YOUR FISTS. STAY LOOSE, YOU'LL CONSERVE ENERGY.
SURE. LOOSE AS A GOOSE.
I'LL RACE YOU TO THAT LIGHT!
OKAY!
I'M SURE DAD LET ME WIN. THAT WAS FATHERLY LOVE.

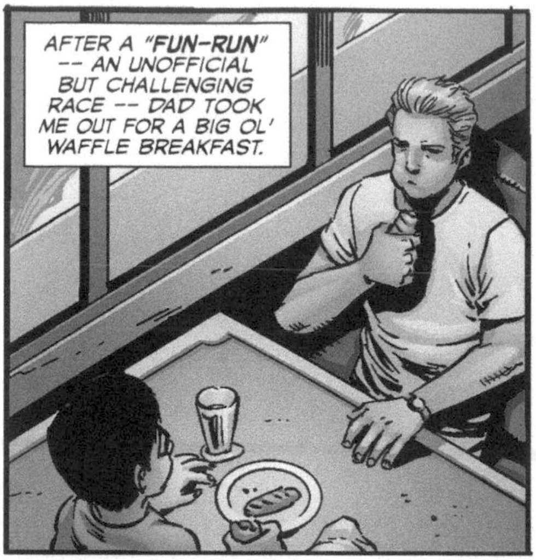
AFTER A "**FUN-RUN**" -- AN UNOFFICIAL BUT CHALLENGING RACE -- DAD TOOK ME OUT FOR A BIG OL' WAFFLE BREAKFAST.

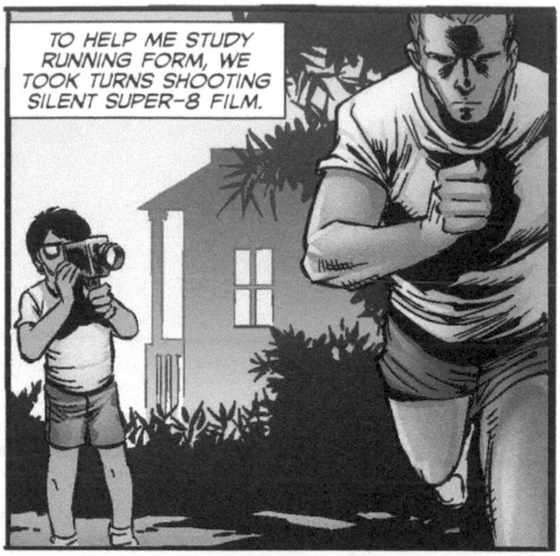
TO HELP ME STUDY RUNNING FORM, WE TOOK TURNS SHOOTING SILENT SUPER-8 FILM.

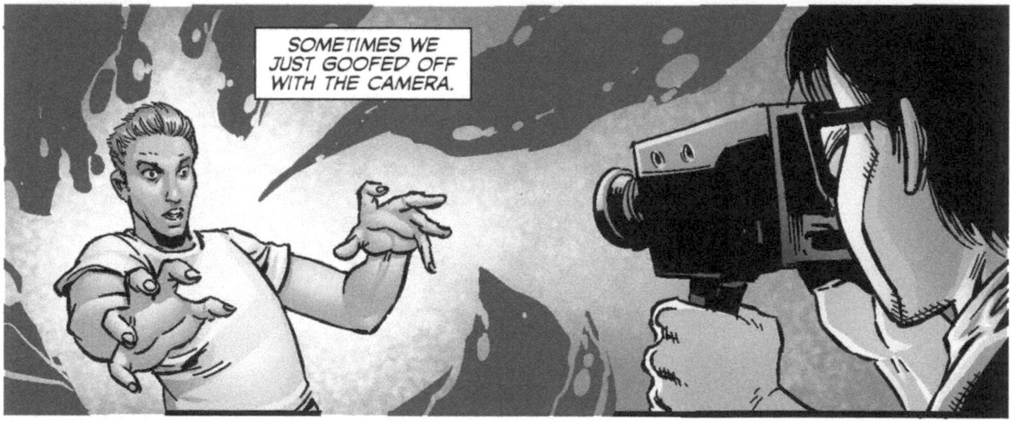
SOMETIMES WE JUST GOOFED OFF WITH THE CAMERA.

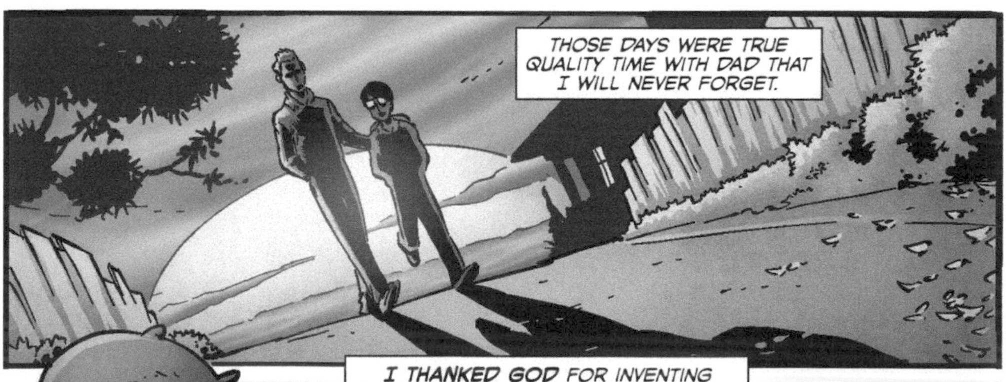
THOSE DAYS WERE TRUE QUALITY TIME WITH DAD THAT I WILL NEVER FORGET.

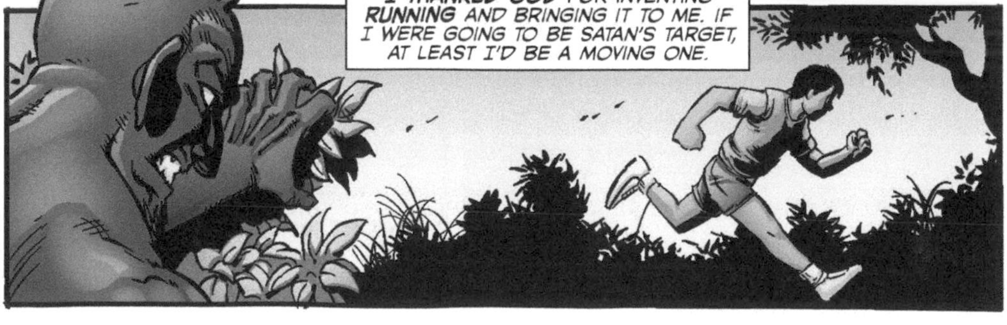
I THANKED GOD FOR INVENTING **RUNNING** AND BRINGING IT TO ME. IF I WERE GOING TO BE SATAN'S TARGET, AT LEAST I'D BE A MOVING ONE.

SOMETIMES DAD WOULD TAKE ME TO DASE'S PLACE.

DASE'S PLACE

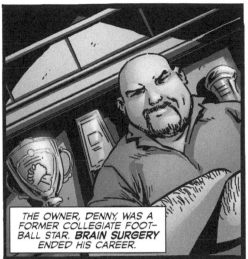

THE OWNER, DENNY, WAS A FORMER COLLEGIATE FOOT-BALL STAR. **BRAIN SURGERY** ENDED HIS CAREER.

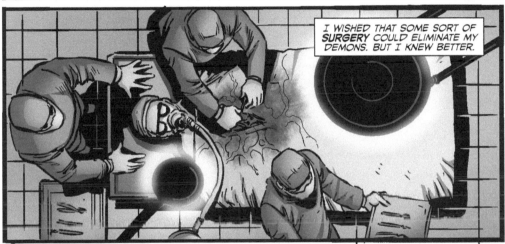

I WISHED THAT SOME SORT OF **SURGERY** COULD ELIMINATE MY DEMONS. BUT I KNEW BETTER.

THE SPORT OF CHOICE AT DASE'S PLACE WAS ARM WRESTLING.

DENNY ONCE BROKE A GUY'S ARM IN A COMPETITION.

COOL!! I WISH I'D SEEN THAT!

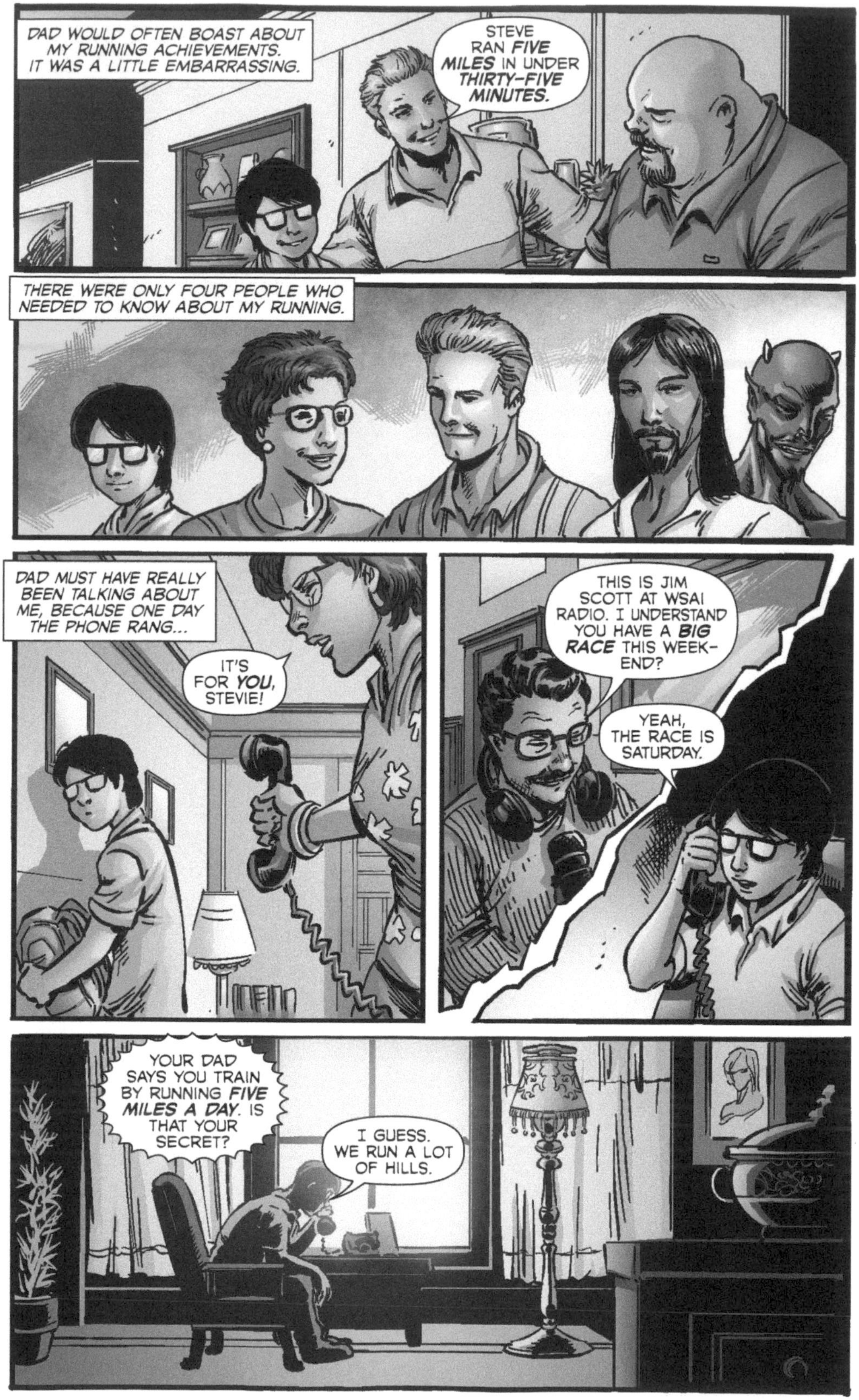
DAD WOULD OFTEN BOAST ABOUT MY RUNNING ACHIEVEMENTS. IT WAS A LITTLE EMBARRASSING.
STEVE RAN FIVE MILES IN UNDER THIRTY-FIVE MINUTES.
THERE WERE ONLY FOUR PEOPLE WHO NEEDED TO KNOW ABOUT MY RUNNING.
DAD MUST HAVE REALLY BEEN TALKING ABOUT ME, BECAUSE ONE DAY THE PHONE RANG...
IT'S FOR YOU, STEVIE!
THIS IS JIM SCOTT AT WSAI RADIO. I UNDERSTAND YOU HAVE A BIG RACE THIS WEEK-END?
YEAH, THE RACE IS SATURDAY.
YOUR DAD SAYS YOU TRAIN BY RUNNING FIVE MILES A DAY. IS THAT YOUR SECRET?
I GUESS. WE RUN A LOT OF HILLS.

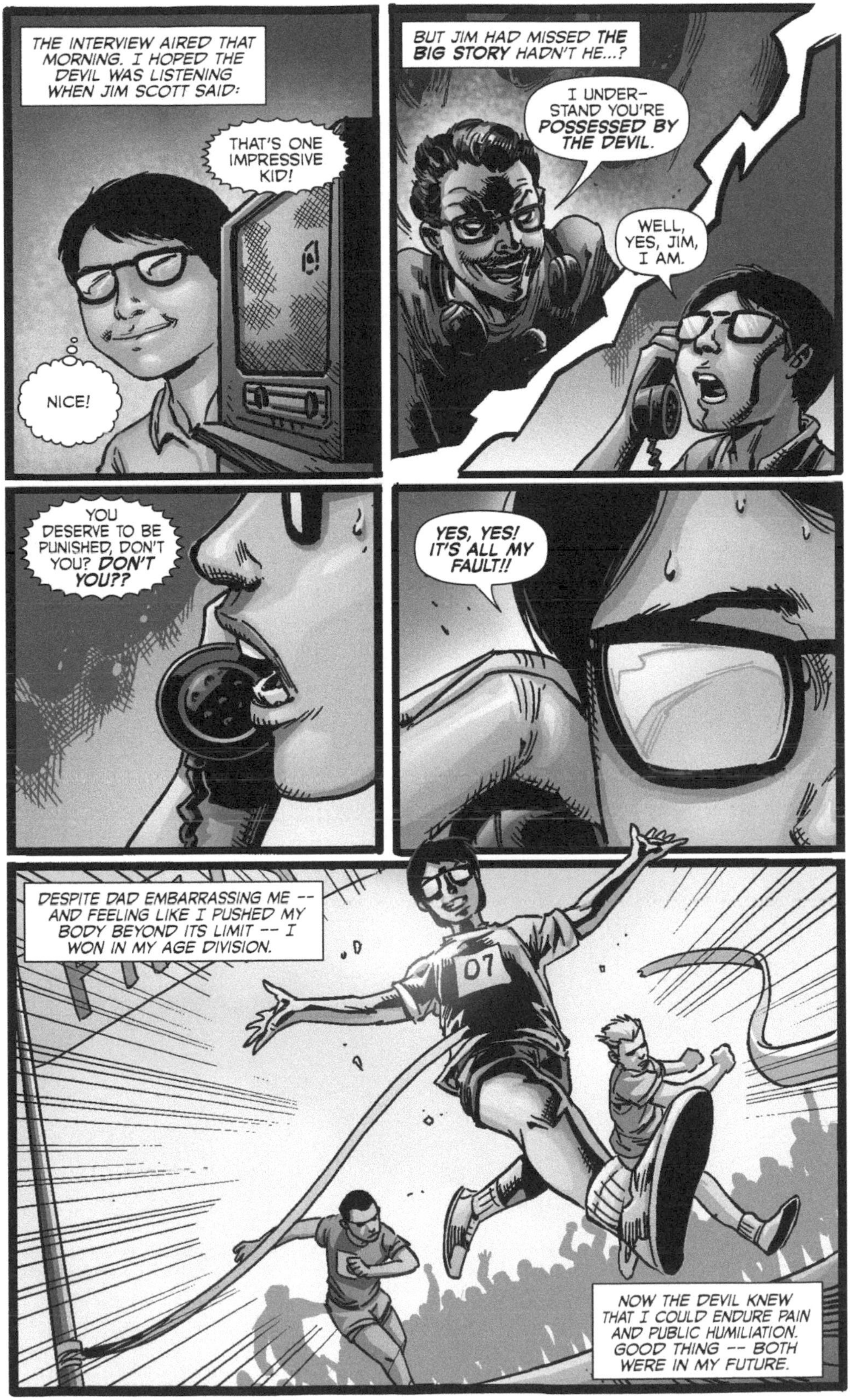
THE INTERVIEW AIRED THAT MORNING. I HOPED THE DEVIL WAS LISTENING WHEN JIM SCOTT SAID:
THAT'S ONE IMPRESSIVE KID!
NICE!
BUT JIM HAD MISSED THE BIG STORY HADN'T HE...?
I UNDER-STAND YOU'RE POSSESSED BY THE DEVIL.
WELL, YES, JIM, I AM.
YOU DESERVE TO BE PUNISHED, DON'T YOU? DON'T YOU??
YES, YES! IT'S ALL MY FAULT!!
DESPITE DAD EMBARRASSING ME -- AND FEELING LIKE I PUSHED MY BODY BEYOND ITS LIMIT -- I WON IN MY AGE DIVISION.
07
NOW THE DEVIL KNEW THAT I COULD ENDURE PAIN AND PUBLIC HUMILIATION. GOOD THING -- BOTH WERE IN MY FUTURE.

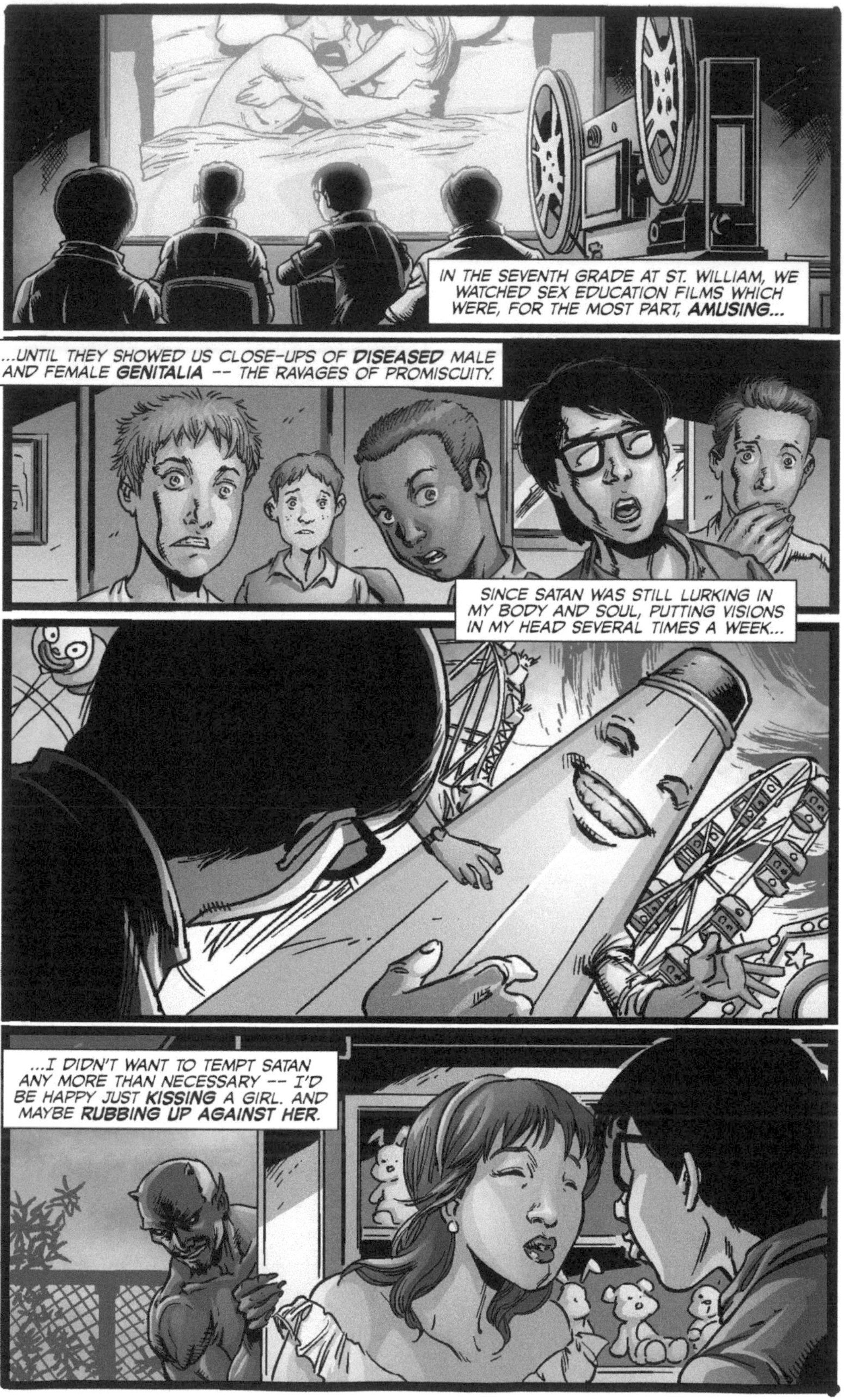
IN THE SEVENTH GRADE AT ST. WILLIAM, WE WATCHED SEX EDUCATION FILMS WHICH WERE, FOR THE MOST PART, **AMUSING...**
...UNTIL THEY SHOWED US CLOSE-UPS OF **DISEASED** MALE AND FEMALE **GENITALIA** -- THE RAVAGES OF PROMISCUITY.
SINCE SATAN WAS STILL LURKING IN MY BODY AND SOUL, PUTTING VISIONS IN MY HEAD SEVERAL TIMES A WEEK...
...I DIDN'T WANT TO TEMPT SATAN ANY MORE THAN NECESSARY -- I'D BE HAPPY JUST **KISSING** A GIRL. AND MAYBE **RUBBING UP AGAINST HER.**

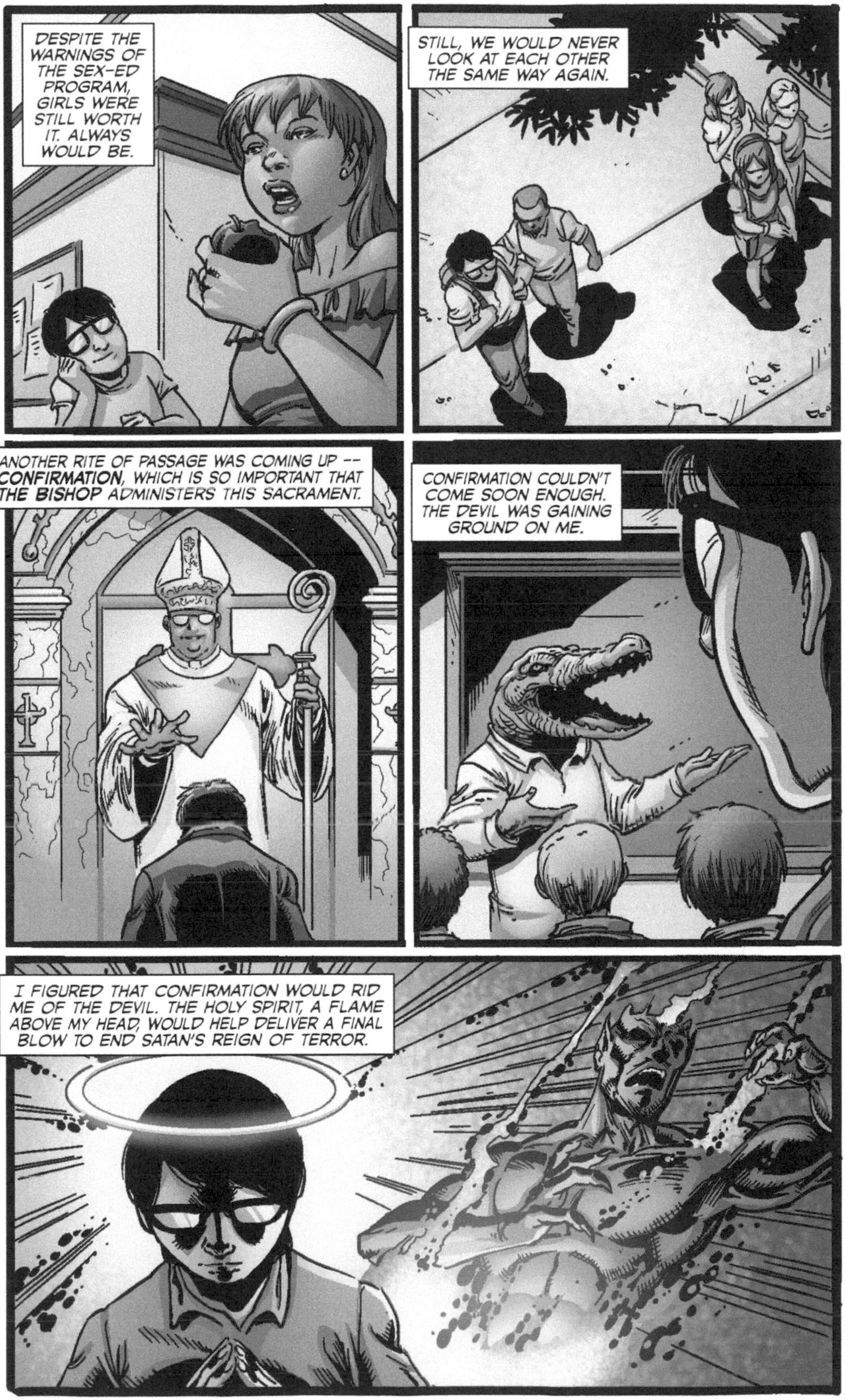
DESPITE THE WARNINGS OF THE SEX-ED PROGRAM, GIRLS WERE STILL WORTH IT. ALWAYS WOULD BE.
STILL, WE WOULD NEVER LOOK AT EACH OTHER THE SAME WAY AGAIN.
ANOTHER RITE OF PASSAGE WAS COMING UP -- **CONFIRMATION**, WHICH IS SO IMPORTANT THAT **THE BISHOP** ADMINISTERS THIS SACRAMENT.
CONFIRMATION COULDN'T COME SOON ENOUGH. THE DEVIL WAS GAINING GROUND ON ME.
I FIGURED THAT CONFIRMATION WOULD RID ME OF THE DEVIL. THE HOLY SPIRIT, A FLAME ABOVE MY HEAD, WOULD HELP DELIVER A FINAL BLOW TO END SATAN'S REIGN OF TERROR.

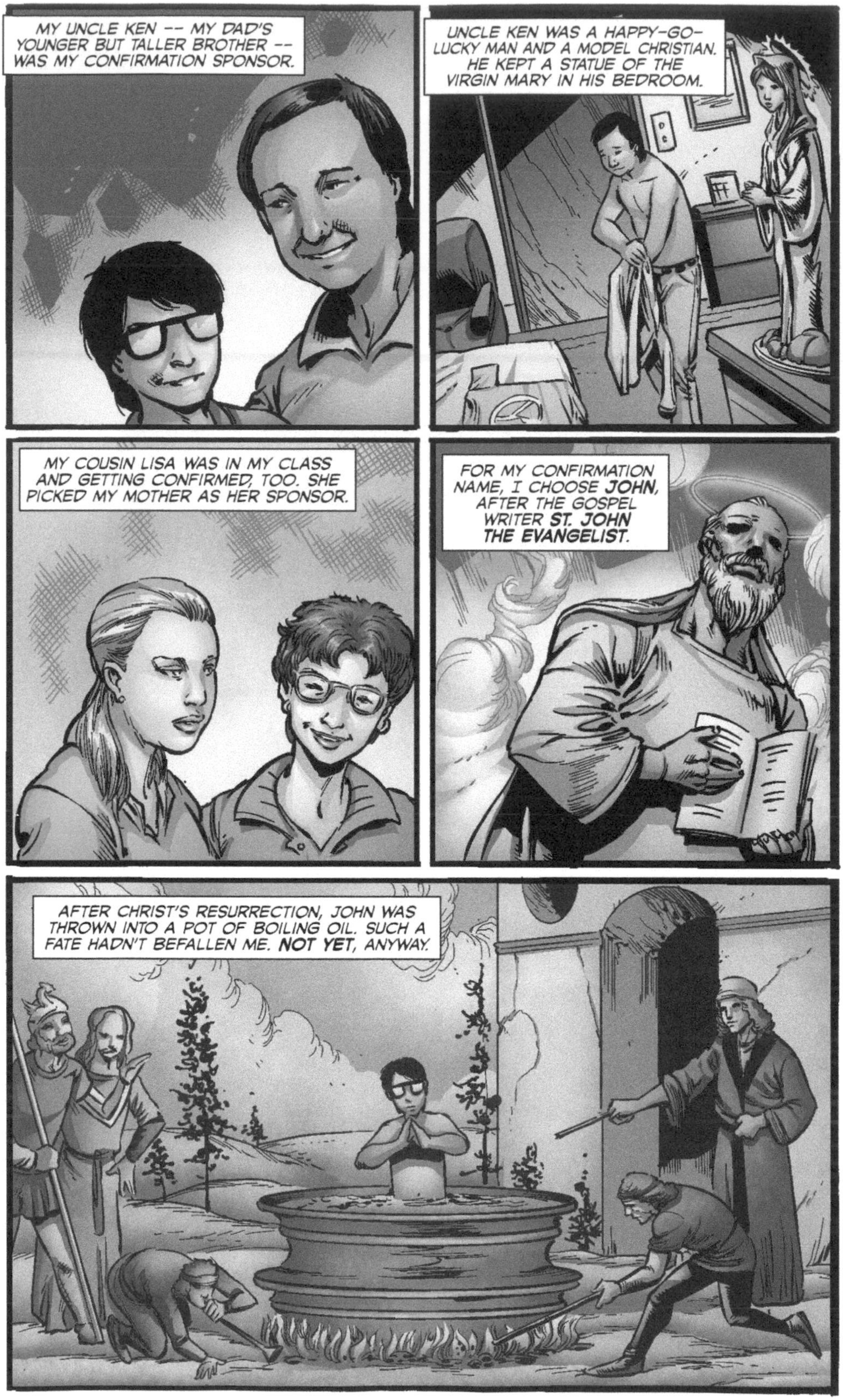
MY UNCLE KEN -- MY DAD'S YOUNGER BUT TALLER BROTHER -- WAS MY CONFIRMATION SPONSOR.
UNCLE KEN WAS A HAPPY-GO-LUCKY MAN AND A MODEL CHRISTIAN. HE KEPT A STATUE OF THE VIRGIN MARY IN HIS BEDROOM.
MY COUSIN LISA WAS IN MY CLASS AND GETTING CONFIRMED, TOO. SHE PICKED MY MOTHER AS HER SPONSOR.
FOR MY CONFIRMATION NAME, I CHOOSE **JOHN**, AFTER THE GOSPEL WRITER **ST. JOHN THE EVANGELIST**.
AFTER CHRIST'S RESURRECTION, JOHN WAS THROWN INTO A POT OF BOILING OIL. SUCH A FATE HADN'T BEFALLEN ME. **NOT YET**, ANYWAY.

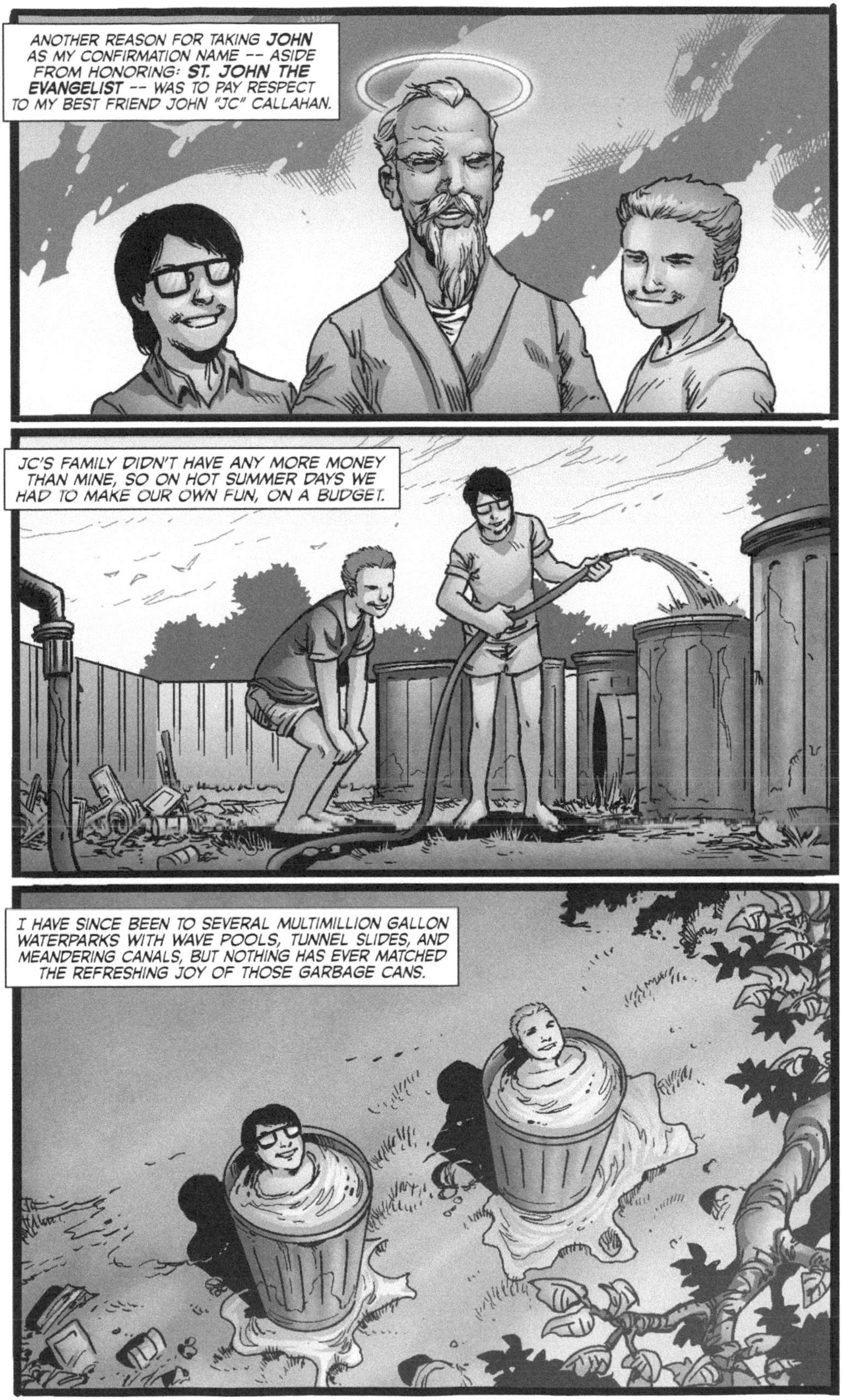
ANOTHER REASON FOR TAKING JOHN AS MY CONFIRMATION NAME -- ASIDE FROM HONORING: ST. JOHN THE EVANGELIST -- WAS TO PAY RESPECT TO MY BEST FRIEND JOHN "JC" CALLAHAN.
JC'S FAMILY DIDN'T HAVE ANY MORE MONEY THAN MINE, SO ON HOT SUMMER DAYS WE HAD TO MAKE OUR OWN FUN, ON A BUDGET.
I HAVE SINCE BEEN TO SEVERAL MULTIMILLION GALLON WATERPARKS WITH WAVE POOLS, TUNNEL SLIDES, AND MEANDERING CANALS, BUT NOTHING HAS EVER MATCHED THE REFRESHING JOY OF THOSE GARBAGE CANS.

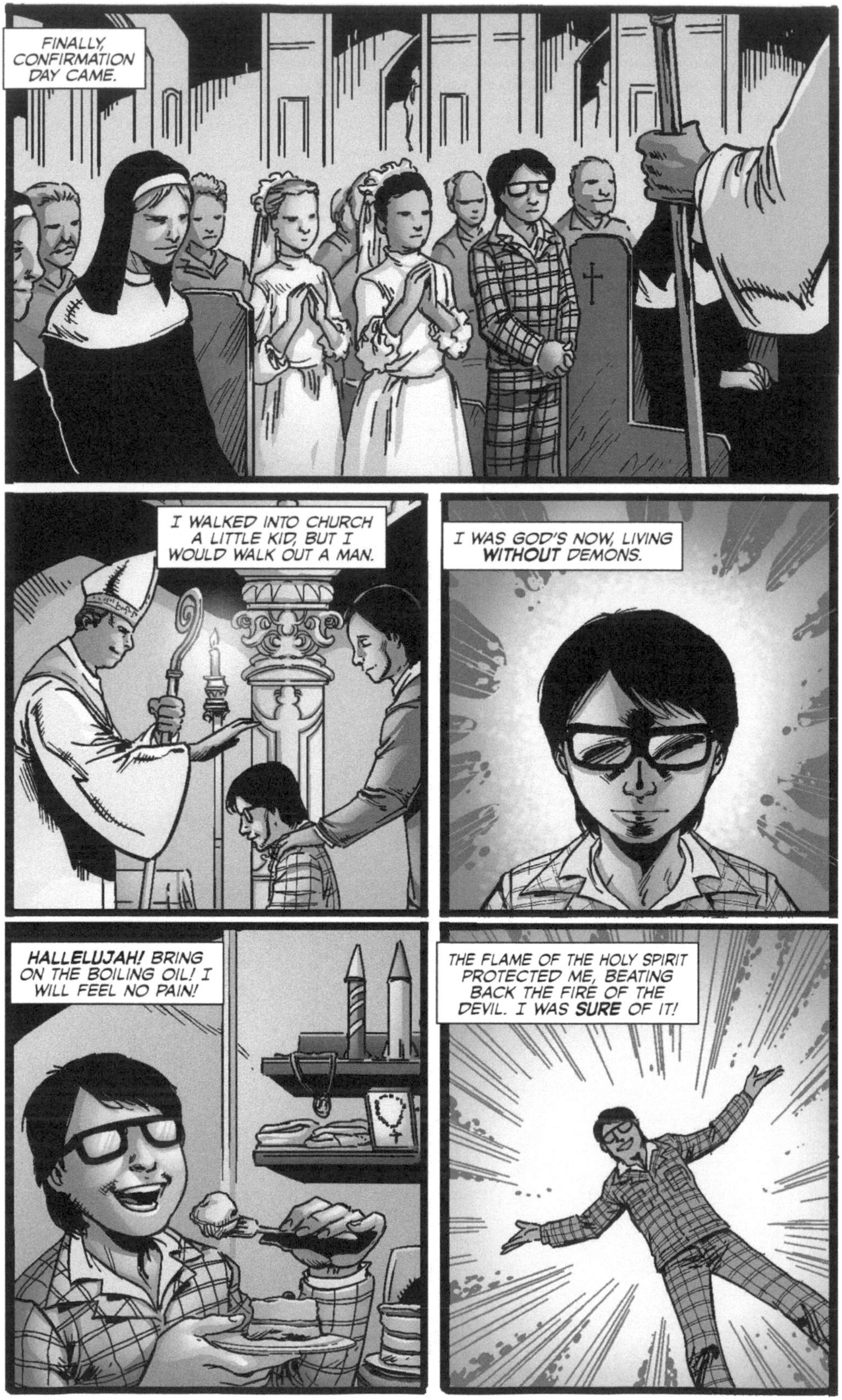
FINALLY, CONFIRMATION DAY CAME.
I WALKED INTO CHURCH A LITTLE KID, BUT I WOULD WALK OUT A MAN.
I WAS GOD'S NOW, LIVING WITHOUT DEMONS.
HALLELUJAH! BRING ON THE BOILING OIL! I WILL FEEL NO PAIN!
THE FLAME OF THE HOLY SPIRIT PROTECTED ME, BEATING BACK THE FIRE OF THE DEVIL. I WAS SURE OF IT!

IN MIND, BODY, AND SPIRIT, I WAS *GOLDEN...WINNING THE MILE RUN* AT THE FIRST TRACK MEET IN THE SEVENTH GRADE.

...GETTING MY *BEST GRADES EVER* IN CLASS...

...AND KEEPING *PRAYER, SERVICE,* AND *CONFESSION* IN HEAVY ROTATION.

BUT, LESS THAN A WEEK AFTER CONFIRMATION...

...I FOUND OUT IT WAS STILL *SATAN* WHO WAS SETTING THE PACE.

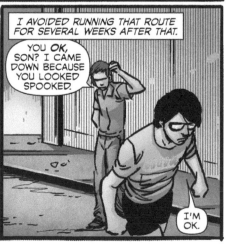

I AVOIDED RUNNING THAT ROUTE FOR SEVERAL WEEKS AFTER THAT.

YOU *OK,* SON? I CAME DOWN BECAUSE YOU LOOKED SPOOKED.

I'M OK.

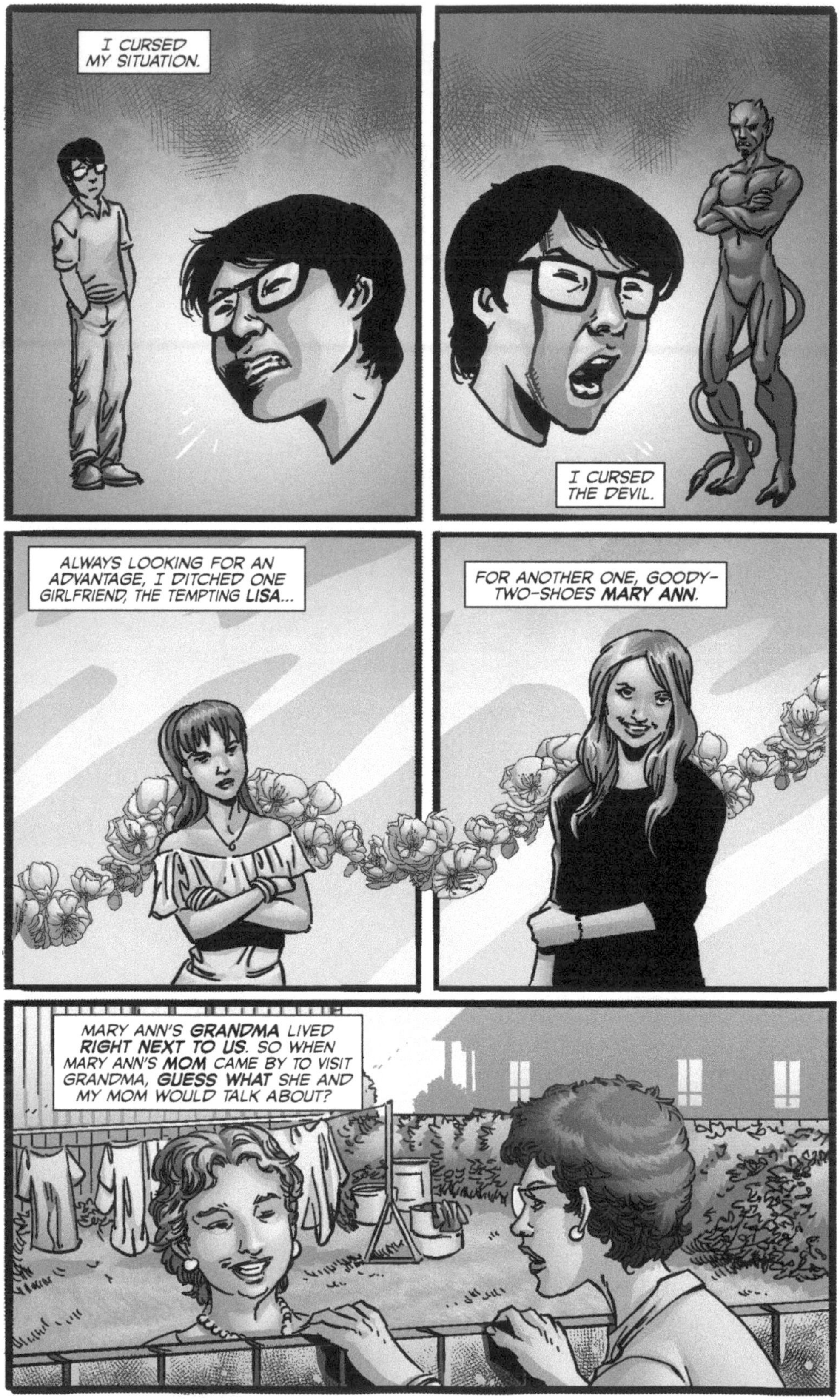
I CURSED MY SITUATION.
I CURSED THE DEVIL.
ALWAYS LOOKING FOR AN ADVANTAGE, I DITCHED ONE GIRLFRIEND, THE TEMPTING **LISA**...
FOR ANOTHER ONE, GOODY-TWO-SHOES **MARY ANN**.
MARY ANN'S **GRANDMA** LIVED **RIGHT NEXT TO US**. SO WHEN MARY ANN'S **MOM** CAME BY TO VISIT GRANDMA, **GUESS WHAT** SHE AND MY MOM WOULD TALK ABOUT?

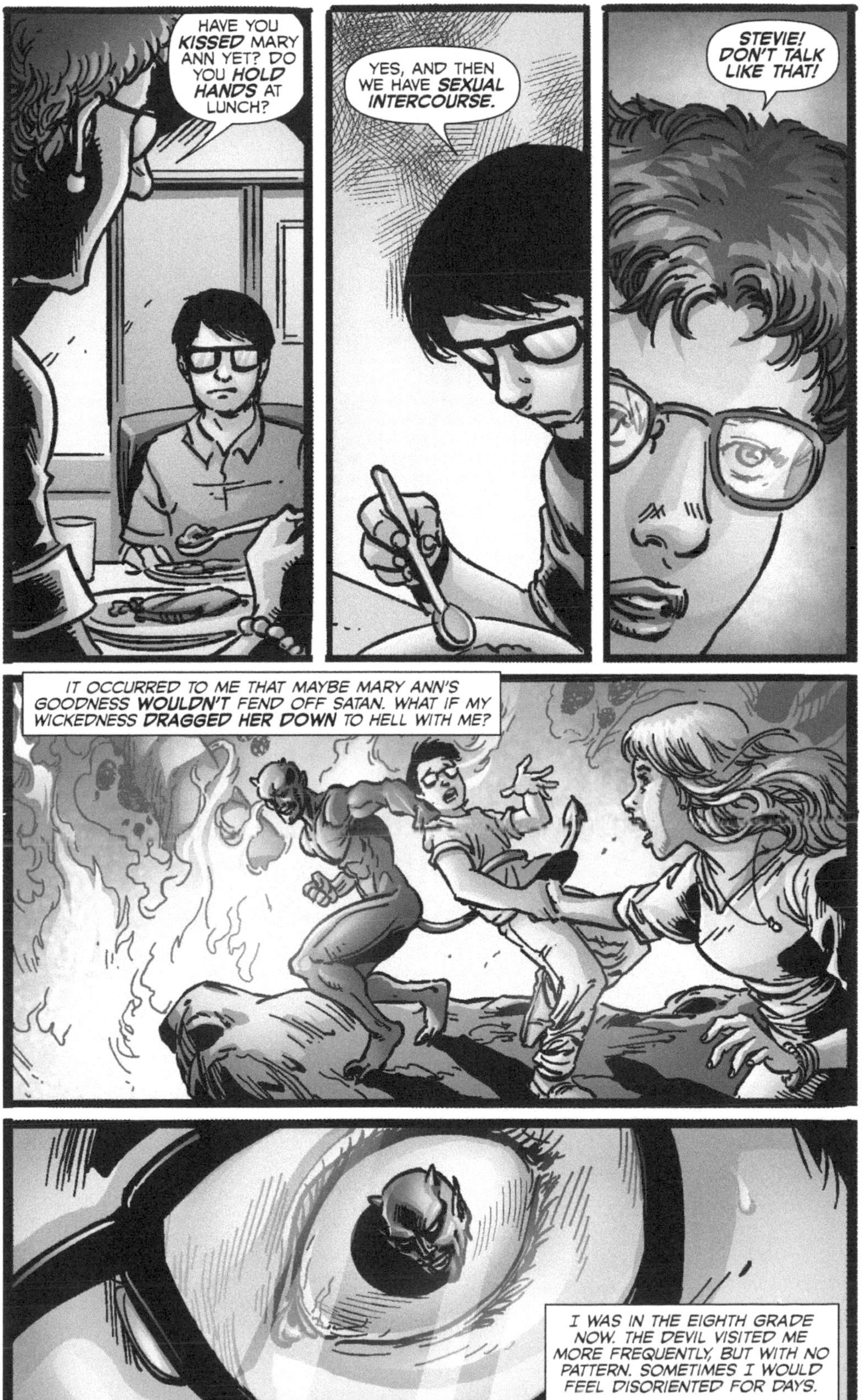
HAVE YOU KISSED MARY ANN YET? DO YOU HOLD HANDS AT LUNCH?
YES, AND THEN WE HAVE SEXUAL INTERCOURSE.
STEVIE! DON'T TALK LIKE THAT!
IT OCCURRED TO ME THAT MAYBE MARY ANN'S GOODNESS WOULDN'T FEND OFF SATAN. WHAT IF MY WICKEDNESS DRAGGED HER DOWN TO HELL WITH ME?
I WAS IN THE EIGHTH GRADE NOW. THE DEVIL VISITED ME MORE FREQUENTLY, BUT WITH NO PATTERN. SOMETIMES I WOULD FEEL DISORIENTED FOR DAYS.

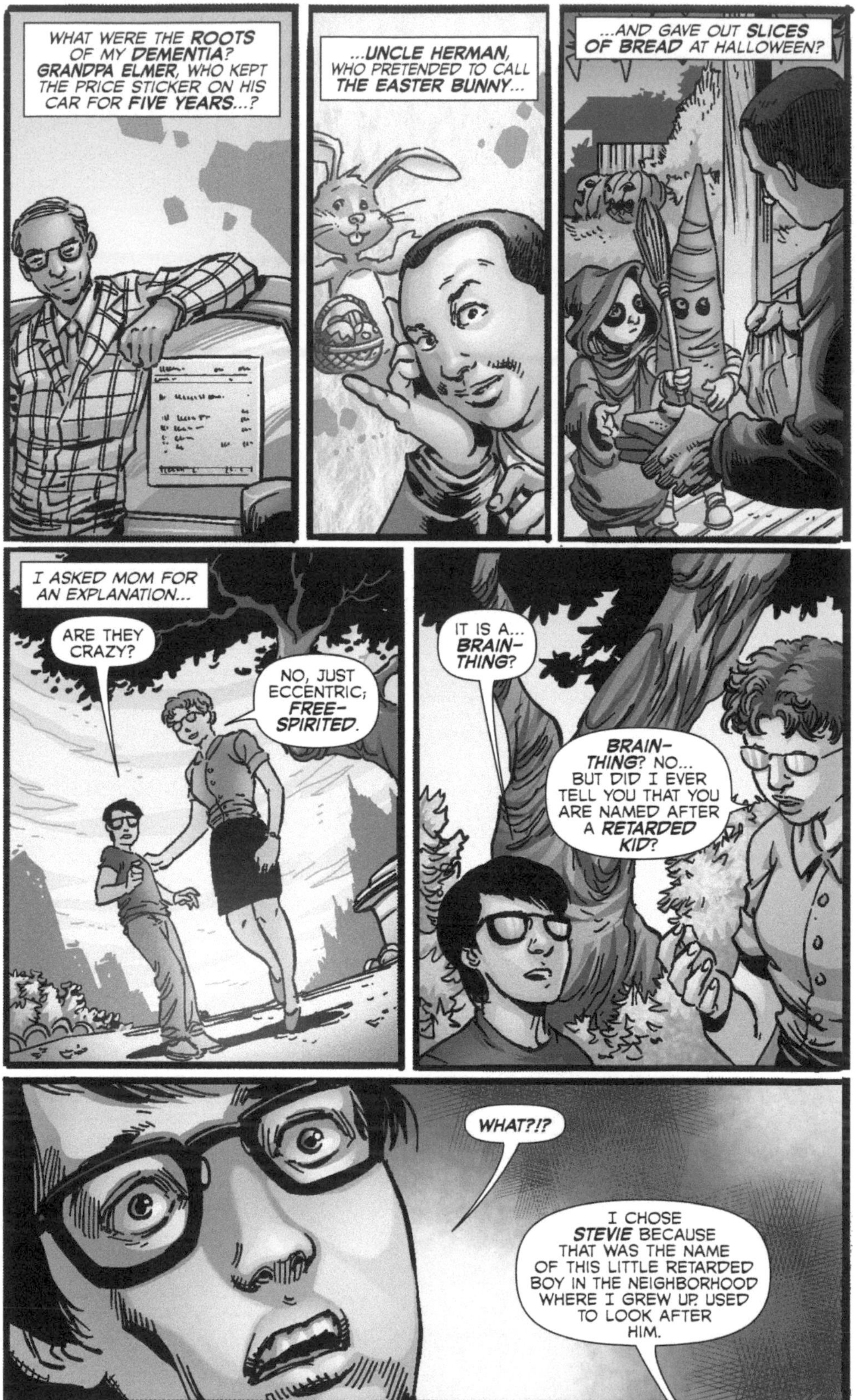
WHAT WERE THE ROOTS OF MY DEMENTIA? GRANDPA ELMER, WHO KEPT THE PRICE STICKER ON HIS CAR FOR FIVE YEARS...?
...UNCLE HERMAN, WHO PRETENDED TO CALL THE EASTER BUNNY...
...AND GAVE OUT SLICES OF BREAD AT HALLOWEEN?
I ASKED MOM FOR AN EXPLANATION...
ARE THEY CRAZY?
NO, JUST ECCENTRIC; FREE-SPIRITED.
IT IS A... BRAIN-THING?
BRAIN-THING? NO... BUT DID I EVER TELL YOU THAT YOU ARE NAMED AFTER A RETARDED KID?
WHAT?!?
I CHOSE STEVIE BECAUSE THAT WAS THE NAME OF THIS LITTLE RETARDED BOY IN THE NEIGHBORHOOD WHERE I GREW UP. I USED TO LOOK AFTER HIM.

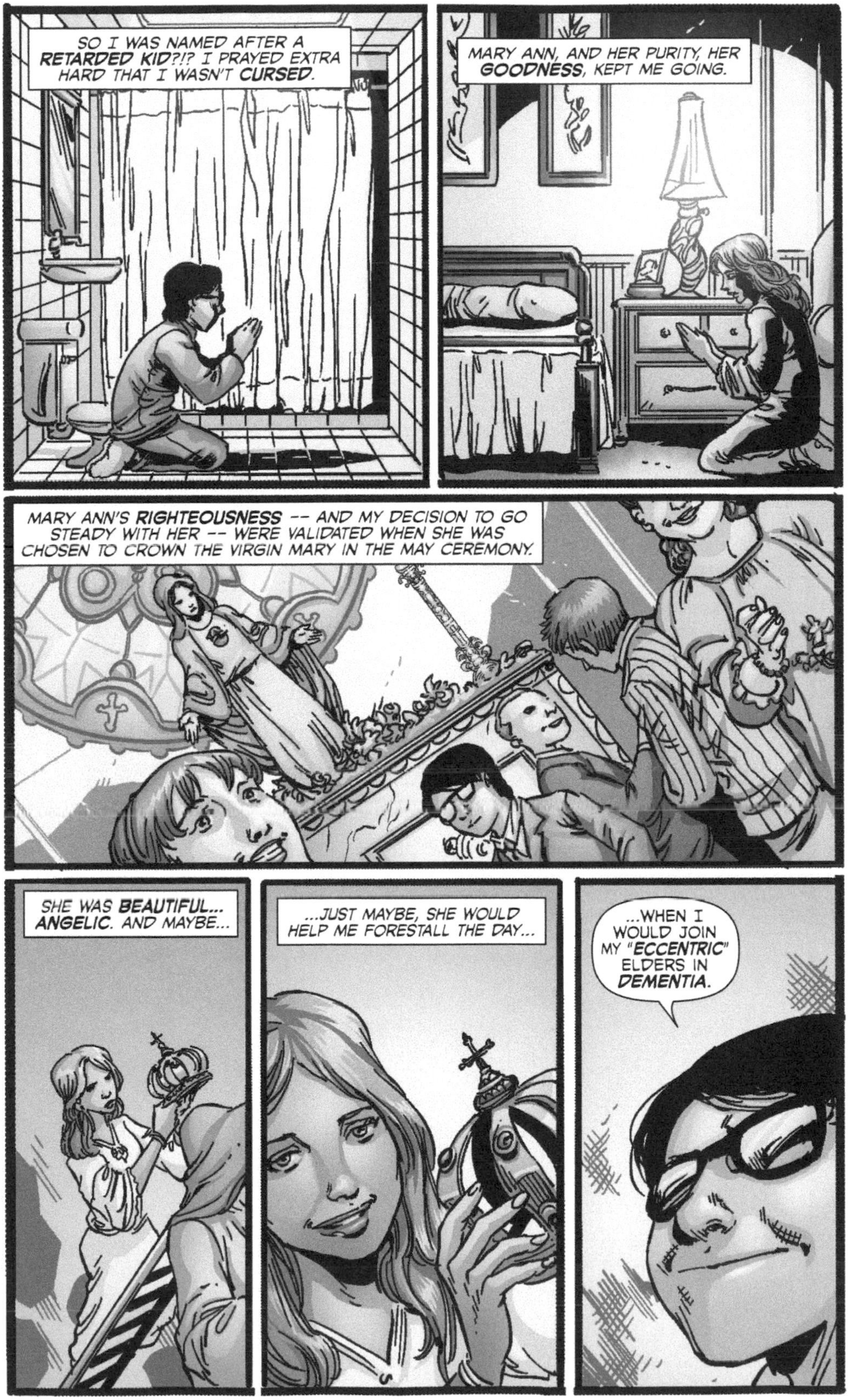
SO I WAS NAMED AFTER A RETARDED KID?!? I PRAYED EXTRA HARD THAT I WASN'T CURSED.
MARY ANN, AND HER PURITY, HER GOODNESS, KEPT ME GOING.
MARY ANN'S RIGHTEOUSNESS -- AND MY DECISION TO GO STEADY WITH HER -- WERE VALIDATED WHEN SHE WAS CHOSEN TO CROWN THE VIRGIN MARY IN THE MAY CEREMONY.
SHE WAS BEAUTIFUL... ANGELIC. AND MAYBE...
...JUST MAYBE, SHE WOULD HELP ME FORESTALL THE DAY...
...WHEN I WOULD JOIN MY "ECCENTRIC" ELDERS IN DEMENTIA.

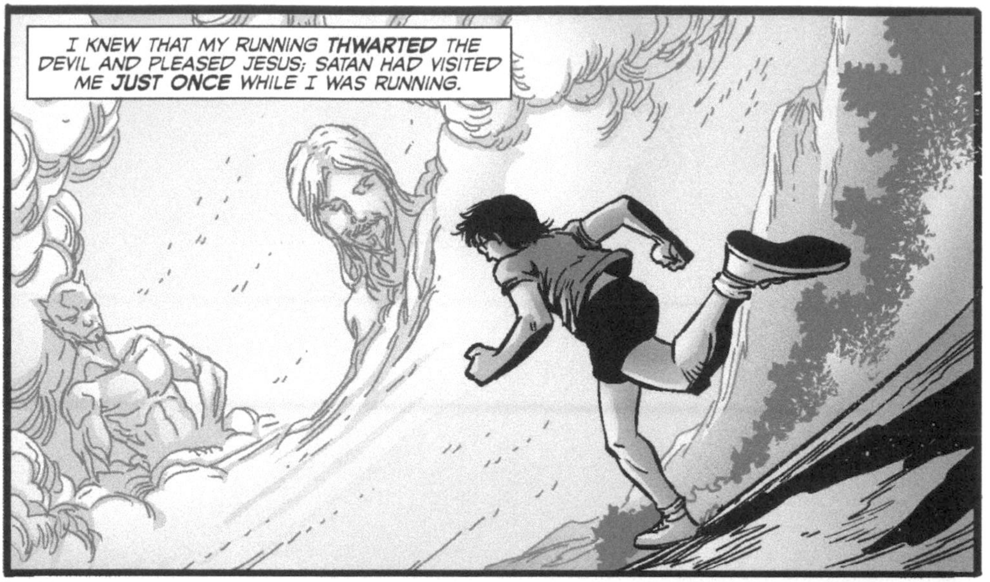
I KNEW THAT MY RUNNING **THWARTED** THE DEVIL AND PLEASED JESUS; SATAN HAD VISITED ME **JUST ONCE** WHILE I WAS RUNNING.

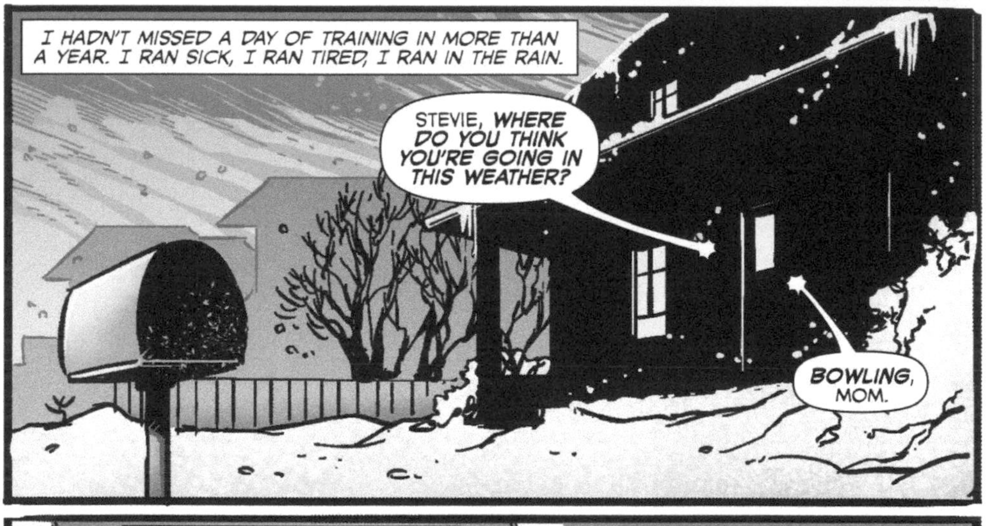
I HADN'T MISSED A DAY OF TRAINING IN MORE THAN A YEAR. I RAN SICK, I RAN TIRED, I RAN IN THE RAIN.
STEVIE, **WHERE DO YOU THINK YOU'RE GOING IN THIS WEATHER?**
BOWLING, MOM.

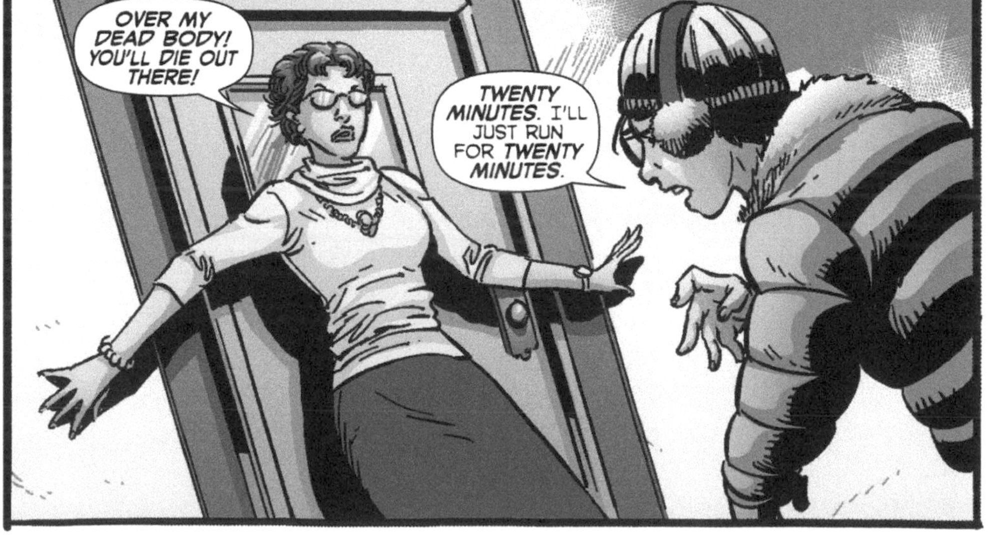
OVER MY DEAD BODY! YOU'LL DIE OUT THERE!
TWENTY MINUTES. I'LL JUST RUN FOR **TWENTY MINUTES**.

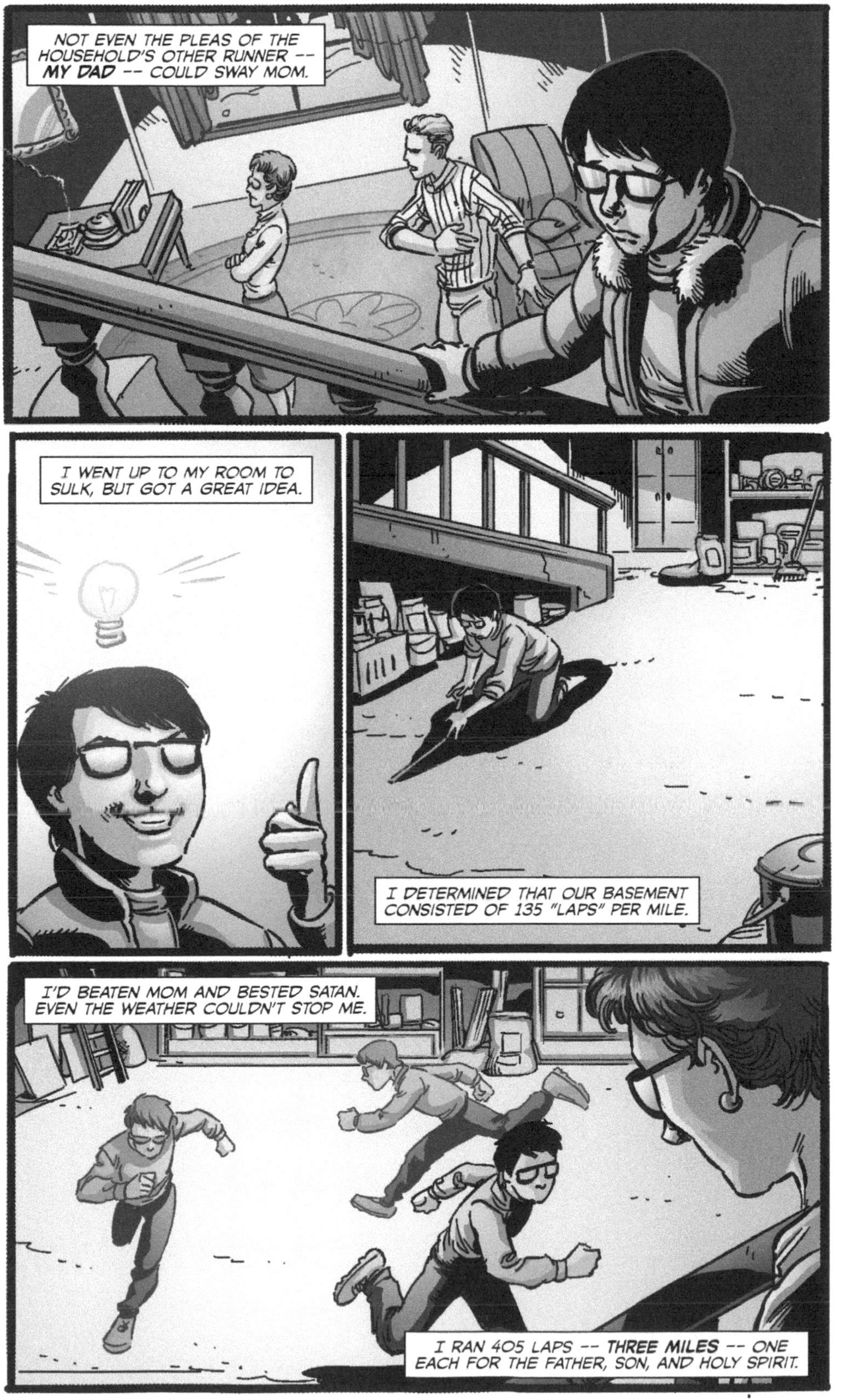
NOT EVEN THE PLEAS OF THE HOUSEHOLD'S OTHER RUNNER -- **MY DAD** -- COULD SWAY MOM.
I WENT UP TO MY ROOM TO SULK, BUT GOT A GREAT IDEA.
I DETERMINED THAT OUR BASEMENT CONSISTED OF 135 "LAPS" PER MILE.
I'D BEATEN MOM AND BESTED SATAN. EVEN THE WEATHER COULDN'T STOP ME.
I RAN 405 LAPS -- **THREE MILES** -- ONE EACH FOR THE FATHER, SON, AND HOLY SPIRIT.

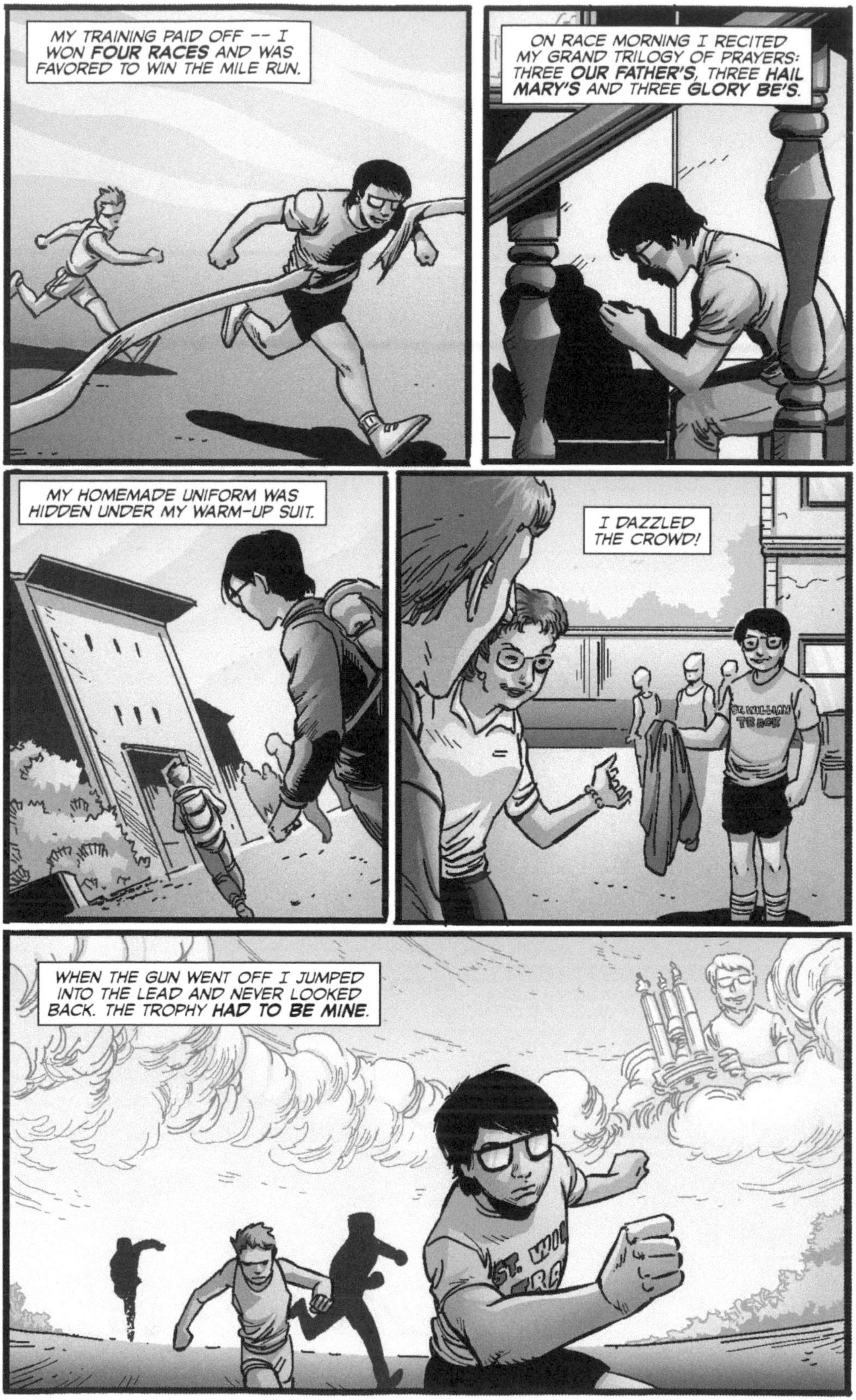
MY TRAINING PAID OFF -- I WON **FOUR RACES** AND WAS FAVORED TO WIN THE MILE RUN.
ON RACE MORNING I RECITED MY GRAND TRILOGY OF PRAYERS: THREE **OUR FATHER'S**, THREE **HAIL MARY'S** AND THREE **GLORY BE'S**.
MY HOMEMADE UNIFORM WAS HIDDEN UNDER MY WARM-UP SUIT.
I DAZZLED THE CROWD!
ST. WILLIAM TRACK
WHEN THE GUN WENT OFF I JUMPED INTO THE LEAD AND NEVER LOOKED BACK. THE TROPHY **HAD TO BE MINE**.

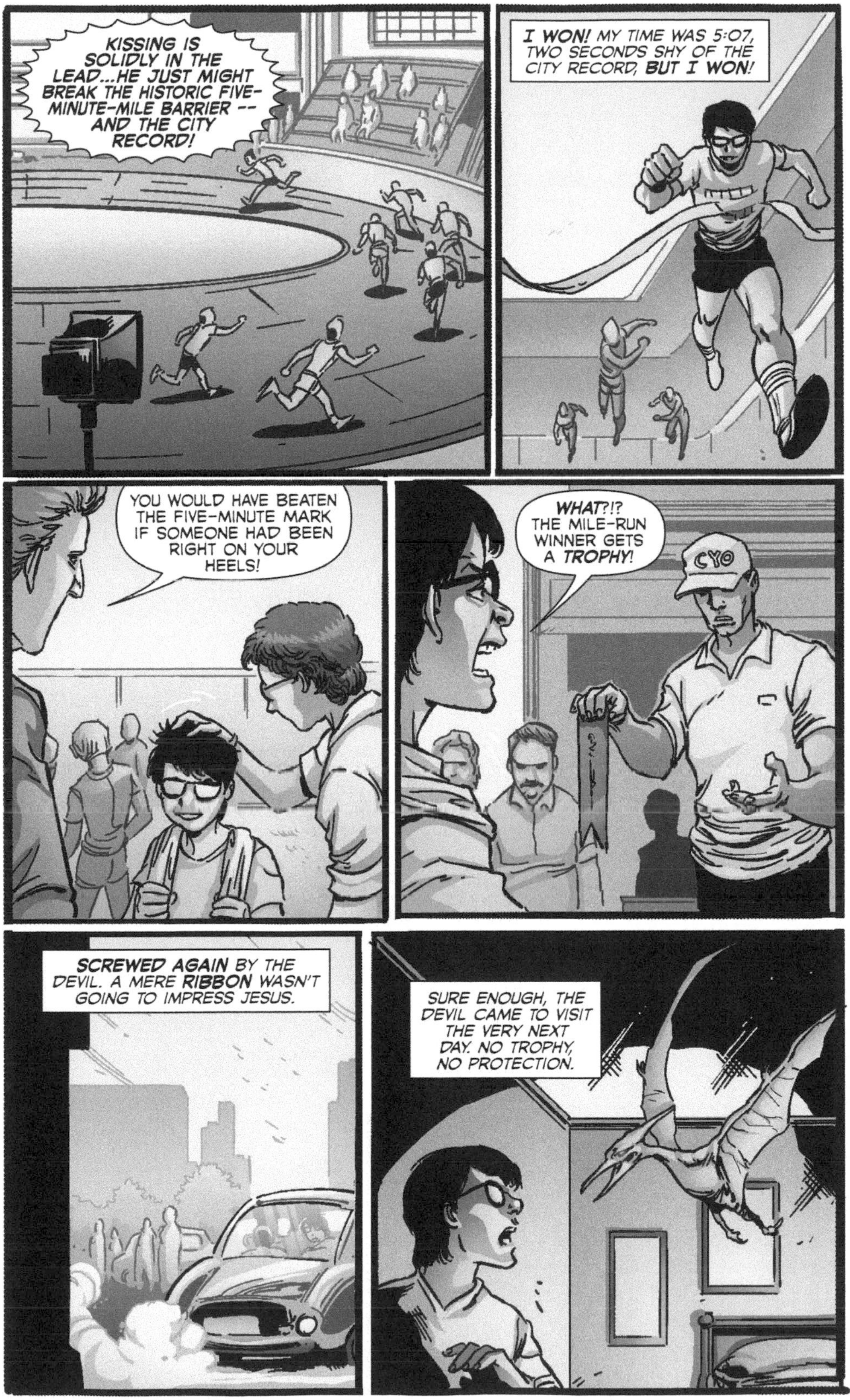
KISSING IS SOLIDLY IN THE LEAD...HE JUST MIGHT BREAK THE HISTORIC FIVE-MINUTE-MILE BARRIER -- AND THE CITY RECORD!
I WON! MY TIME WAS 5:07, TWO SECONDS SHY OF THE CITY RECORD, BUT I WON!
YOU WOULD HAVE BEATEN THE FIVE-MINUTE MARK IF SOMEONE HAD BEEN RIGHT ON YOUR HEELS!
WHAT?!? THE MILE-RUN WINNER GETS A TROPHY!
CYO
SCREWED AGAIN BY THE DEVIL. A MERE RIBBON WASN'T GOING TO IMPRESS JESUS.
SURE ENOUGH, THE DEVIL CAME TO VISIT THE VERY NEXT DAY. NO TROPHY, NO PROTECTION.

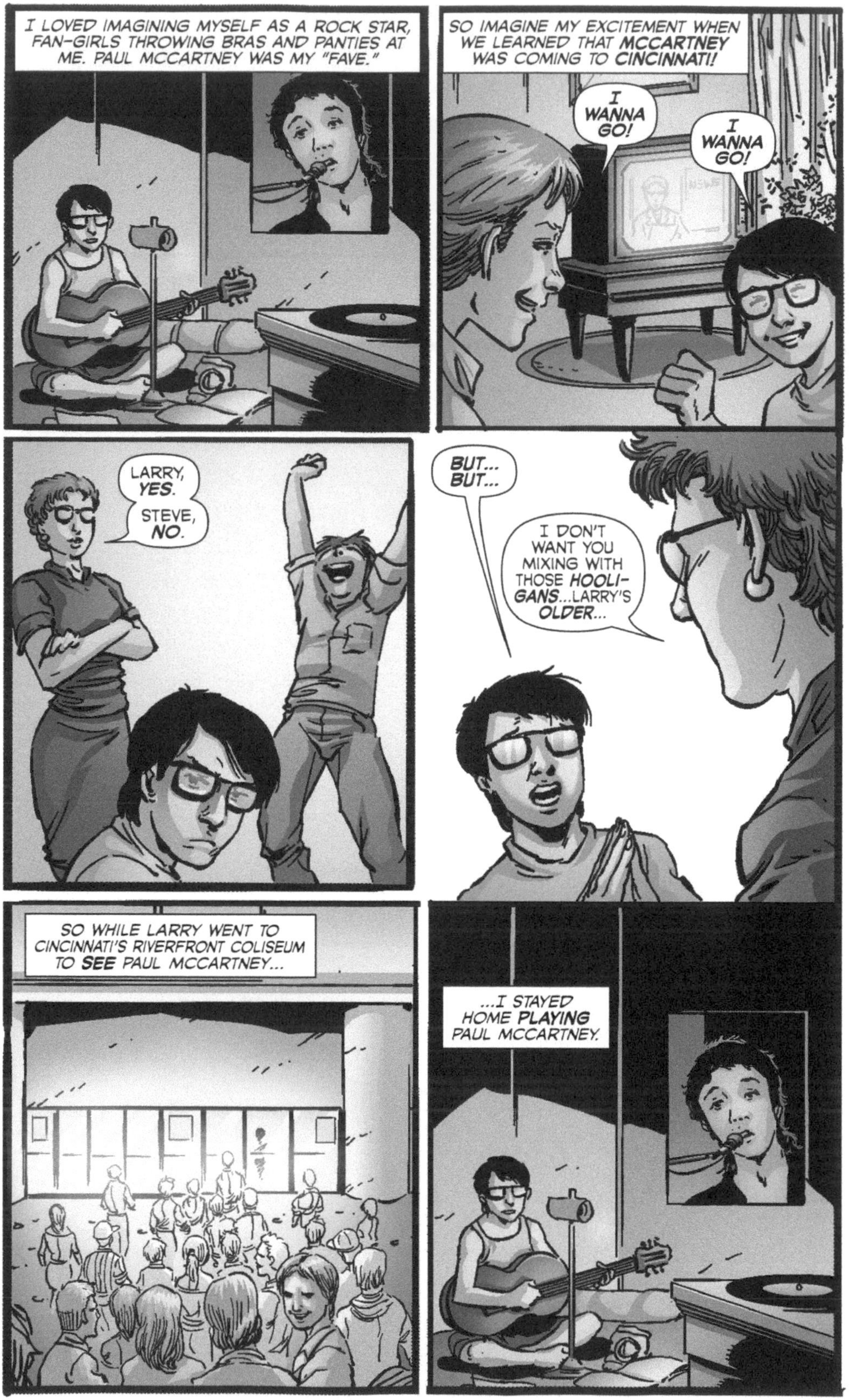
I LOVED IMAGINING MYSELF AS A ROCK STAR, FAN-GIRLS THROWING BRAS AND PANTIES AT ME. PAUL MCCARTNEY WAS MY "FAVE."
SO IMAGINE MY EXCITEMENT WHEN WE LEARNED THAT MCCARTNEY WAS COMING TO CINCINNATI!
I WANNA GO!
I WANNA GO!
LARRY, YES.
STEVE, NO.
BUT... BUT...
I DON'T WANT YOU MIXING WITH THOSE HOOLI-GANS...LARRY'S OLDER...
SO WHILE LARRY WENT TO CINCINNATI'S RIVERFRONT COLISEUM TO SEE PAUL MCCARTNEY...
...I STAYED HOME PLAYING PAUL MCCARTNEY.

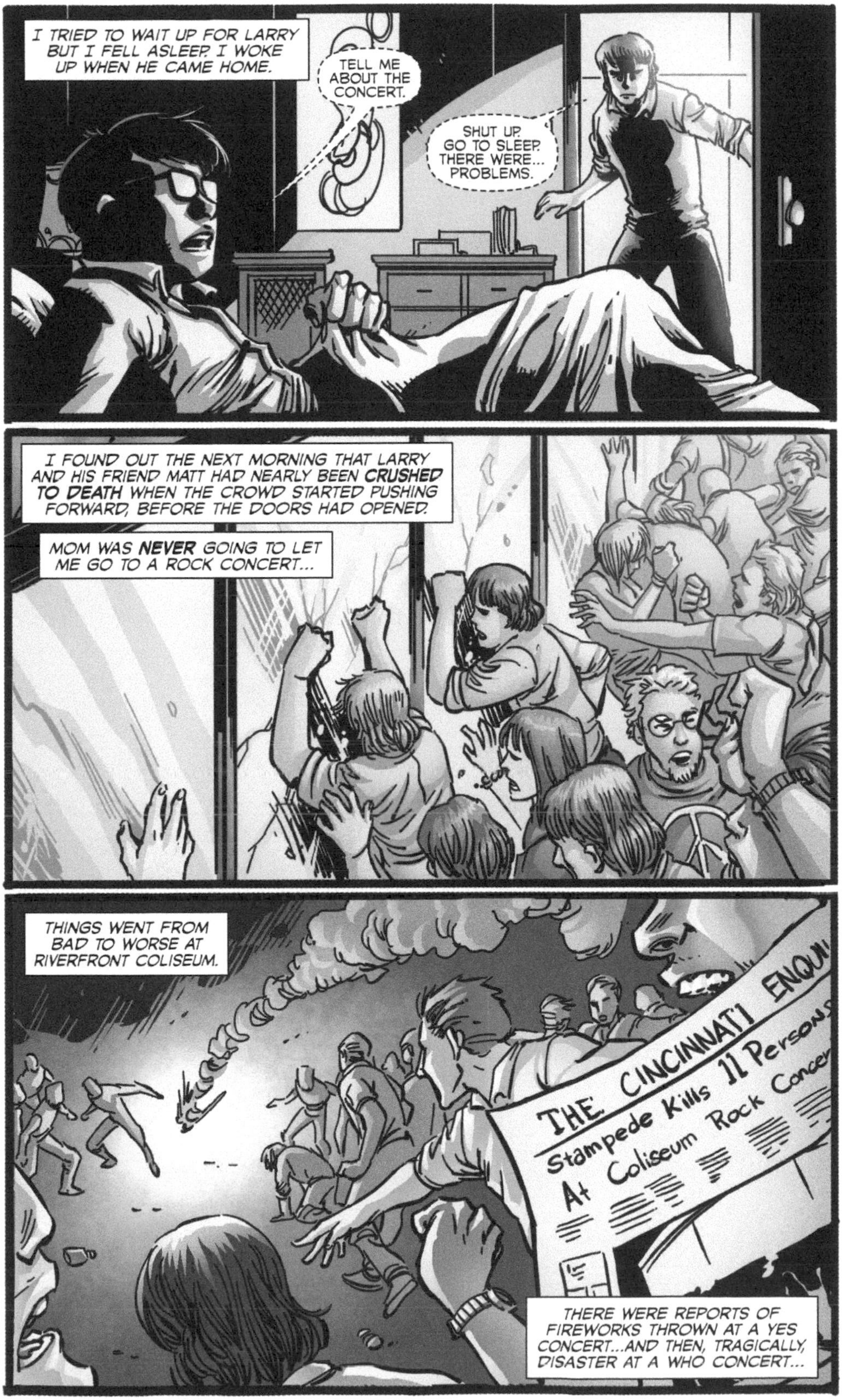
I TRIED TO WAIT UP FOR LARRY BUT I FELL ASLEEP. I WOKE UP WHEN HE CAME HOME.
TELL ME ABOUT THE CONCERT.
SHUT UP. GO TO SLEEP. THERE WERE... PROBLEMS.
I FOUND OUT THE NEXT MORNING THAT LARRY AND HIS FRIEND MATT HAD NEARLY BEEN **CRUSHED TO DEATH** WHEN THE CROWD STARTED PUSHING FORWARD, BEFORE THE DOORS HAD OPENED.
MOM WAS **NEVER** GOING TO LET ME GO TO A ROCK CONCERT...
THINGS WENT FROM BAD TO WORSE AT RIVERFRONT COLISEUM.
THE CINCINNATI ENQU
Stampede Kills 11 Persons
At Coliseum Rock Concer
THERE WERE REPORTS OF FIREWORKS THROWN AT A YES CONCERT...AND THEN, TRAGICALLY, DISASTER AT A WHO CONCERT...

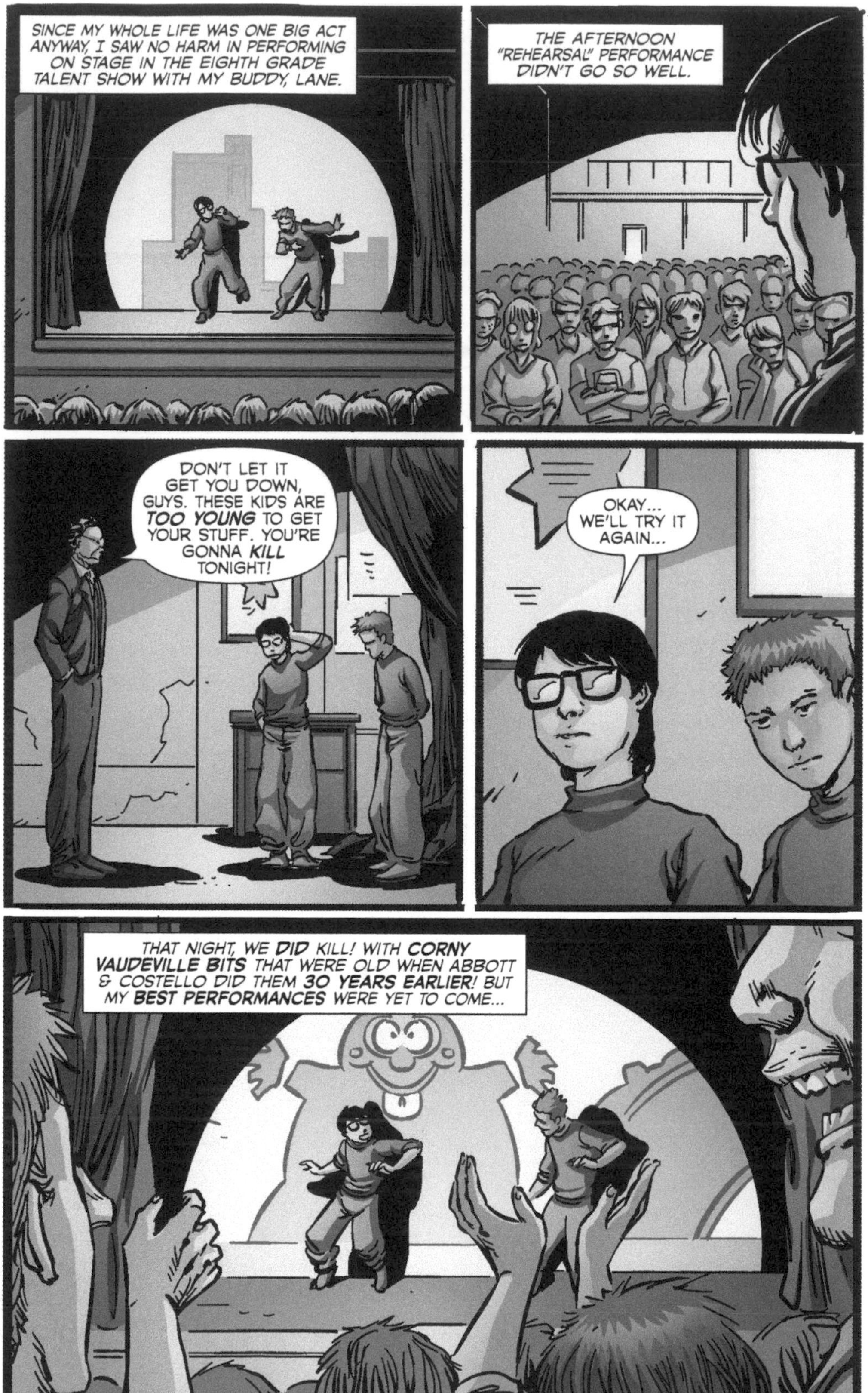
SINCE MY WHOLE LIFE WAS ONE BIG ACT ANYWAY, I SAW NO HARM IN PERFORMING ON STAGE IN THE EIGHTH GRADE TALENT SHOW WITH MY BUDDY, LANE.
THE AFTERNOON "REHEARSAL" PERFORMANCE DIDN'T GO SO WELL.
DON'T LET IT GET YOU DOWN, GUYS. THESE KIDS ARE **TOO YOUNG** TO GET YOUR STUFF. YOU'RE GONNA **KILL** TONIGHT!
OKAY... WE'LL TRY IT AGAIN...
THAT NIGHT, WE **DID** KILL! WITH **CORNY VAUDEVILLE BITS** THAT WERE OLD WHEN ABBOTT & COSTELLO DID THEM **30 YEARS EARLIER**! BUT MY **BEST PERFORMANCES** WERE YET TO COME...

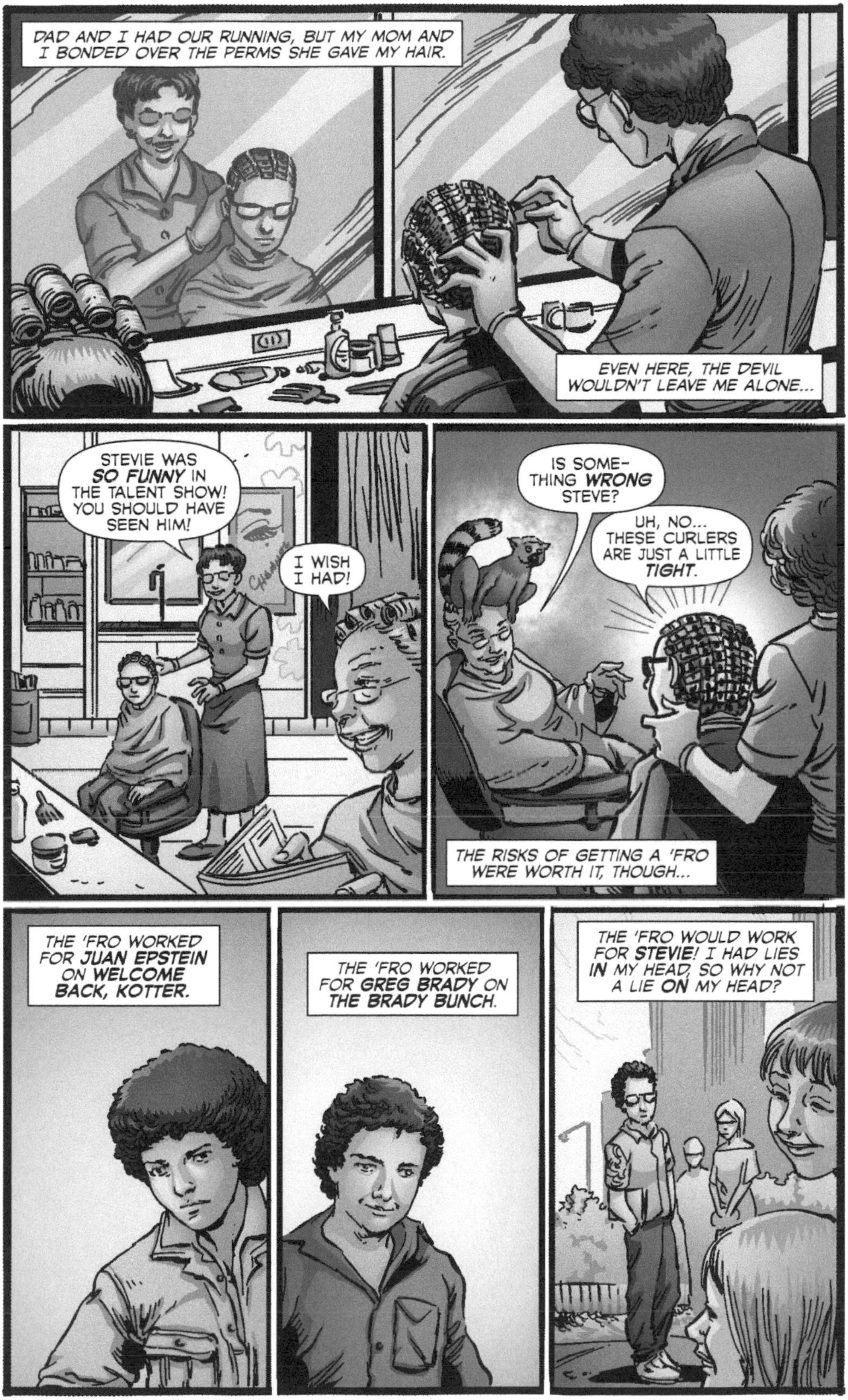
DAD AND I HAD OUR RUNNING, BUT MY MOM AND I BONDED OVER THE PERMS SHE GAVE MY HAIR.
EVEN HERE, THE DEVIL WOULDN'T LEAVE ME ALONE...
STEVIE WAS SO FUNNY IN THE TALENT SHOW! YOU SHOULD HAVE SEEN HIM!
I WISH I HAD!
IS SOME-THING WRONG STEVE?
UH, NO... THESE CURLERS ARE JUST A LITTLE TIGHT.
THE RISKS OF GETTING A 'FRO WERE WORTH IT, THOUGH...
THE 'FRO WORKED FOR JUAN EPSTEIN ON WELCOME BACK, KOTTER.
THE 'FRO WORKED FOR GREG BRADY ON THE BRADY BUNCH.
THE 'FRO WOULD WORK FOR STEVIE! I HAD LIES IN MY HEAD, SO WHY NOT A LIE ON MY HEAD?

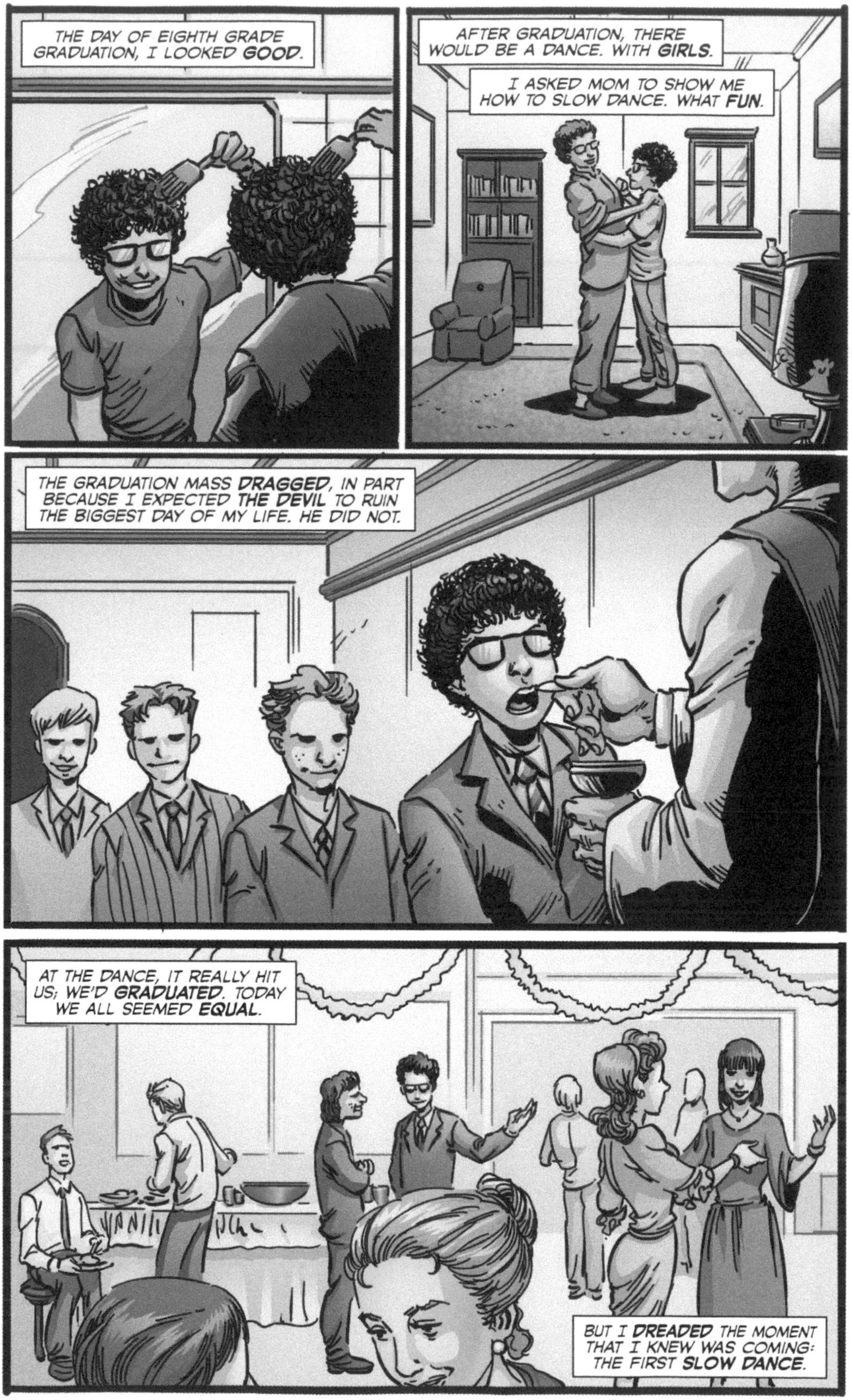
THE DAY OF EIGHTH GRADE GRADUATION, I LOOKED GOOD.
AFTER GRADUATION, THERE WOULD BE A DANCE. WITH GIRLS.
I ASKED MOM TO SHOW ME HOW TO SLOW DANCE. WHAT FUN.
THE GRADUATION MASS DRAGGED, IN PART BECAUSE I EXPECTED THE DEVIL TO RUIN THE BIGGEST DAY OF MY LIFE. HE DID NOT.
AT THE DANCE, IT REALLY HIT US; WE'D GRADUATED. TODAY WE ALL SEEMED EQUAL.
BUT I DREADED THE MOMENT THAT I KNEW WAS COMING: THE FIRST SLOW DANCE.

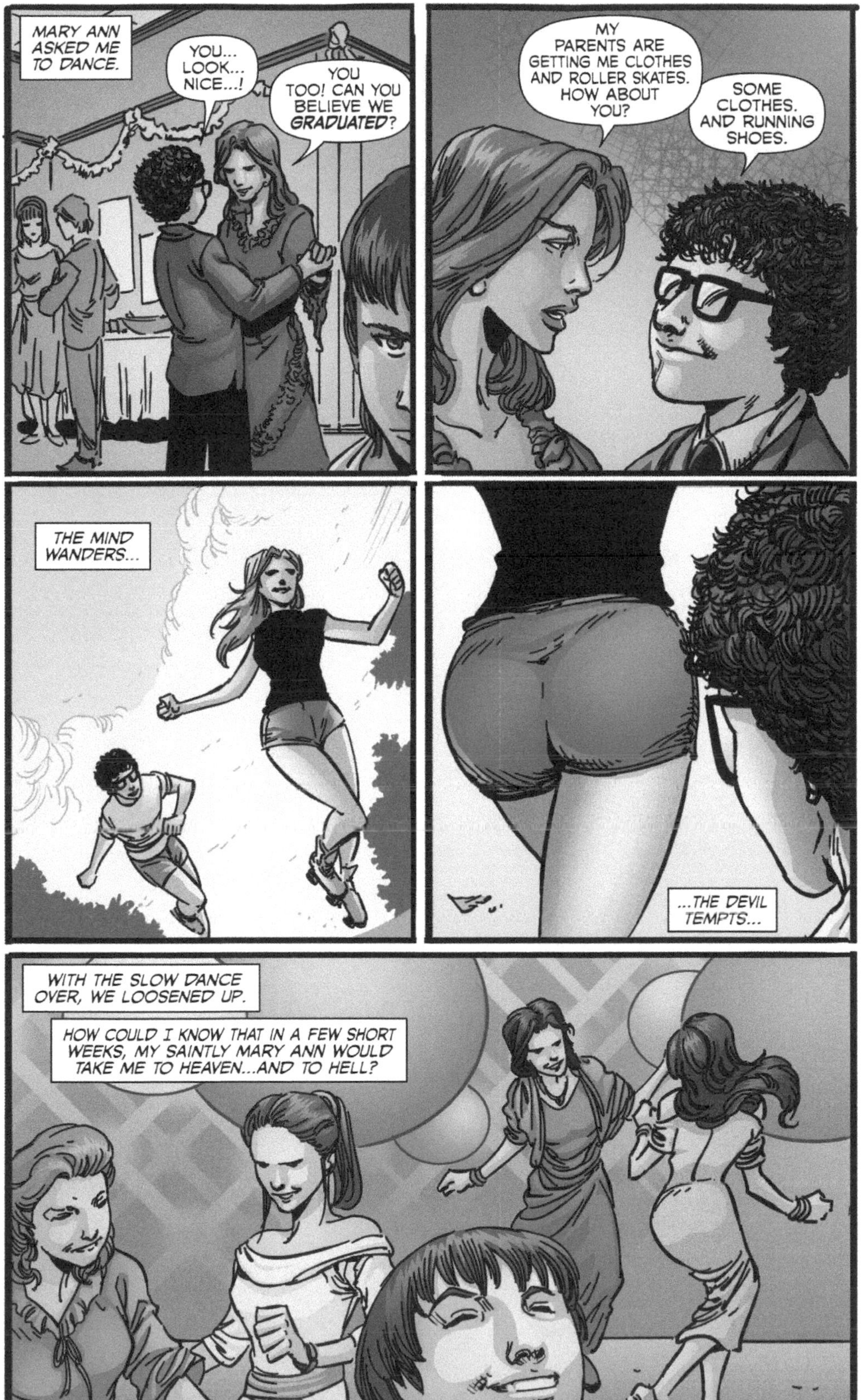
MARY ANN ASKED ME TO DANCE.
YOU... LOOK... NICE...!
YOU TOO! CAN YOU BELIEVE WE GRADUATED?
MY PARENTS ARE GETTING ME CLOTHES AND ROLLER SKATES. HOW ABOUT YOU?
SOME CLOTHES. AND RUNNING SHOES.
THE MIND WANDERS...
...THE DEVIL TEMPTS...
WITH THE SLOW DANCE OVER, WE LOOSENED UP.
HOW COULD I KNOW THAT IN A FEW SHORT WEEKS, MY SAINTLY MARY ANN WOULD TAKE ME TO HEAVEN...AND TO HELL?

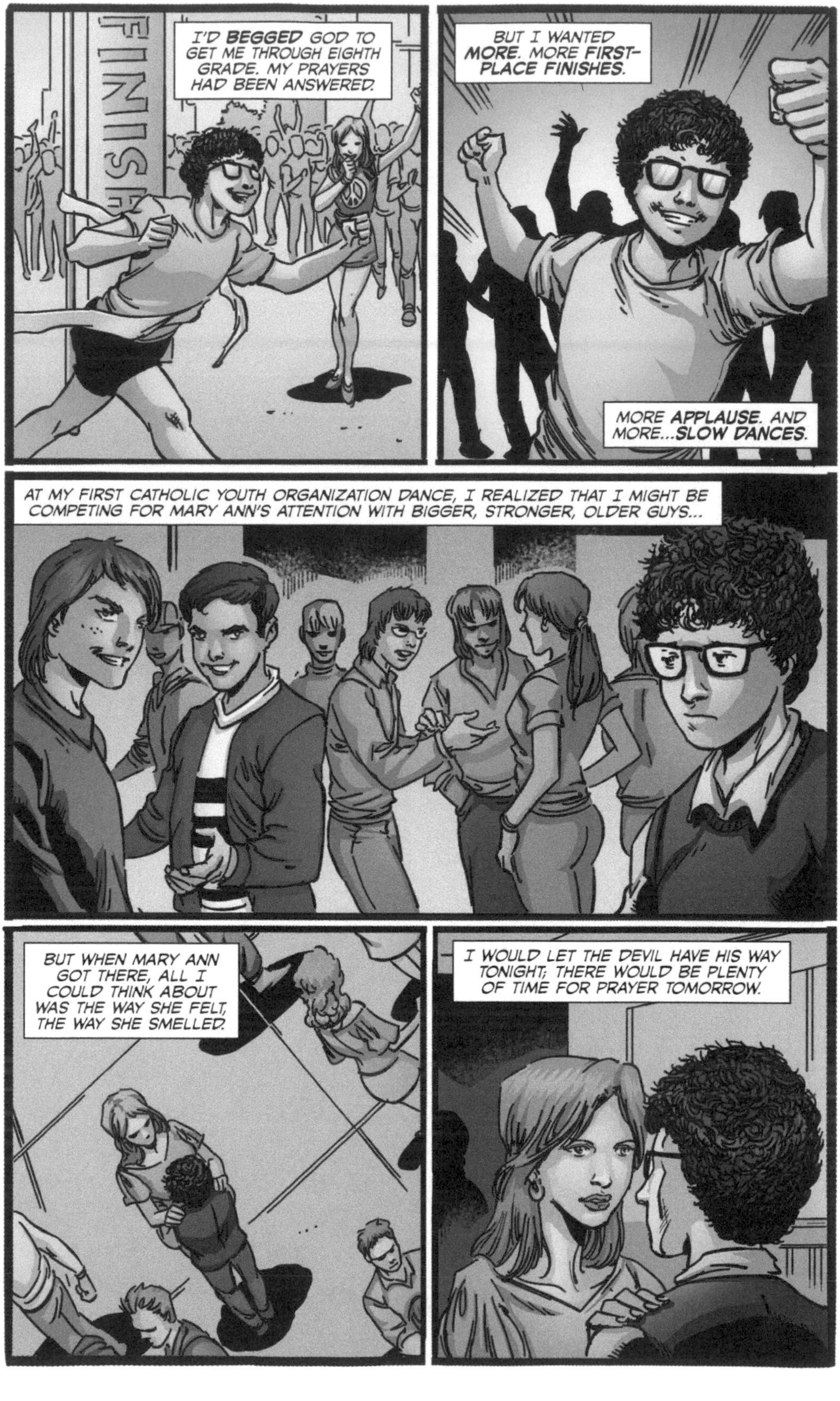
I'D **BEGGED** GOD TO GET ME THROUGH EIGHTH GRADE. MY PRAYERS HAD BEEN ANSWERED.
BUT I WANTED **MORE**. MORE **FIRST-PLACE FINISHES**.
MORE **APPLAUSE**. AND MORE...**SLOW DANCES**.
AT MY FIRST CATHOLIC YOUTH ORGANIZATION DANCE, I REALIZED THAT I MIGHT BE COMPETING FOR MARY ANN'S ATTENTION WITH BIGGER, STRONGER, OLDER GUYS...
BUT WHEN MARY ANN GOT THERE, ALL I COULD THINK ABOUT WAS THE WAY SHE FELT, THE WAY SHE SMELLED.
I WOULD LET THE DEVIL HAVE HIS WAY TONIGHT; THERE WOULD BE PLENTY OF TIME FOR PRAYER TOMORROW.

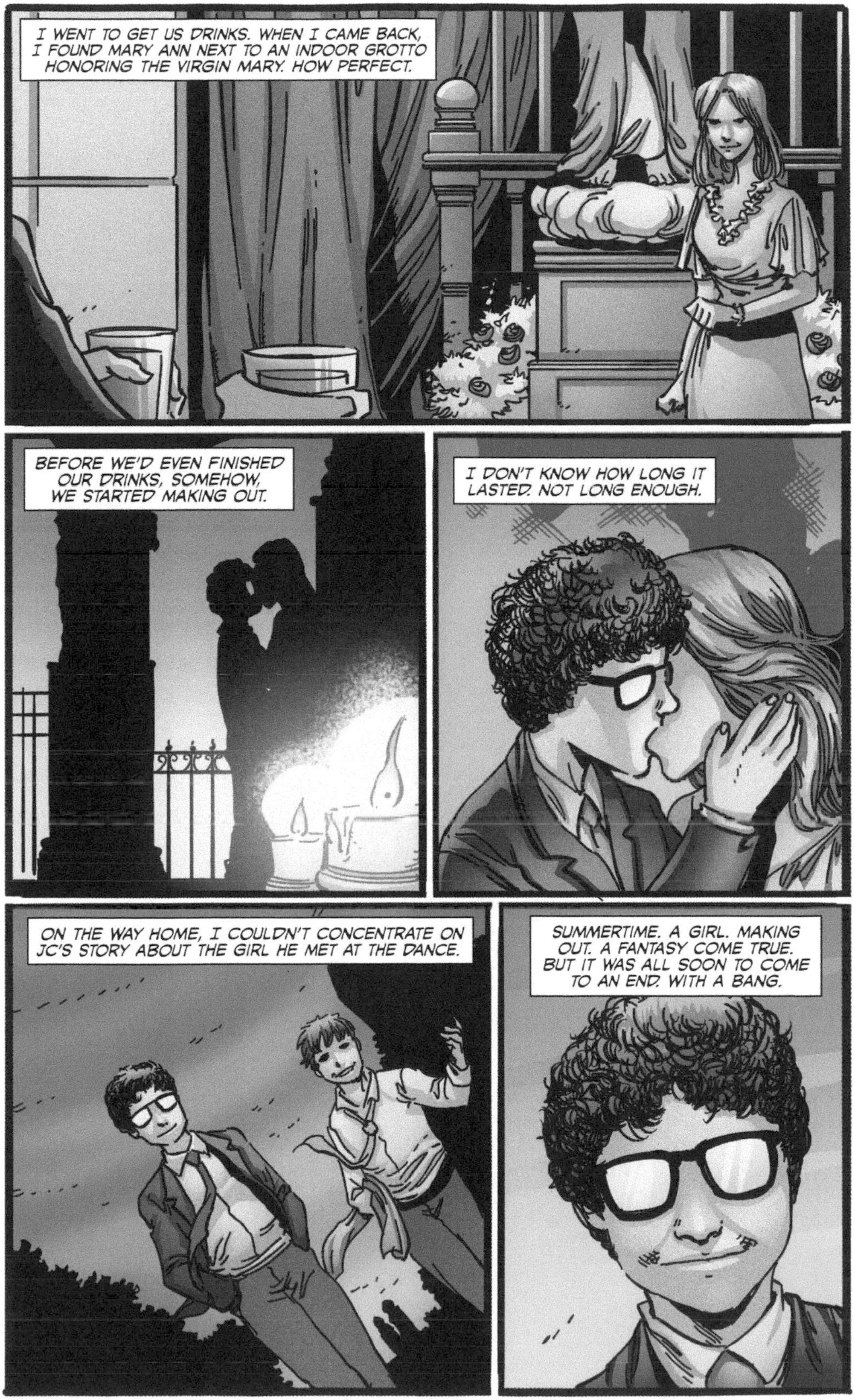
I WENT TO GET US DRINKS. WHEN I CAME BACK, I FOUND MARY ANN NEXT TO AN INDOOR GROTTO HONORING THE VIRGIN MARY. HOW PERFECT.
BEFORE WE'D EVEN FINISHED OUR DRINKS, SOMEHOW, WE STARTED MAKING OUT.
I DON'T KNOW HOW LONG IT LASTED. NOT LONG ENOUGH.
ON THE WAY HOME, I COULDN'T CONCENTRATE ON JC'S STORY ABOUT THE GIRL HE MET AT THE DANCE.
SUMMERTIME. A GIRL. MAKING OUT. A FANTASY COME TRUE. BUT IT WAS ALL SOON TO COME TO AN END. WITH A BANG.

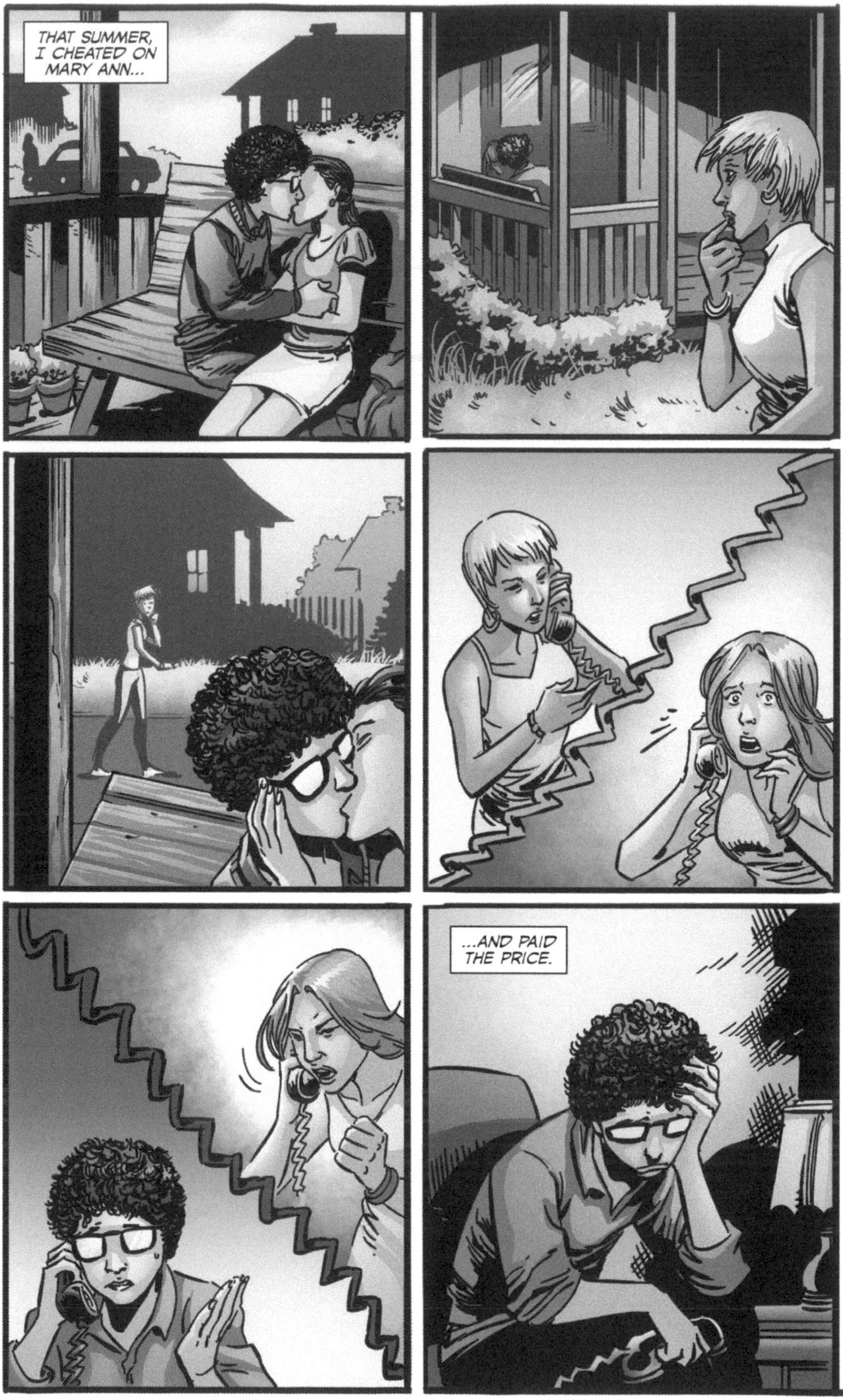
THAT SUMMER, I CHEATED ON MARY ANN...
...AND PAID THE PRICE.

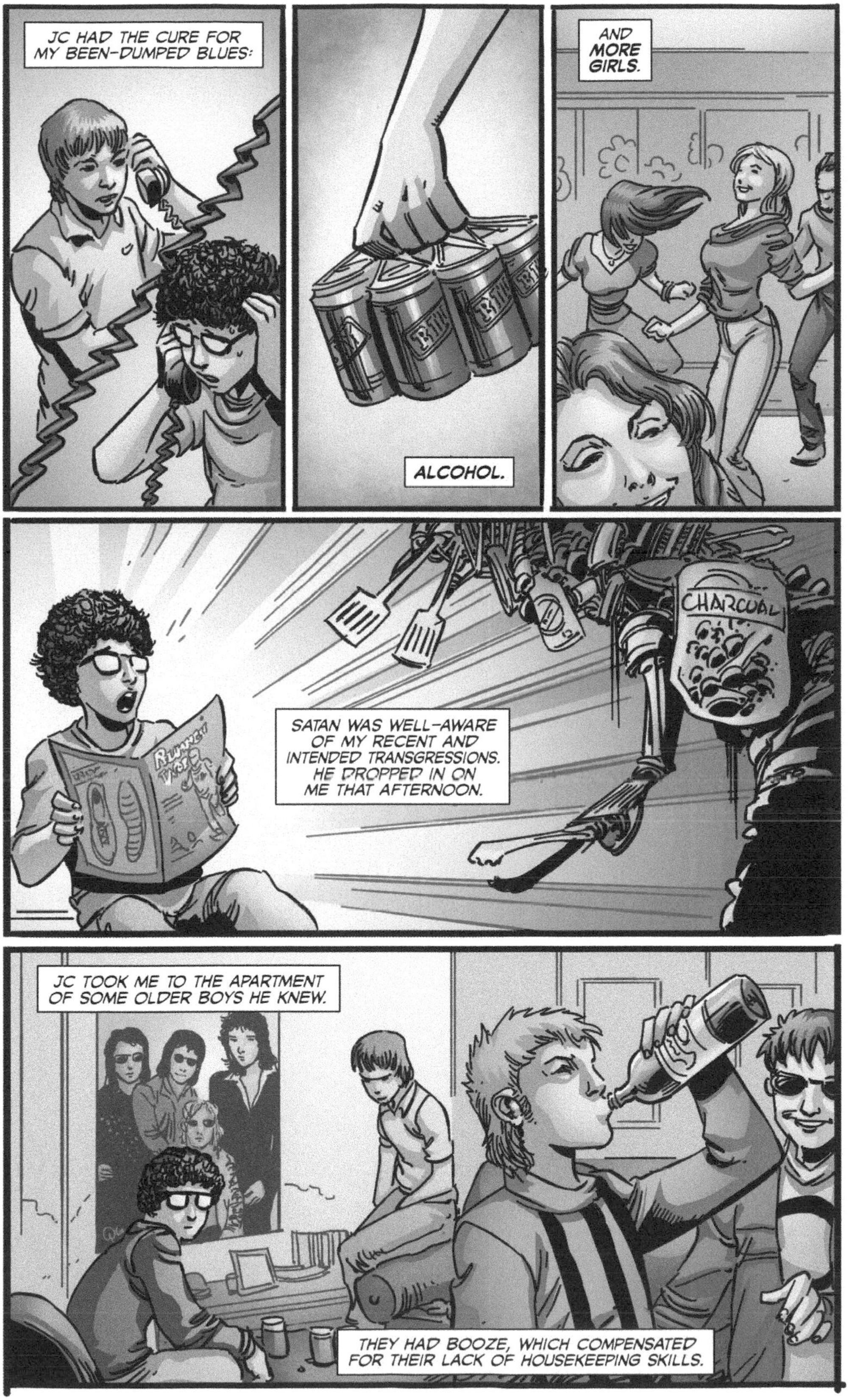
JC HAD THE CURE FOR MY BEEN-DUMPED BLUES:
ALCOHOL.
AND MORE GIRLS.
CHARCOAL
SATAN WAS WELL-AWARE OF MY RECENT AND INTENDED TRANSGRESSIONS. HE DROPPED IN ON ME THAT AFTERNOON.
JC TOOK ME TO THE APARTMENT OF SOME OLDER BOYS HE KNEW.
THEY HAD BOOZE, WHICH COMPENSATED FOR THEIR LACK OF HOUSEKEEPING SKILLS.

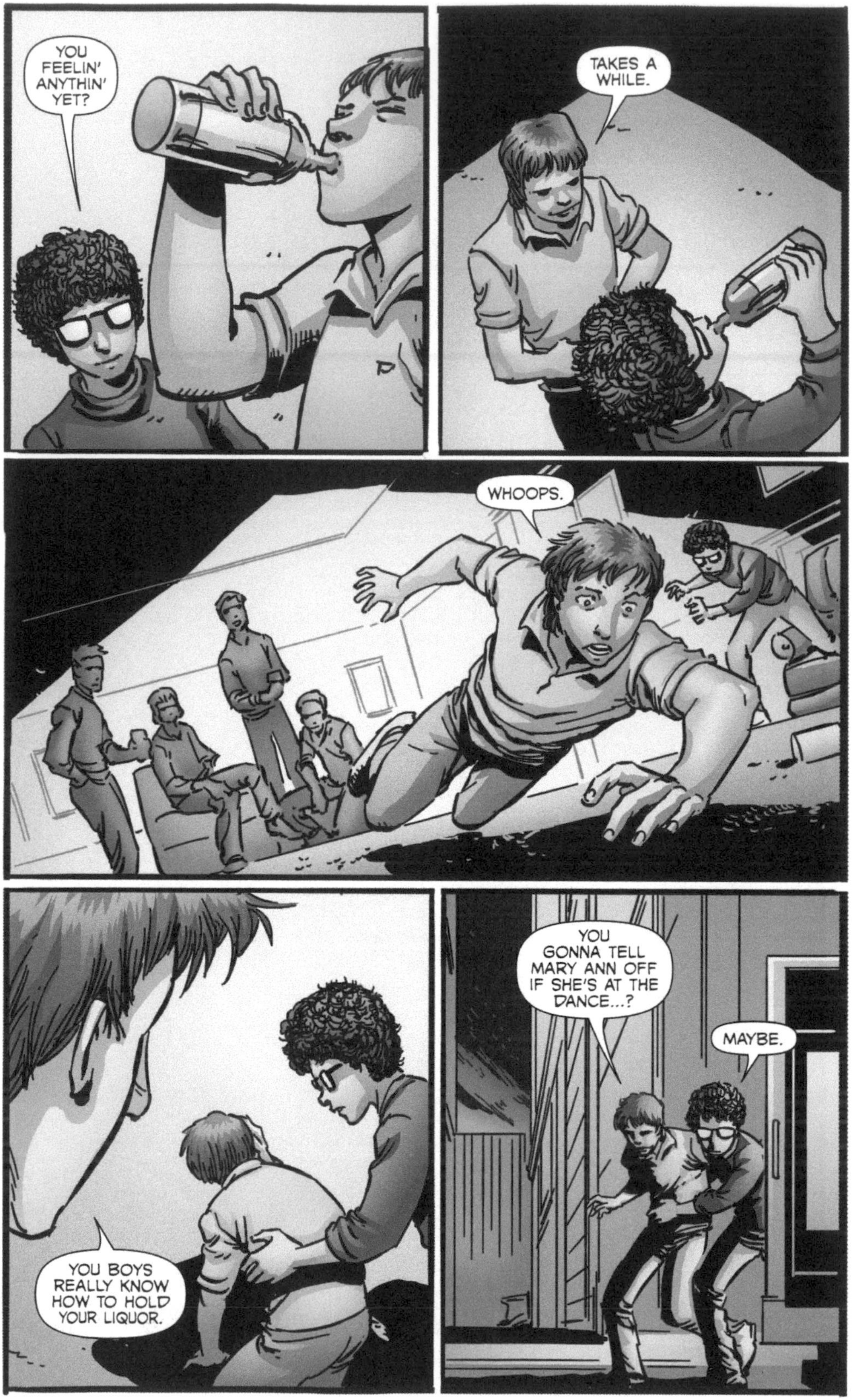
YOU FEELIN' ANYTHIN' YET?
TAKES A WHILE.
WHOOPS.
YOU BOYS REALLY KNOW HOW TO HOLD YOUR LIQUOR.
YOU GONNA TELL MARY ANN OFF IF SHE'S AT THE DANCE...?
MAYBE.

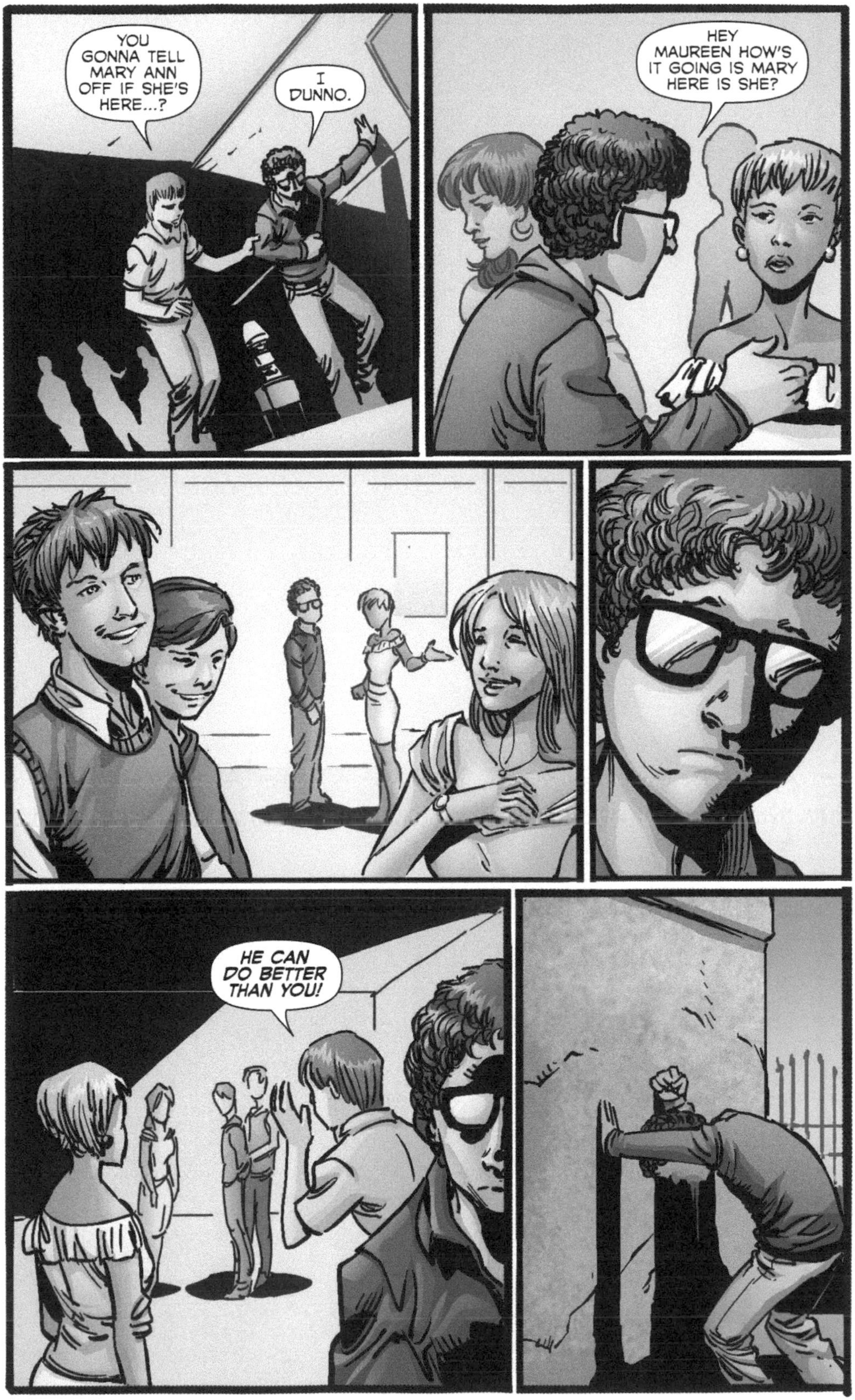
YOU GONNA TELL MARY ANN OFF IF SHE'S HERE...?
I DUNNO.
HEY MAUREEN HOW'S IT GOING IS MARY HERE IS SHE?
HE CAN DO BETTER THAN YOU!

JC AND I JOINED THE **ST. WILLIAM YOUTH CLUB**. MOSTLY TO MEET GIRLS, BUT I ALSO HOPED TO SCORE POINTS WITH THE "BIG MAN UPSTAIRS."
OPEN HOUSE ST. WILLIAM YOUTH CLUB!
I HOPED THAT JESUS WOULD FORGIVE MY CARNAL DESIRES AND THE DEVIL WOULD WITHER IN THE FACE OF MY DEDICATION TO **ALL THINGS RELIGIOUS.**
SO WHEN THEY ASKED FOR **VOLUNTEERS** -- WHO WOULD NO DOUBT BECOME FUTURE **CLUB LEADERS** -- I DID NOT HESITATE.
I GOT THE PLUM ASSIGNMENT OF CREATING POSTERS FOR THE NEXT FUND-RAISER.
OPEN HOUSE
ST. WILLIAM

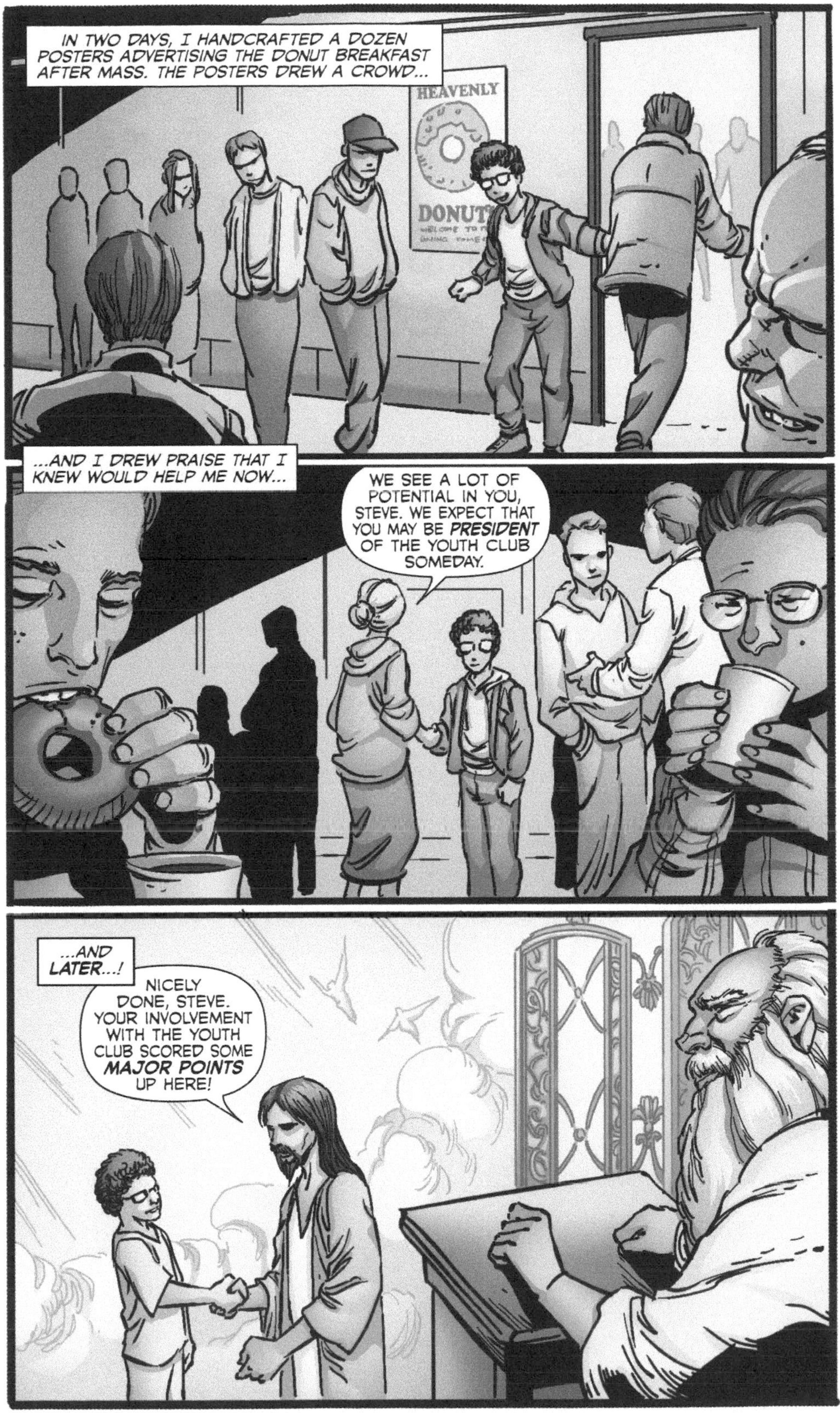
IN TWO DAYS, I HANDCRAFTED A DOZEN POSTERS ADVERTISING THE DONUT BREAKFAST AFTER MASS. THE POSTERS DREW A CROWD...
HEAVENLY
DONUT
...AND I DREW PRAISE THAT I KNEW WOULD HELP ME NOW...
WE SEE A LOT OF POTENTIAL IN YOU, STEVE. WE EXPECT THAT YOU MAY BE **PRESIDENT** OF THE YOUTH CLUB SOMEDAY.
...AND **LATER**...!
NICELY DONE, STEVE. YOUR INVOLVEMENT WITH THE YOUTH CLUB SCORED SOME **MAJOR POINTS** UP HERE!

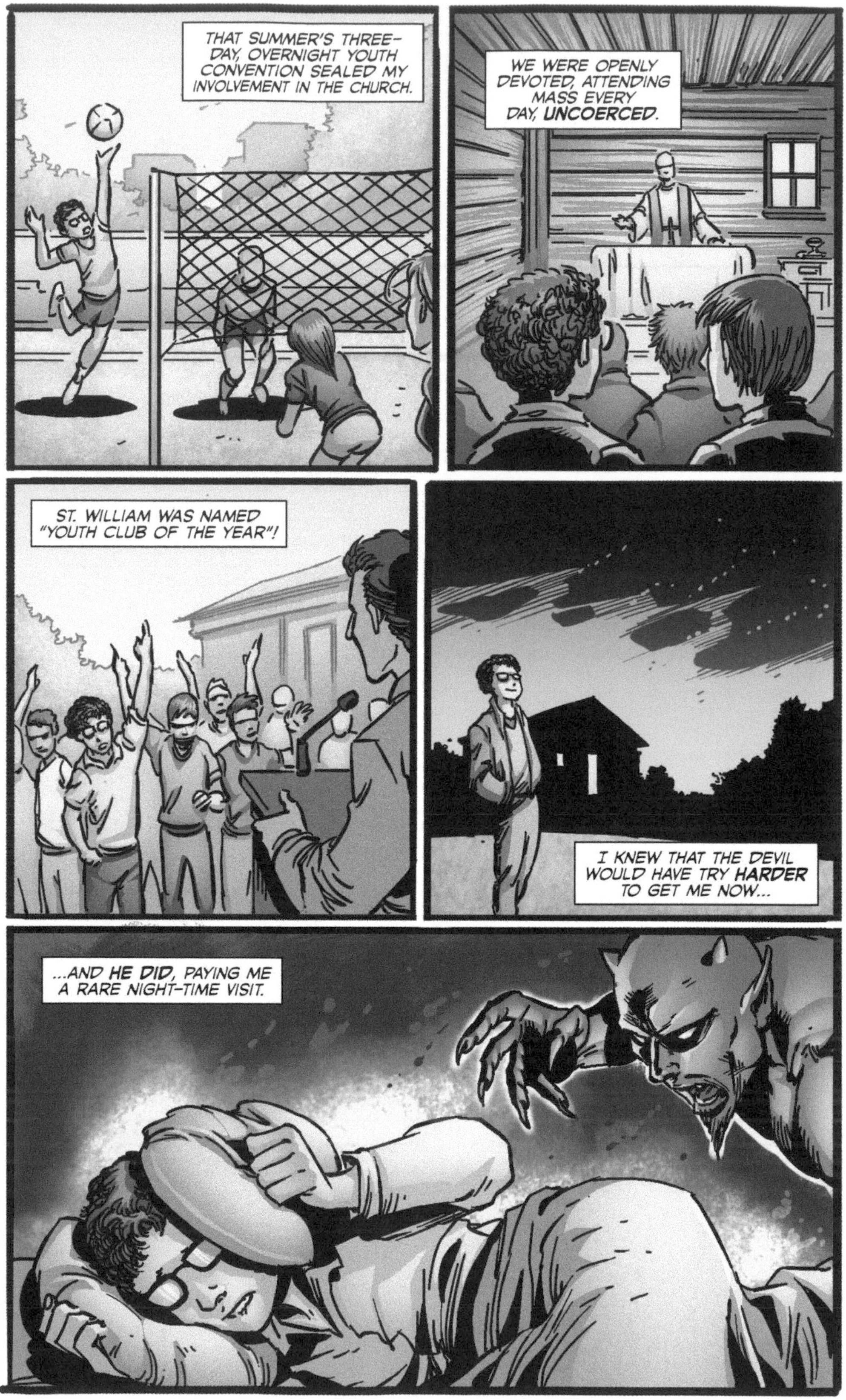
THAT SUMMER'S THREE-DAY, OVERNIGHT YOUTH CONVENTION SEALED MY INVOLVEMENT IN THE CHURCH.
WE WERE OPENLY DEVOTED, ATTENDING MASS EVERY DAY, UNCOERCED.
ST. WILLIAM WAS NAMED "YOUTH CLUB OF THE YEAR"!
I KNEW THAT THE DEVIL WOULD HAVE TRY HARDER TO GET ME NOW...
...AND HE DID, PAYING ME A RARE NIGHT-TIME VISIT.

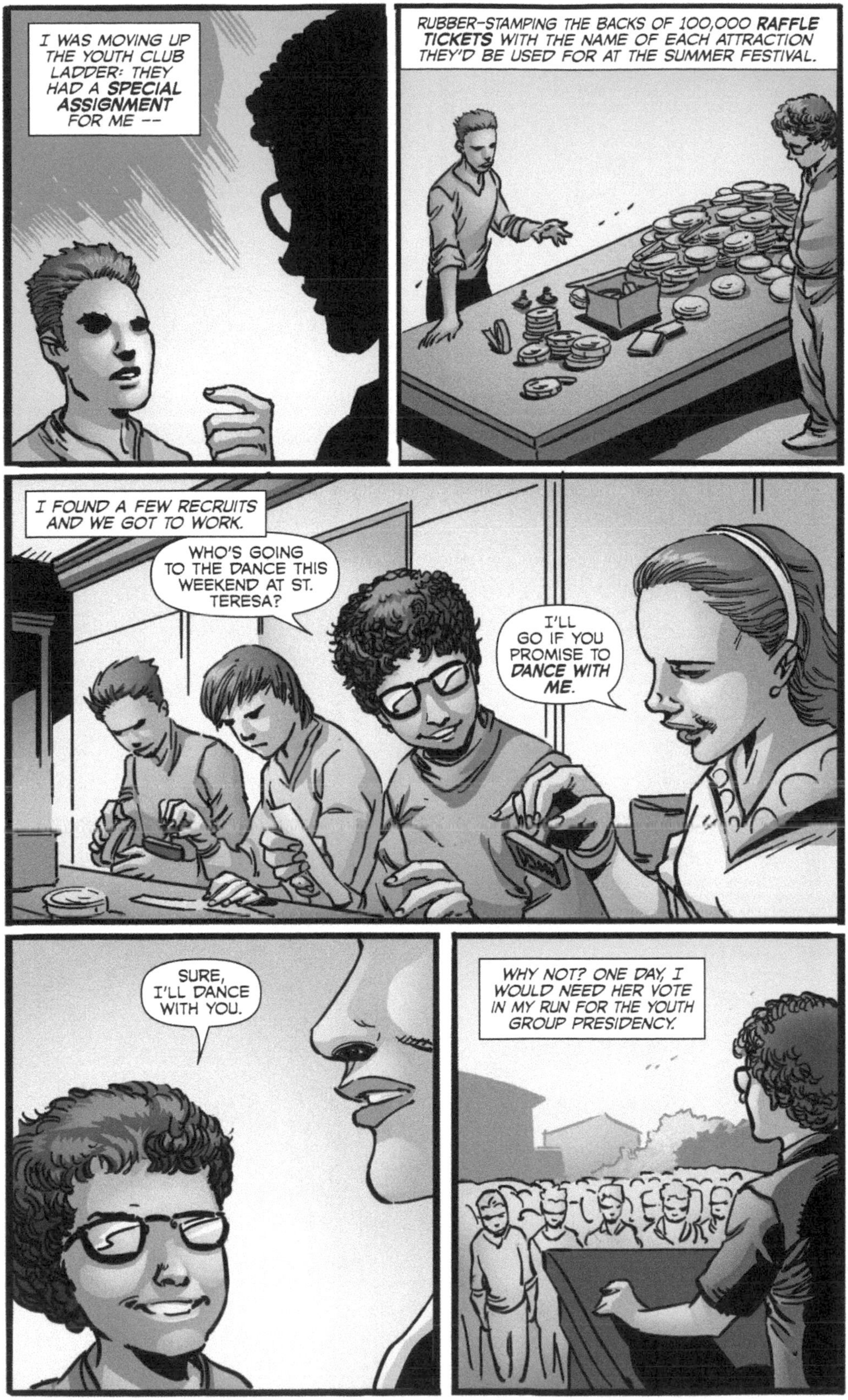
I WAS MOVING UP THE YOUTH CLUB LADDER: THEY HAD A SPECIAL ASSIGNMENT FOR ME --
RUBBER-STAMPING THE BACKS OF 100,000 RAFFLE TICKETS WITH THE NAME OF EACH ATTRACTION THEY'D BE USED FOR AT THE SUMMER FESTIVAL.
I FOUND A FEW RECRUITS AND WE GOT TO WORK.
WHO'S GOING TO THE DANCE THIS WEEKEND AT ST. TERESA?
I'LL GO IF YOU PROMISE TO DANCE WITH ME.
SURE, I'LL DANCE WITH YOU.
WHY NOT? ONE DAY, I WOULD NEED HER VOTE IN MY RUN FOR THE YOUTH GROUP PRESIDENCY.

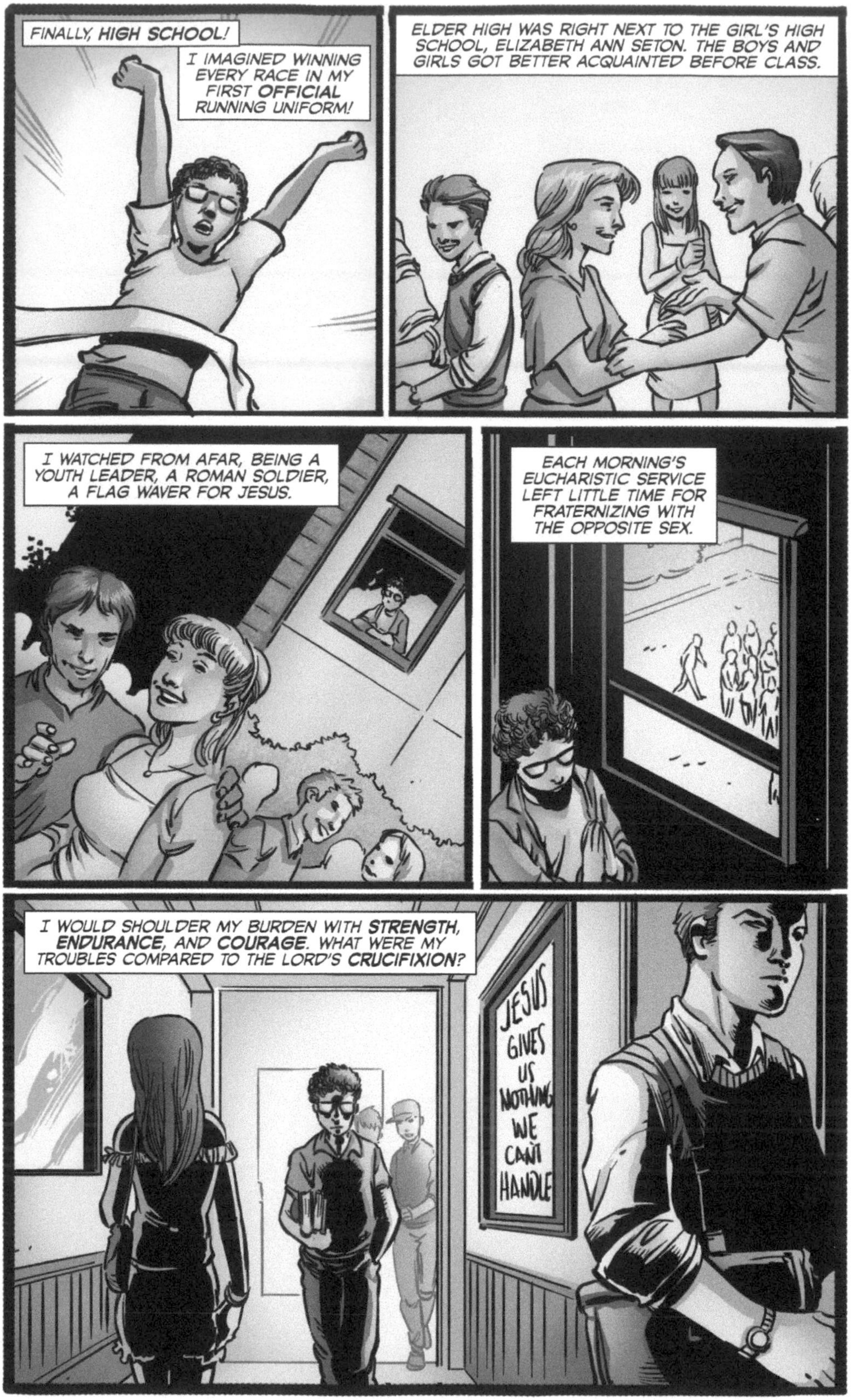
FINALLY, HIGH SCHOOL!
I IMAGINED WINNING EVERY RACE IN MY FIRST OFFICIAL RUNNING UNIFORM!
ELDER HIGH WAS RIGHT NEXT TO THE GIRL'S HIGH SCHOOL, ELIZABETH ANN SETON. THE BOYS AND GIRLS GOT BETTER ACQUAINTED BEFORE CLASS.
I WATCHED FROM AFAR, BEING A YOUTH LEADER, A ROMAN SOLDIER, A FLAG WAVER FOR JESUS.
EACH MORNING'S EUCHARISTIC SERVICE LEFT LITTLE TIME FOR FRATERNIZING WITH THE OPPOSITE SEX.
I WOULD SHOULDER MY BURDEN WITH STRENGTH, ENDURANCE, AND COURAGE. WHAT WERE MY TROUBLES COMPARED TO THE LORD'S CRUCIFIXION?
JESUS GIVES US NOTHING WE CAN'T HANDLE

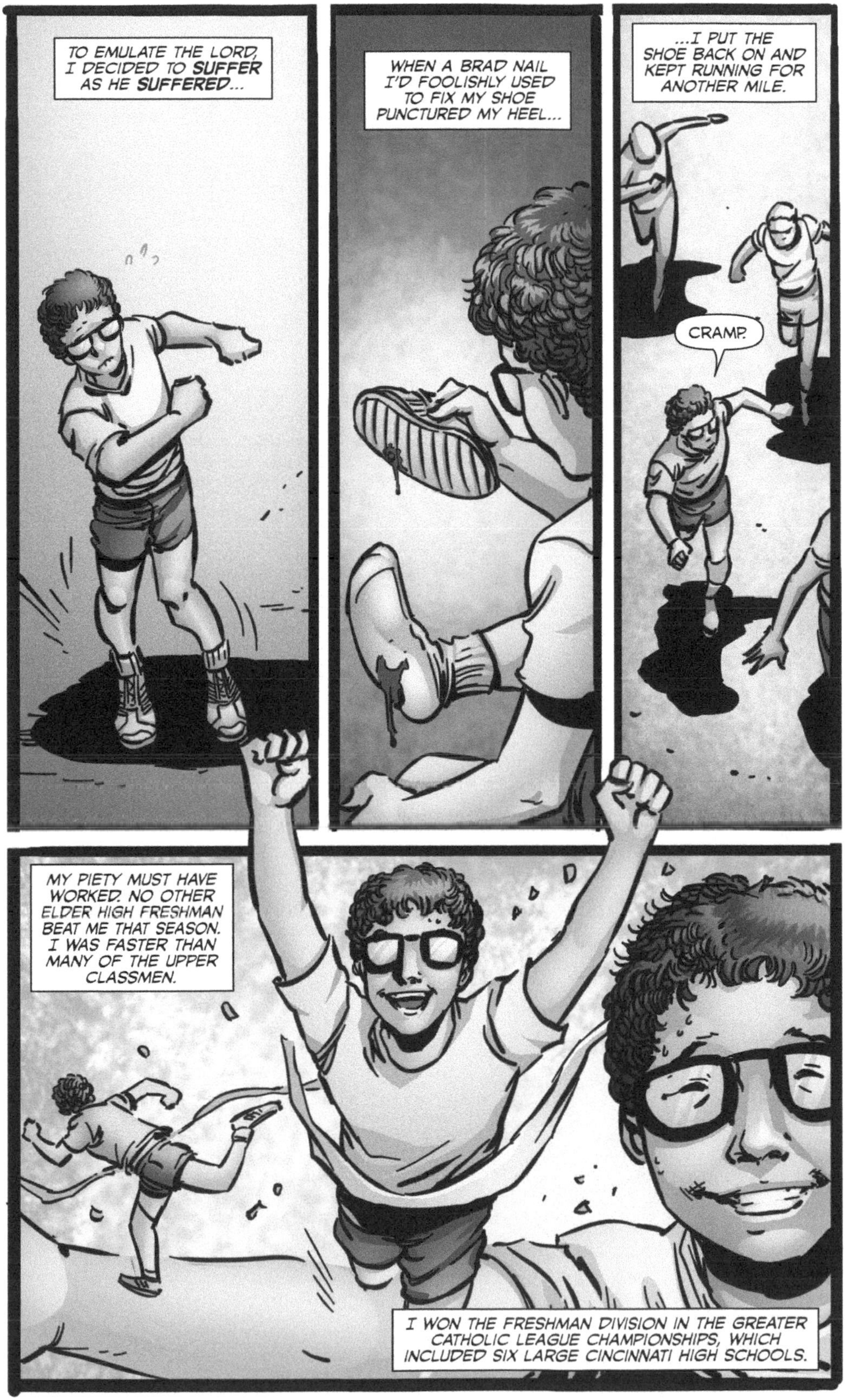
TO EMULATE THE LORD, I DECIDED TO **SUFFER** AS HE **SUFFERED**...
WHEN A BRAD NAIL I'D FOOLISHLY USED TO FIX MY SHOE PUNCTURED MY HEEL...
...I PUT THE SHOE BACK ON AND KEPT RUNNING FOR ANOTHER MILE.
CRAMP.
MY PIETY MUST HAVE WORKED. NO OTHER ELDER HIGH FRESHMAN BEAT ME THAT SEASON. I WAS FASTER THAN MANY OF THE UPPER CLASSMEN.
I WON THE FRESHMAN DIVISION IN THE GREATER CATHOLIC LEAGUE CHAMPIONSHIPS, WHICH INCLUDED SIX LARGE CINCINNATI HIGH SCHOOLS.

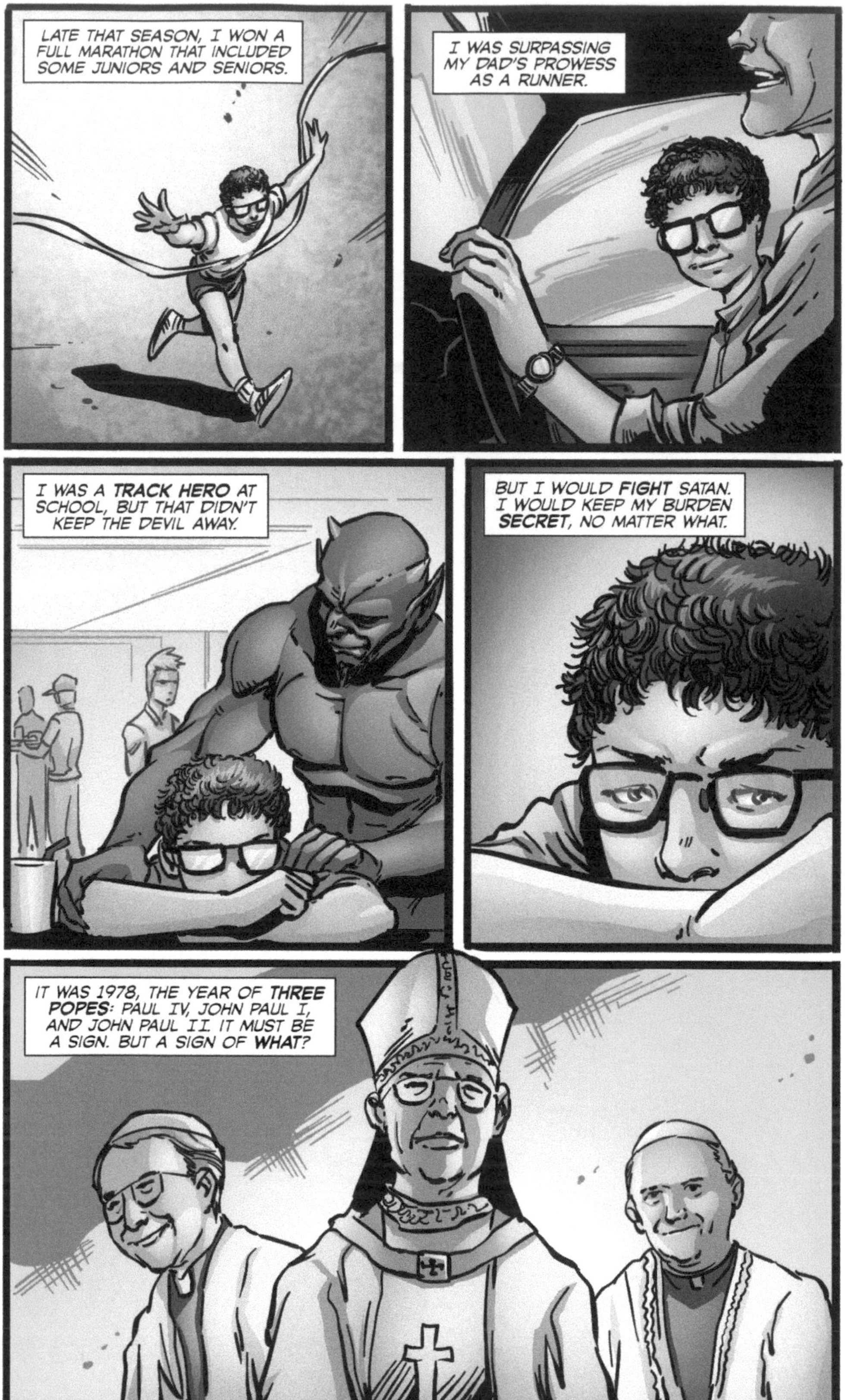
LATE THAT SEASON, I WON A FULL MARATHON THAT INCLUDED SOME JUNIORS AND SENIORS.
I WAS SURPASSING MY DAD'S PROWESS AS A RUNNER.
I WAS A TRACK HERO AT SCHOOL, BUT THAT DIDN'T KEEP THE DEVIL AWAY.
BUT I WOULD FIGHT SATAN. I WOULD KEEP MY BURDEN SECRET, NO MATTER WHAT.
IT WAS 1978, THE YEAR OF THREE POPES: PAUL IV, JOHN PAUL I, AND JOHN PAUL II. IT MUST BE A SIGN. BUT A SIGN OF WHAT?

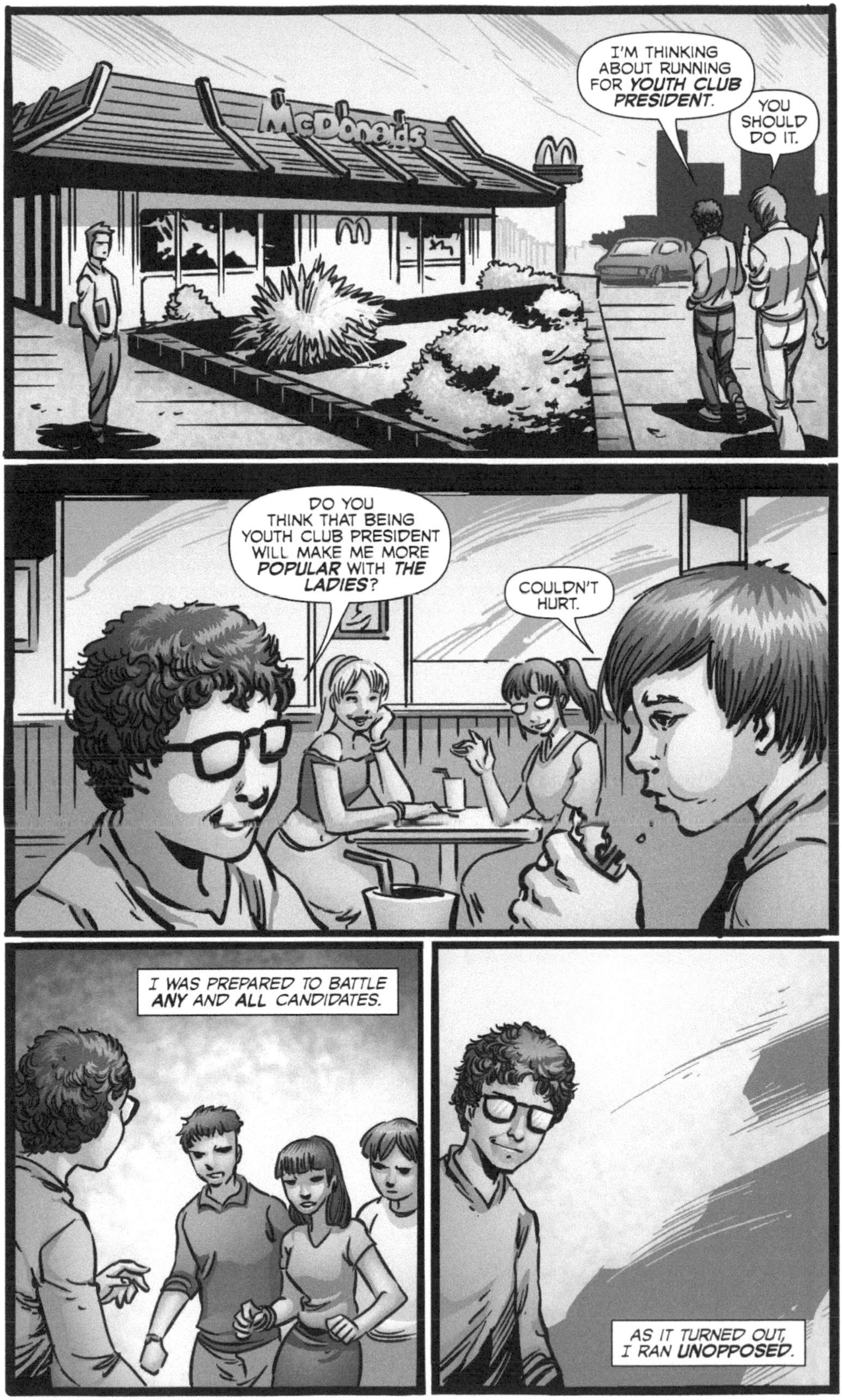
McDonald's
I'M THINKING ABOUT RUNNING FOR YOUTH CLUB PRESIDENT.
YOU SHOULD DO IT.
DO YOU THINK THAT BEING YOUTH CLUB PRESIDENT WILL MAKE ME MORE POPULAR WITH THE LADIES?
COULDN'T HURT.
I WAS PREPARED TO BATTLE ANY AND ALL CANDIDATES.
AS IT TURNED OUT, I RAN UNOPPOSED.

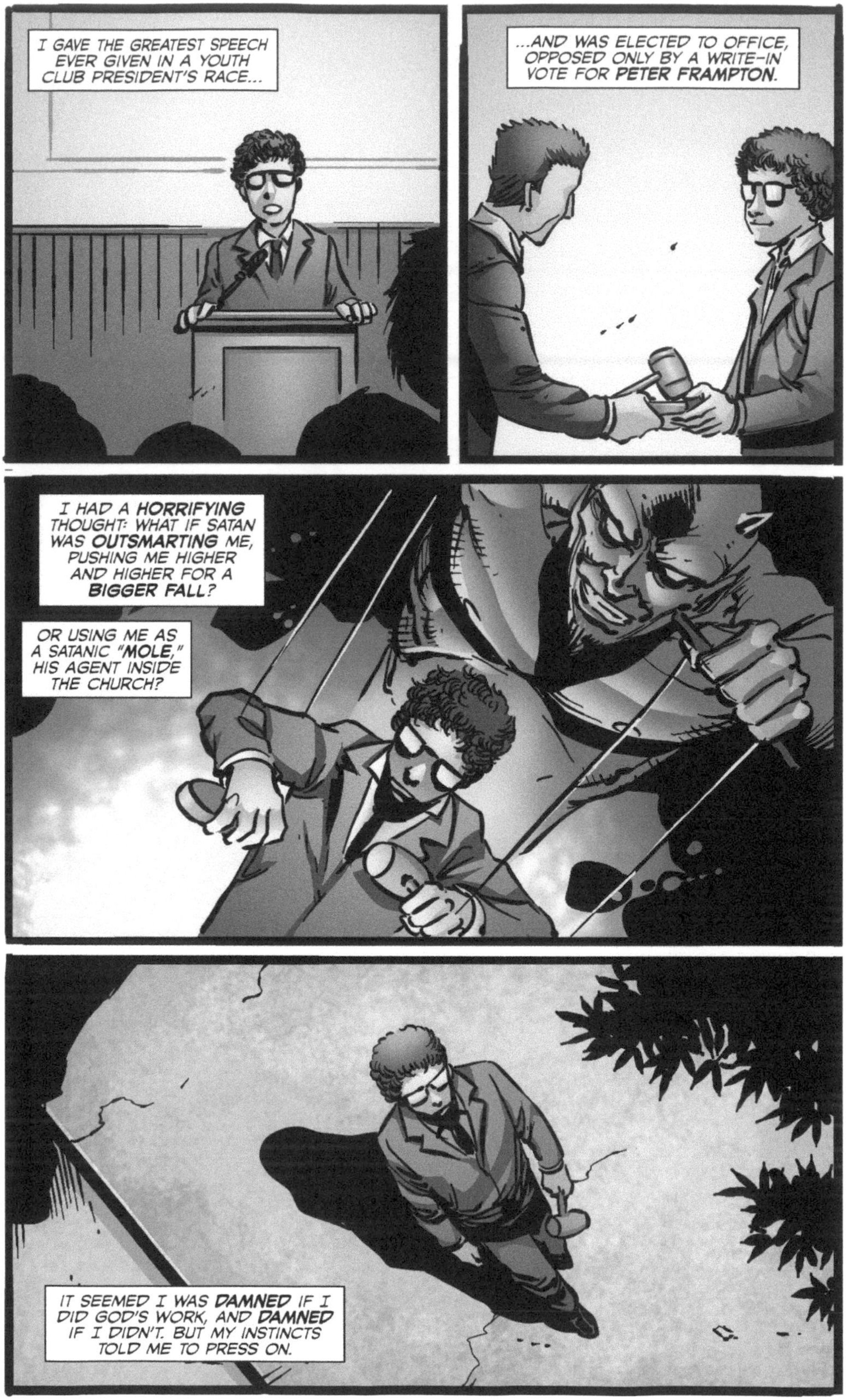
I GAVE THE GREATEST SPEECH EVER GIVEN IN A YOUTH CLUB PRESIDENT'S RACE...
...AND WAS ELECTED TO OFFICE, OPPOSED ONLY BY A WRITE-IN VOTE FOR **PETER FRAMPTON**.
I HAD A **HORRIFYING** THOUGHT: WHAT IF SATAN WAS **OUTSMARTING** ME, PUSHING ME HIGHER AND HIGHER FOR A **BIGGER FALL**?
OR USING ME AS A SATANIC "**MOLE**," HIS AGENT INSIDE THE CHURCH?
IT SEEMED I WAS **DAMNED** IF I DID GOD'S WORK, AND **DAMNED** IF I DIDN'T. BUT MY INSTINCTS TOLD ME TO PRESS ON.

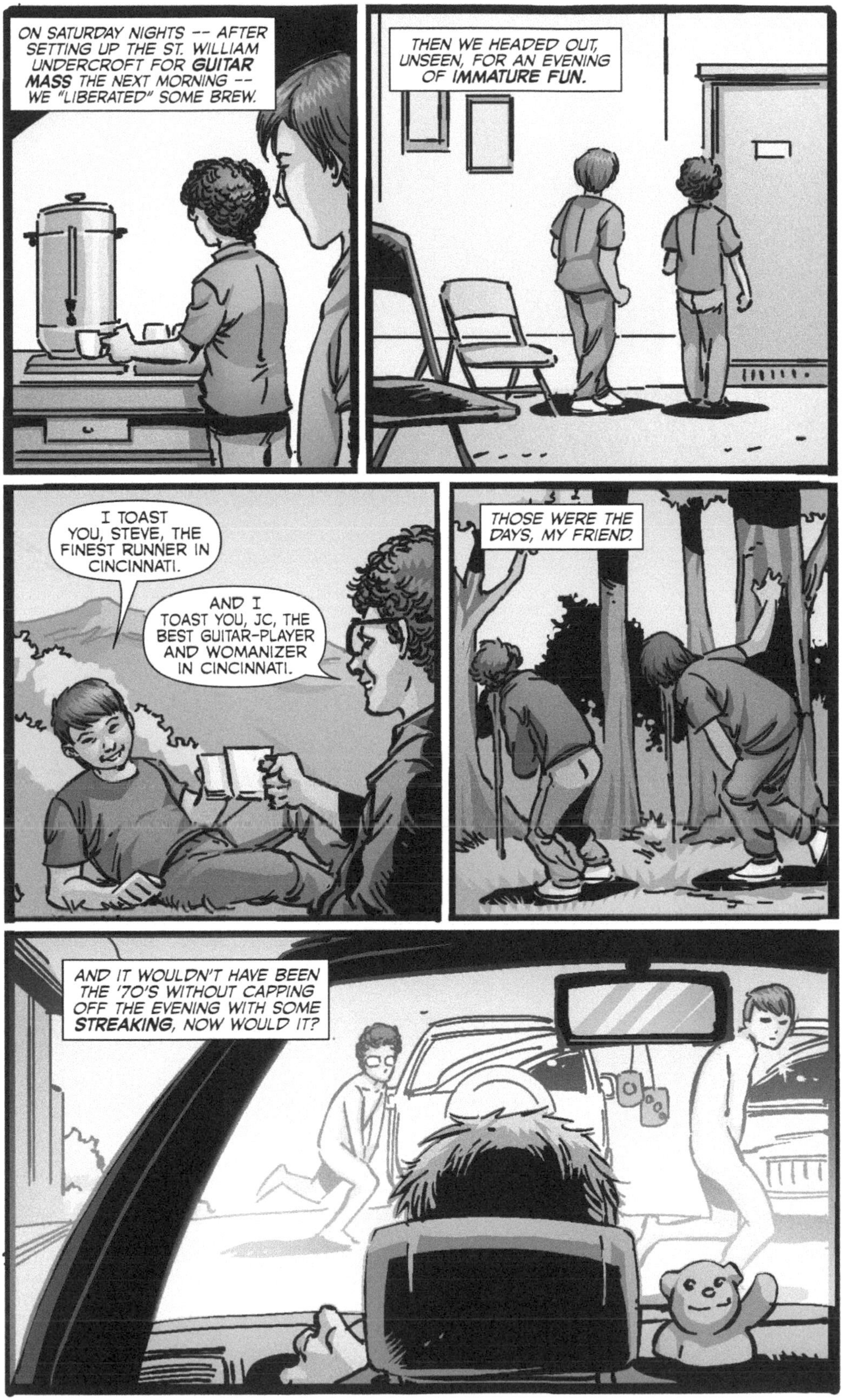
ON SATURDAY NIGHTS -- AFTER SETTING UP THE ST. WILLIAM UNDERCROFT FOR GUITAR MASS THE NEXT MORNING -- WE "LIBERATED" SOME BREW.
THEN WE HEADED OUT, UNSEEN, FOR AN EVENING OF IMMATURE FUN.
I TOAST YOU, STEVE, THE FINEST RUNNER IN CINCINNATI.
AND I TOAST YOU, JC, THE BEST GUITAR-PLAYER AND WOMANIZER IN CINCINNATI.
THOSE WERE THE DAYS, MY FRIEND.
AND IT WOULDN'T HAVE BEEN THE '70'S WITHOUT CAPPING OFF THE EVENING WITH SOME STREAKING, NOW WOULD IT?

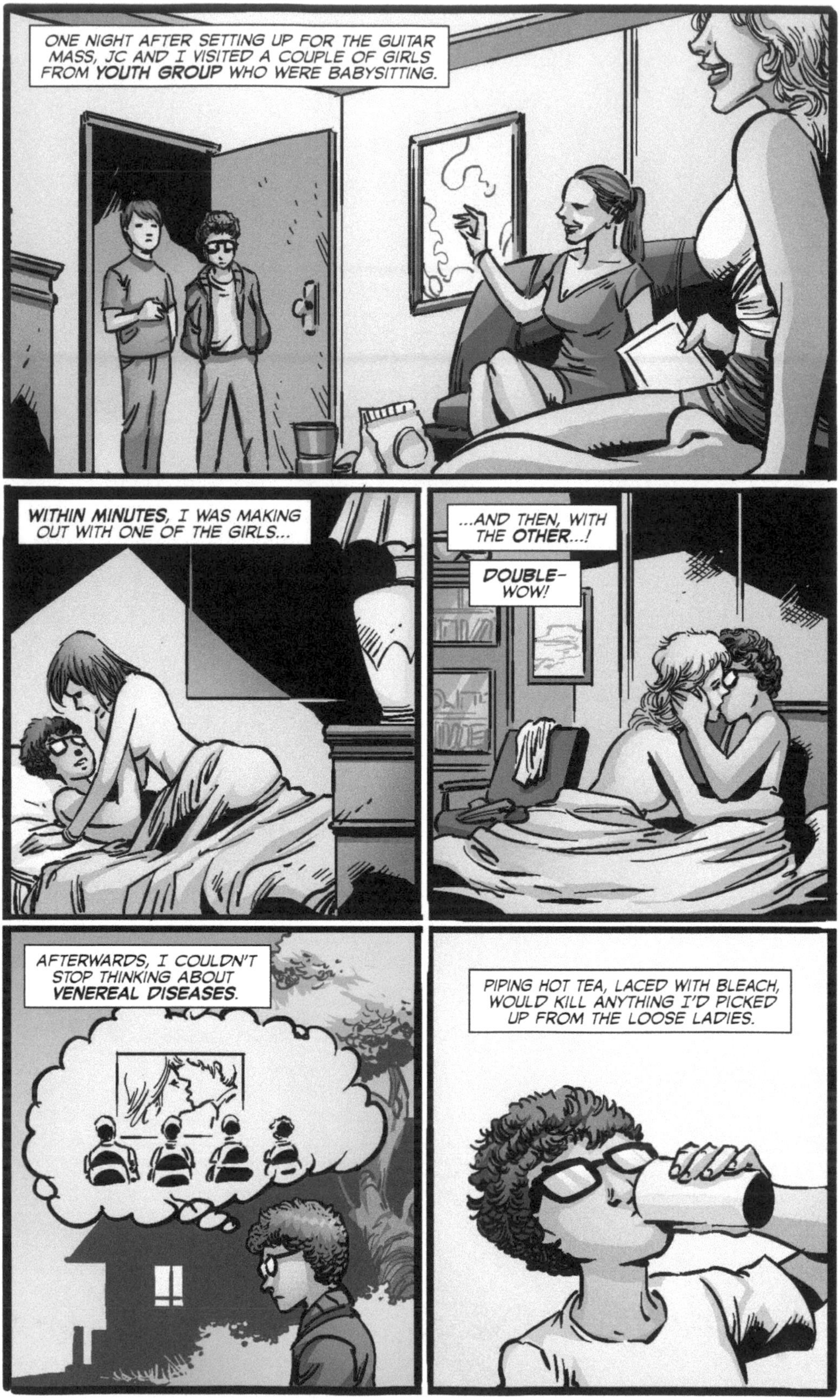
ONE NIGHT AFTER SETTING UP FOR THE GUITAR MASS, JC AND I VISITED A COUPLE OF GIRLS FROM YOUTH GROUP WHO WERE BABYSITTING.
WITHIN MINUTES, I WAS MAKING OUT WITH ONE OF THE GIRLS...
...AND THEN, WITH THE OTHER...!
DOUBLE-WOW!
AFTERWARDS, I COULDN'T STOP THINKING ABOUT VENEREAL DISEASES.
PIPING HOT TEA, LACED WITH BLEACH, WOULD KILL ANYTHING I'D PICKED UP FROM THE LOOSE LADIES.

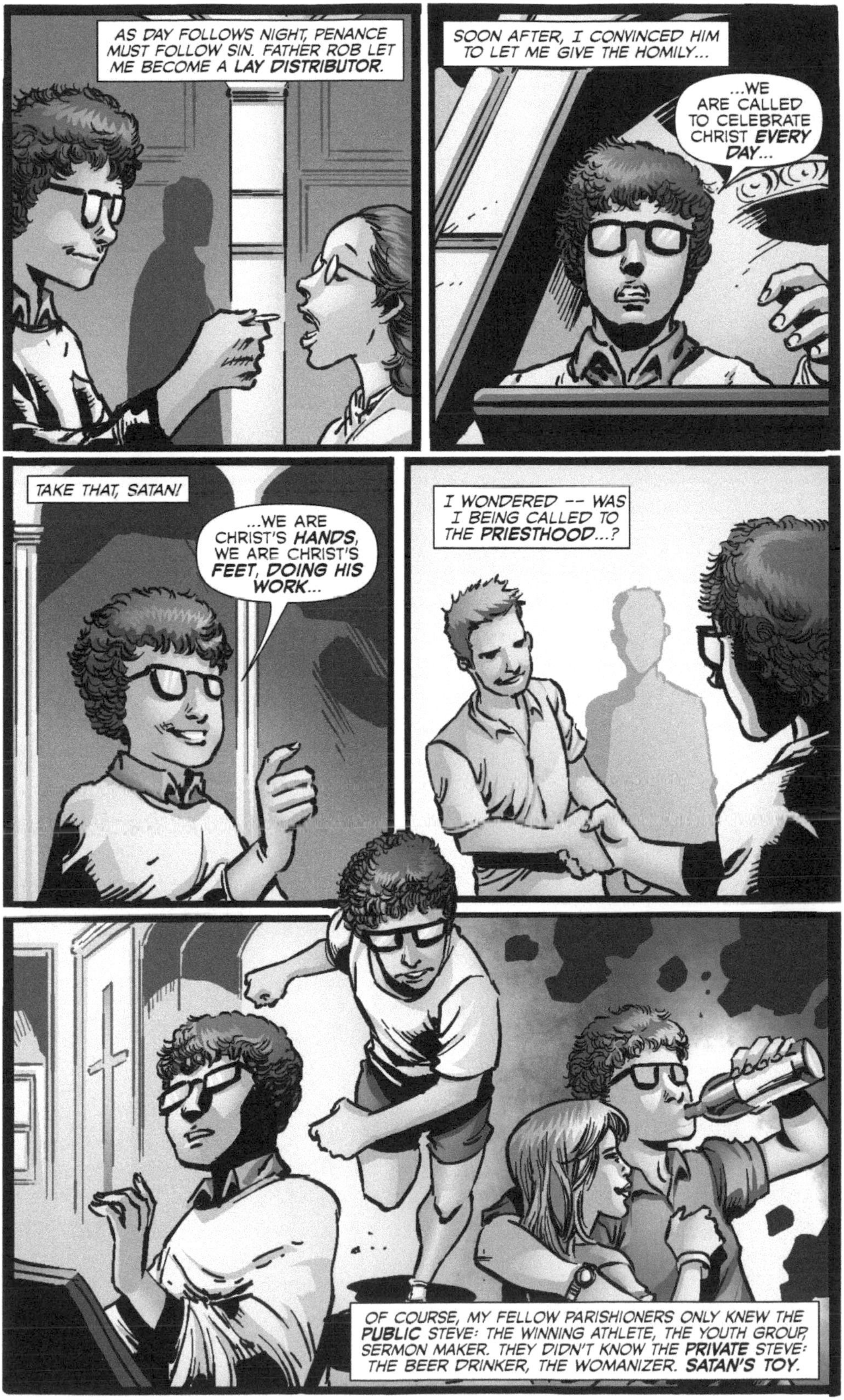
AS DAY FOLLOWS NIGHT, PENANCE MUST FOLLOW SIN. FATHER ROB LET ME BECOME A LAY DISTRIBUTOR.
SOON AFTER, I CONVINCED HIM TO LET ME GIVE THE HOMILY...
...WE ARE CALLED TO CELEBRATE CHRIST EVERY DAY...
TAKE THAT, SATAN!
...WE ARE CHRIST'S HANDS, WE ARE CHRIST'S FEET, DOING HIS WORK...
I WONDERED -- WAS I BEING CALLED TO THE PRIESTHOOD...?
OF COURSE, MY FELLOW PARISHIONERS ONLY KNEW THE PUBLIC STEVE: THE WINNING ATHLETE, THE YOUTH GROUP, SERMON MAKER. THEY DIDN'T KNOW THE PRIVATE STEVE: THE BEER DRINKER, THE WOMANIZER. SATAN'S TOY.

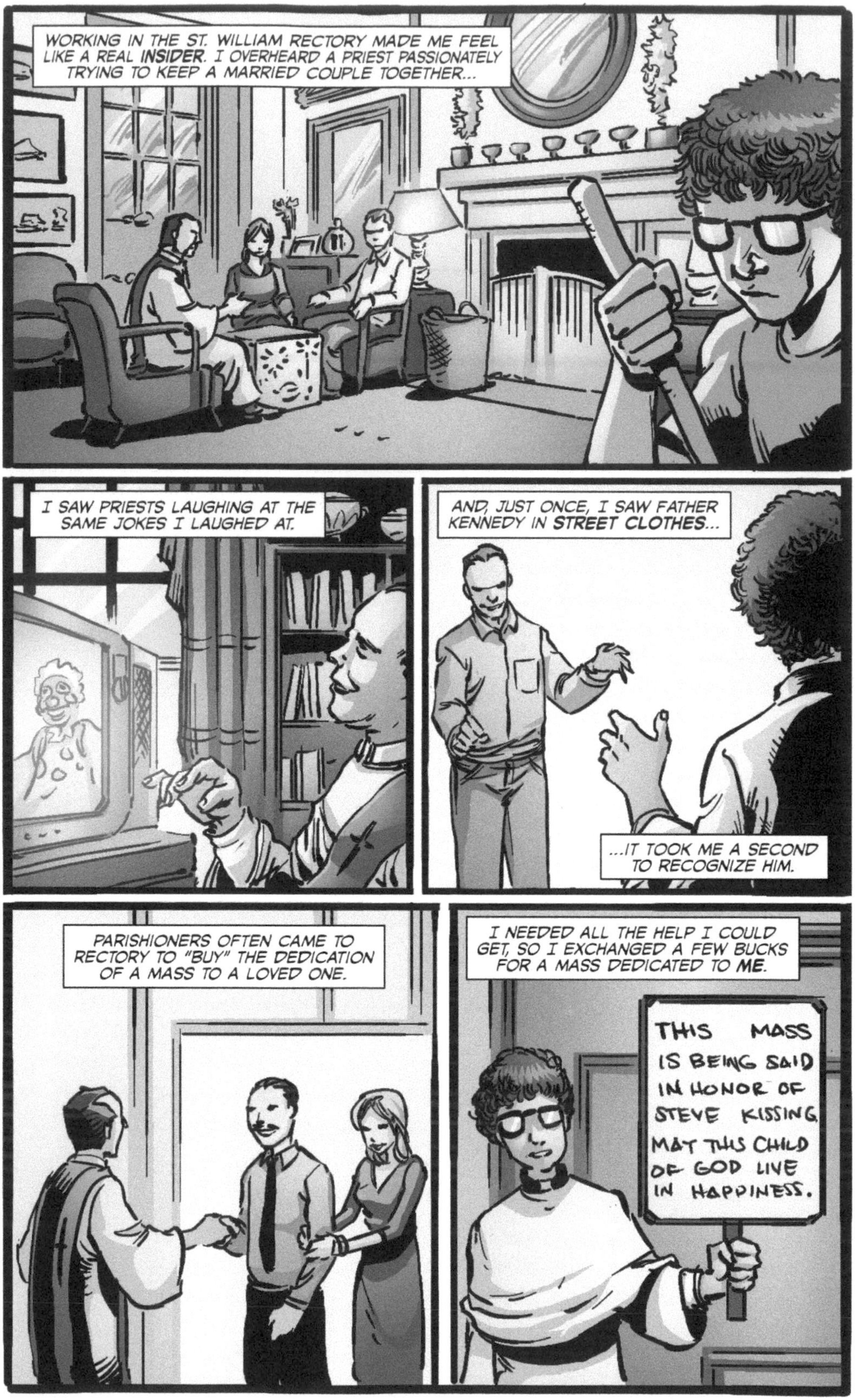
WORKING IN THE ST. WILLIAM RECTORY MADE ME FEEL LIKE A REAL INSIDER. I OVERHEARD A PRIEST PASSIONATELY TRYING TO KEEP A MARRIED COUPLE TOGETHER...
I SAW PRIESTS LAUGHING AT THE SAME JOKES I LAUGHED AT.
AND, JUST ONCE, I SAW FATHER KENNEDY IN STREET CLOTHES...
...IT TOOK ME A SECOND TO RECOGNIZE HIM.
PARISHIONERS OFTEN CAME TO RECTORY TO "BUY" THE DEDICATION OF A MASS TO A LOVED ONE.
I NEEDED ALL THE HELP I COULD GET, SO I EXCHANGED A FEW BUCKS FOR A MASS DEDICATED TO ME.
THIS MASS IS BEING SAID IN HONOR OF STEVE KISSING. MAY THIS CHILD OF GOD LIVE IN HAPPINESS.

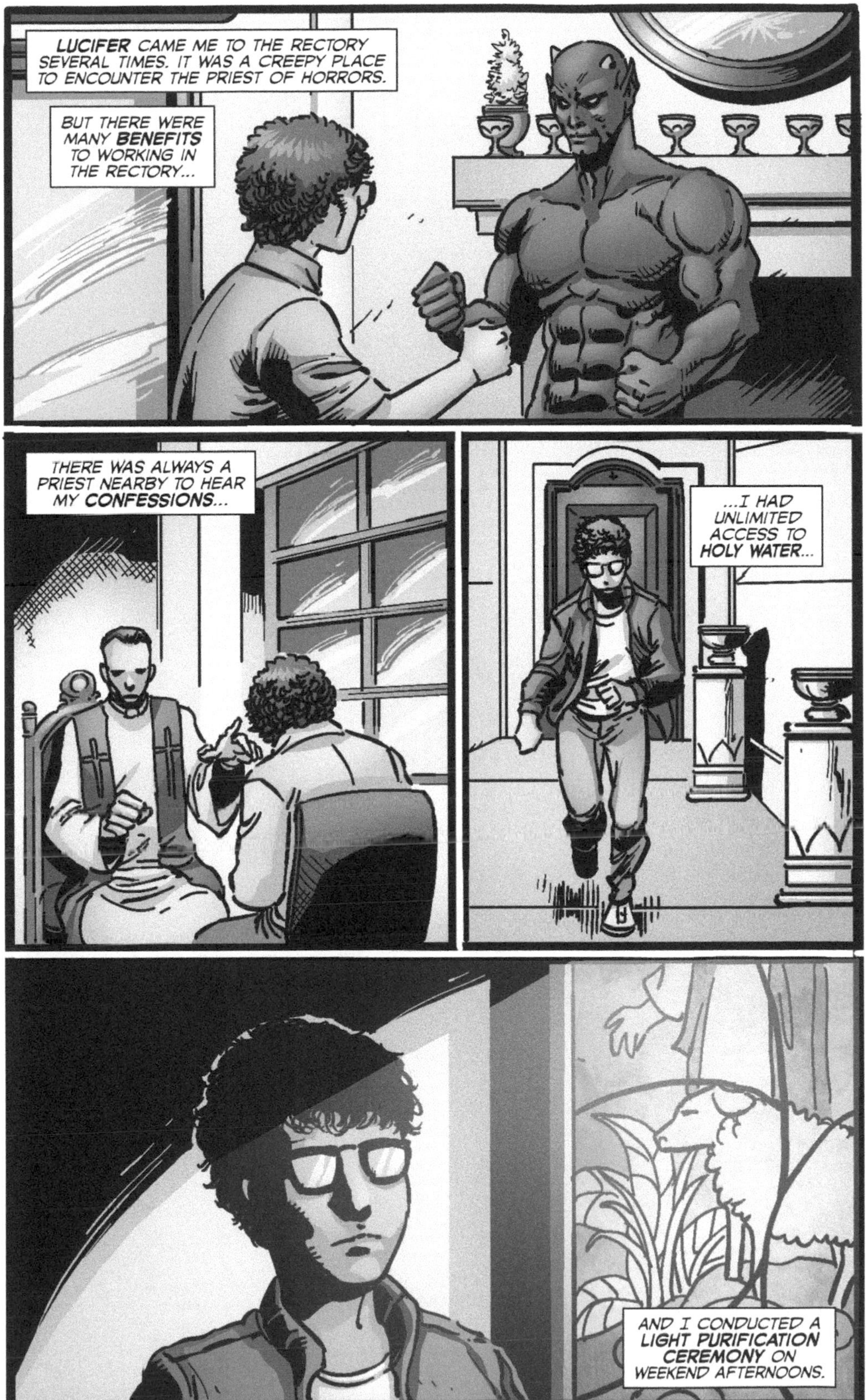
LUCIFER CAME ME TO THE RECTORY SEVERAL TIMES. IT WAS A CREEPY PLACE TO ENCOUNTER THE PRIEST OF HORRORS.
BUT THERE WERE MANY **BENEFITS** TO WORKING IN THE RECTORY...
THERE WAS ALWAYS A PRIEST NEARBY TO HEAR MY **CONFESSIONS**...
...I HAD UNLIMITED ACCESS TO **HOLY WATER**...
AND I CONDUCTED A **LIGHT PURIFICATION CEREMONY** ON WEEKEND AFTERNOONS.

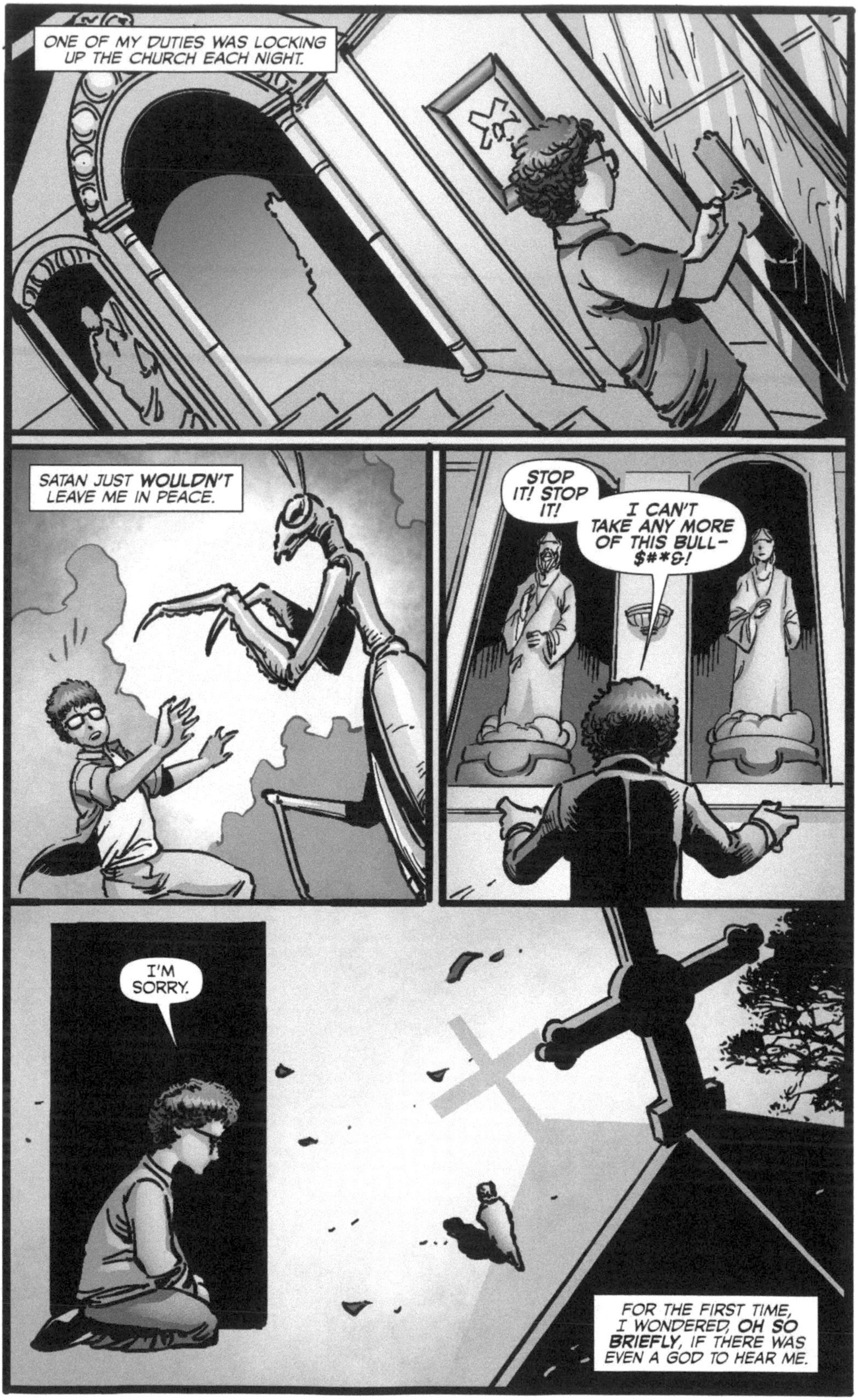
ONE OF MY DUTIES WAS LOCKING UP THE CHURCH EACH NIGHT.
SATAN JUST **WOULDN'T** LEAVE ME IN PEACE.
STOP IT! STOP IT!
I CAN'T TAKE ANY MORE OF THIS BULL-$#*&!
I'M SORRY.
FOR THE FIRST TIME, I WONDERED, **OH SO BRIEFLY**, IF THERE WAS EVEN A GOD TO HEAR ME.

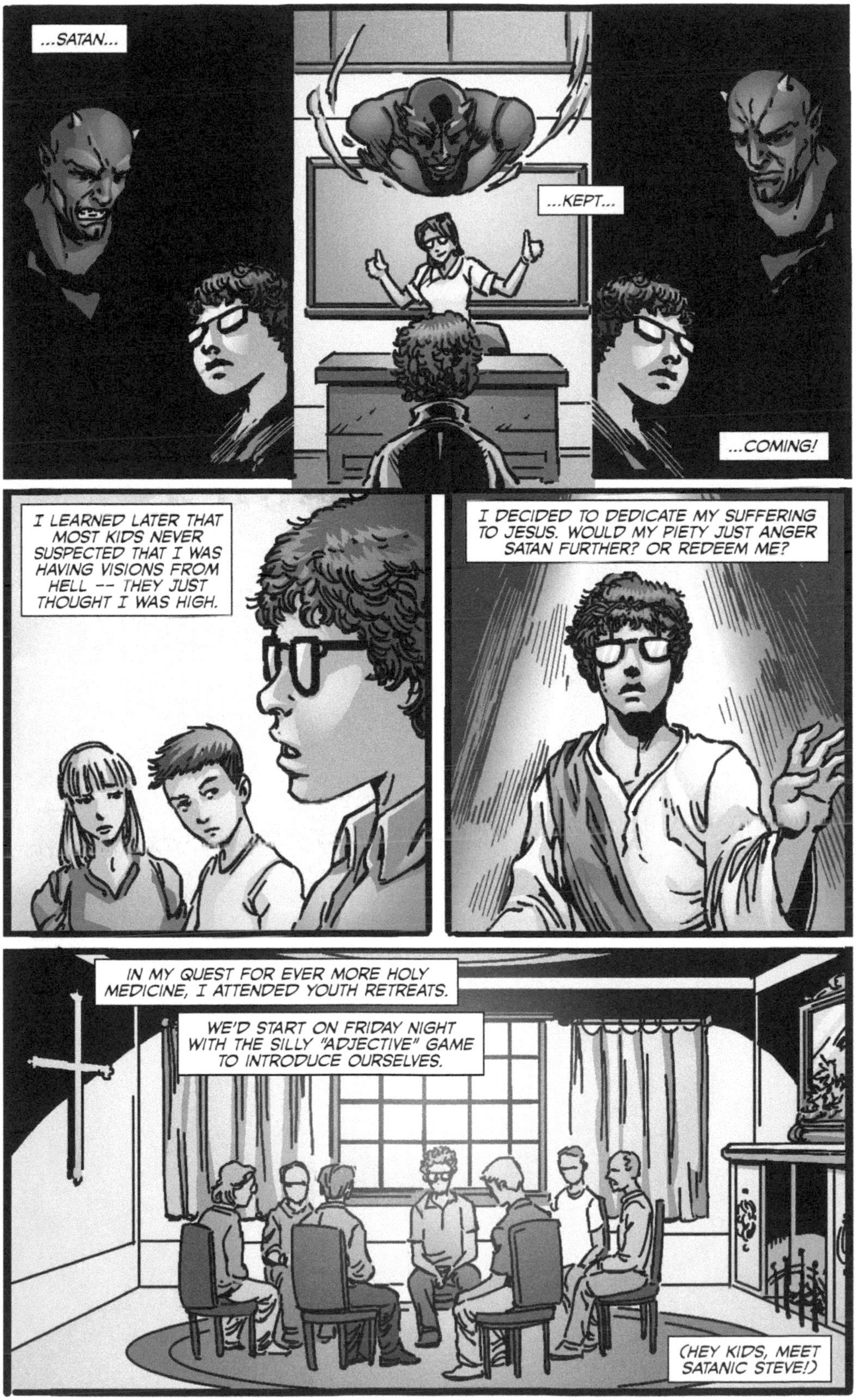
...SATAN...
...KEPT...
...COMING!
I LEARNED LATER THAT MOST KIDS NEVER SUSPECTED THAT I WAS HAVING VISIONS FROM HELL -- THEY JUST THOUGHT I WAS HIGH.
I DECIDED TO DEDICATE MY SUFFERING TO JESUS. WOULD MY PIETY JUST ANGER SATAN FURTHER? OR REDEEM ME?
IN MY QUEST FOR EVER MORE HOLY MEDICINE, I ATTENDED YOUTH RETREATS.
WE'D START ON FRIDAY NIGHT WITH THE SILLY "ADJECTIVE" GAME TO INTRODUCE OURSELVES.
(HEY KIDS, MEET SATANIC STEVE!)

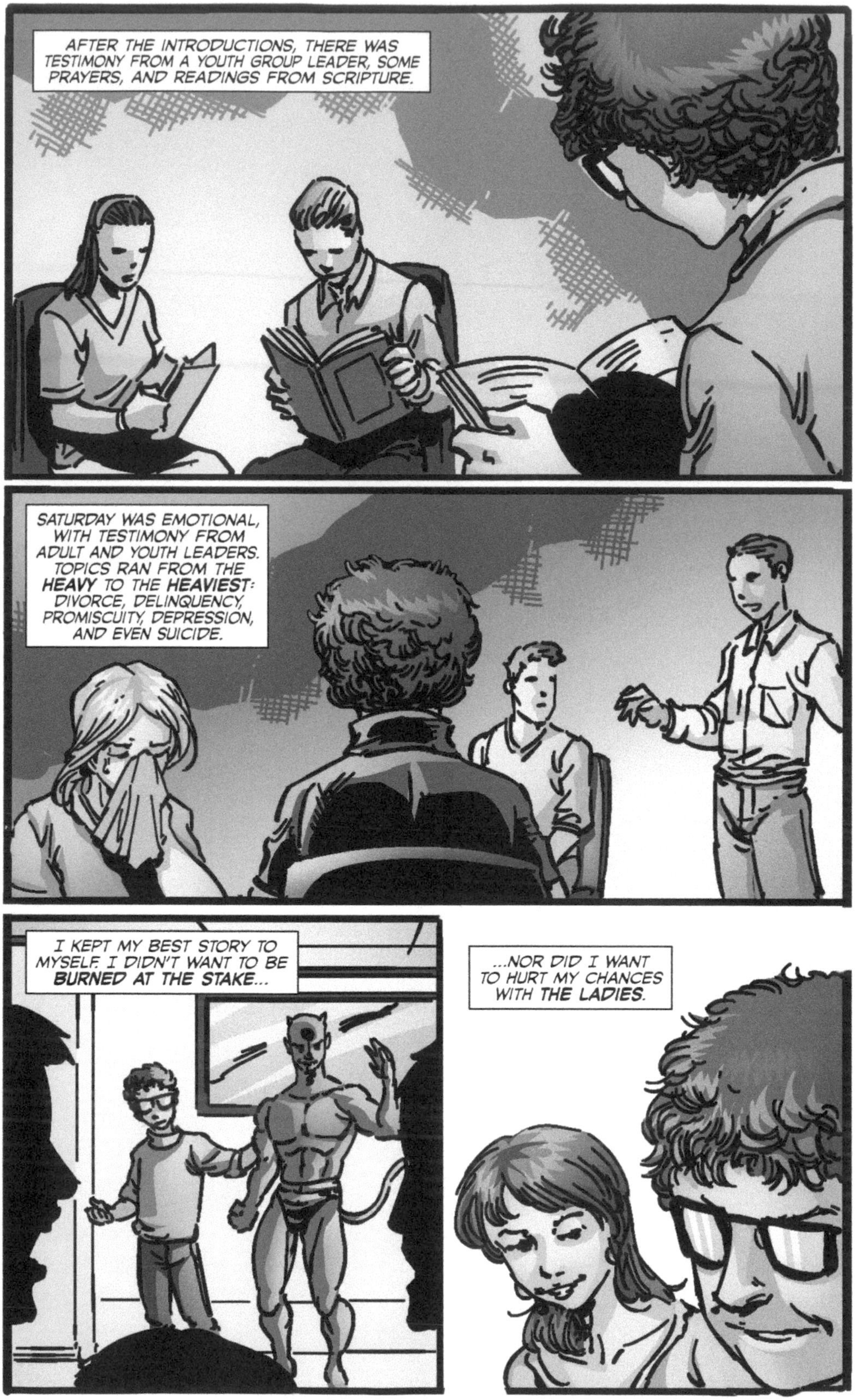
AFTER THE INTRODUCTIONS, THERE WAS TESTIMONY FROM A YOUTH GROUP LEADER, SOME PRAYERS, AND READINGS FROM SCRIPTURE.
SATURDAY WAS EMOTIONAL, WITH TESTIMONY FROM ADULT AND YOUTH LEADERS. TOPICS RAN FROM THE HEAVY TO THE HEAVIEST: DIVORCE, DELINQUENCY, PROMISCUITY, DEPRESSION, AND EVEN SUICIDE.
I KEPT MY BEST STORY TO MYSELF. I DIDN'T WANT TO BE BURNED AT THE STAKE...
...NOR DID I WANT TO HURT MY CHANCES WITH THE LADIES.

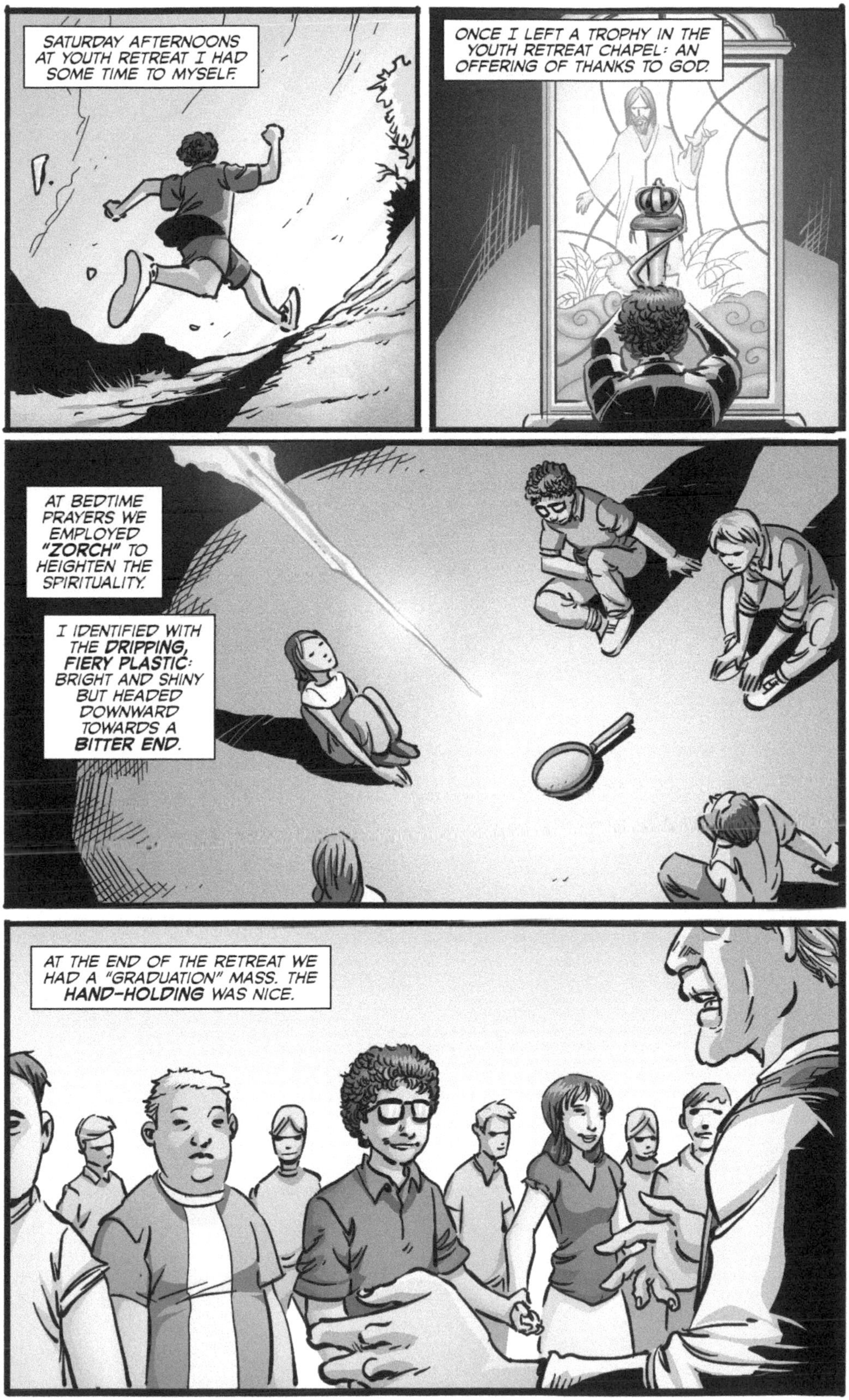
SATURDAY AFTERNOONS AT YOUTH RETREAT I HAD SOME TIME TO MYSELF.
ONCE I LEFT A TROPHY IN THE YOUTH RETREAT CHAPEL: AN OFFERING OF THANKS TO GOD.
AT BEDTIME PRAYERS WE EMPLOYED "ZORCH" TO HEIGHTEN THE SPIRITUALITY.
I IDENTIFIED WITH THE DRIPPING, FIERY PLASTIC: BRIGHT AND SHINY BUT HEADED DOWNWARD TOWARDS A BITTER END.
AT THE END OF THE RETREAT WE HAD A "GRADUATION" MASS. THE HAND-HOLDING WAS NICE.

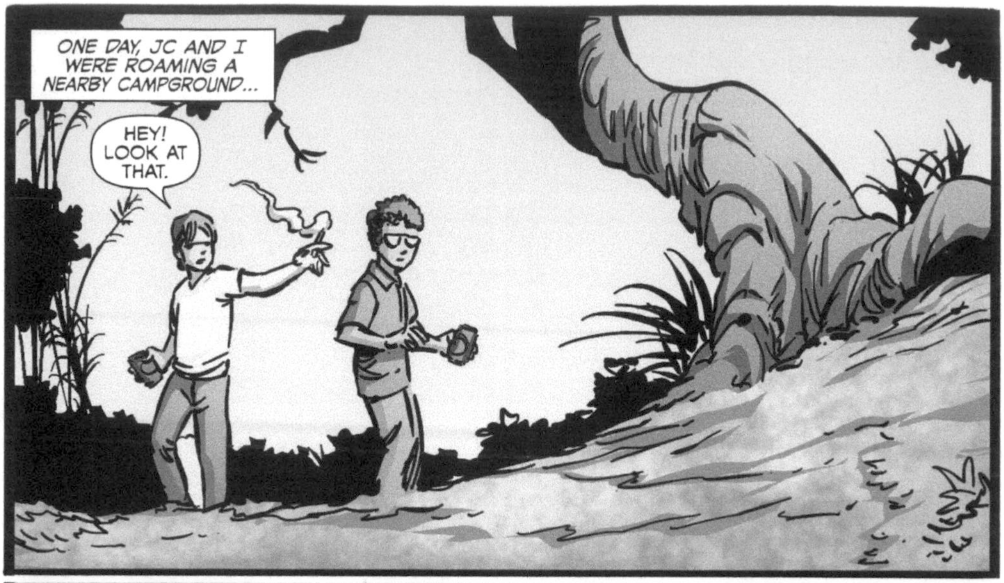
ONE DAY, JC AND I WERE ROAMING A NEARBY CAMPGROUND...
HEY! LOOK AT THAT.
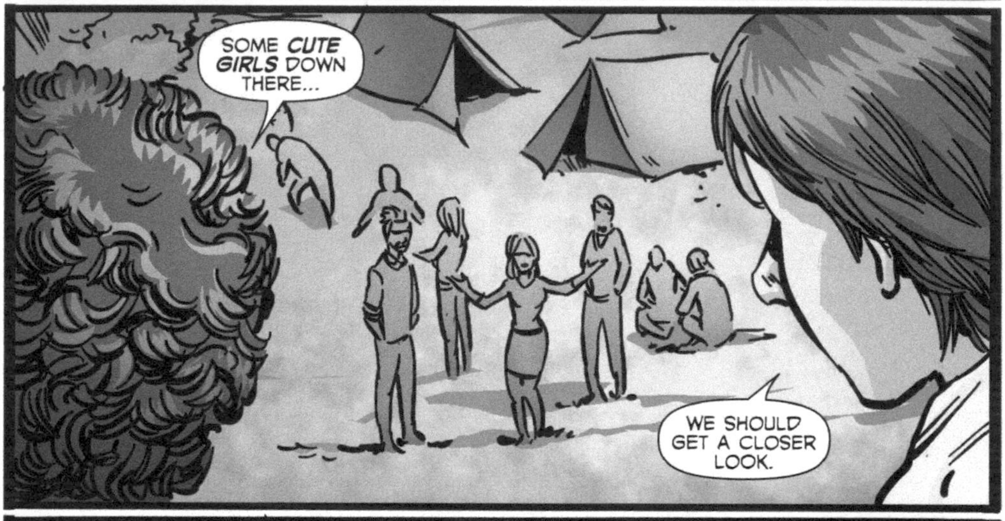
SOME CUTE GIRLS DOWN THERE...
WE SHOULD GET A CLOSER LOOK.
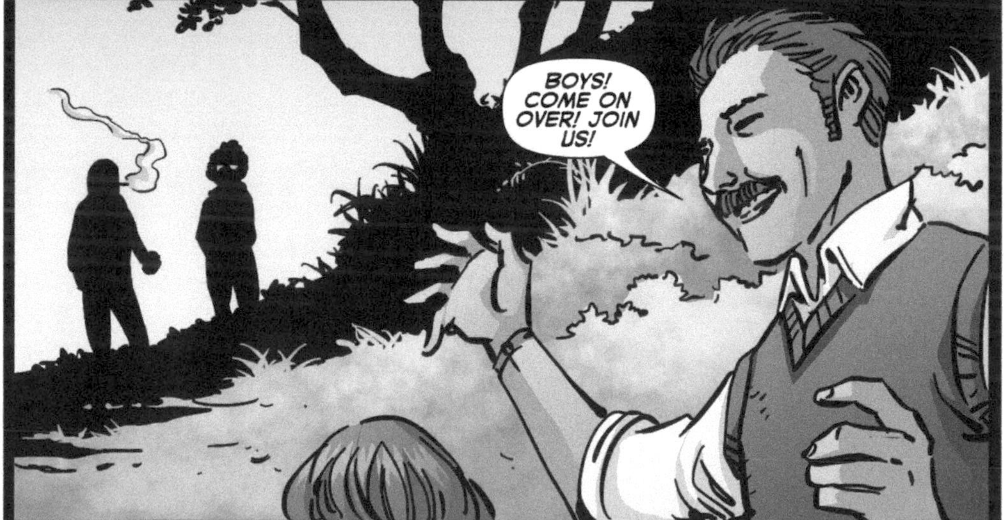
BOYS! COME ON OVER! JOIN US!

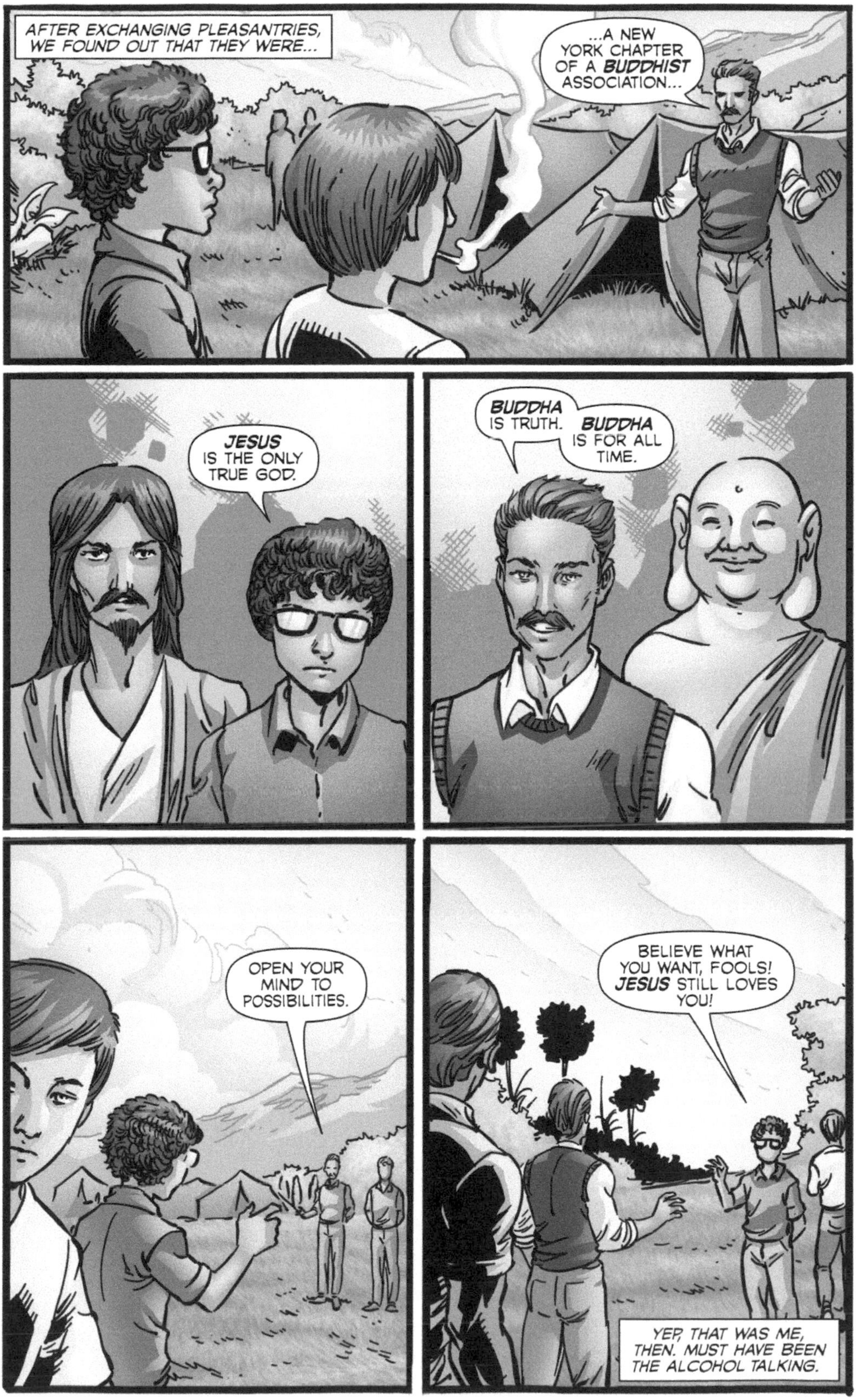
AFTER EXCHANGING PLEASANTRIES, WE FOUND OUT THAT THEY WERE...
...A NEW YORK CHAPTER OF A BUDDHIST ASSOCIATION...
JESUS IS THE ONLY TRUE GOD.
BUDDHA IS TRUTH.
BUDDHA IS FOR ALL TIME.
OPEN YOUR MIND TO POSSIBILITIES.
BELIEVE WHAT YOU WANT, FOOLS! JESUS STILL LOVES YOU!
YEP, THAT WAS ME, THEN. MUST HAVE BEEN THE ALCOHOL TALKING.

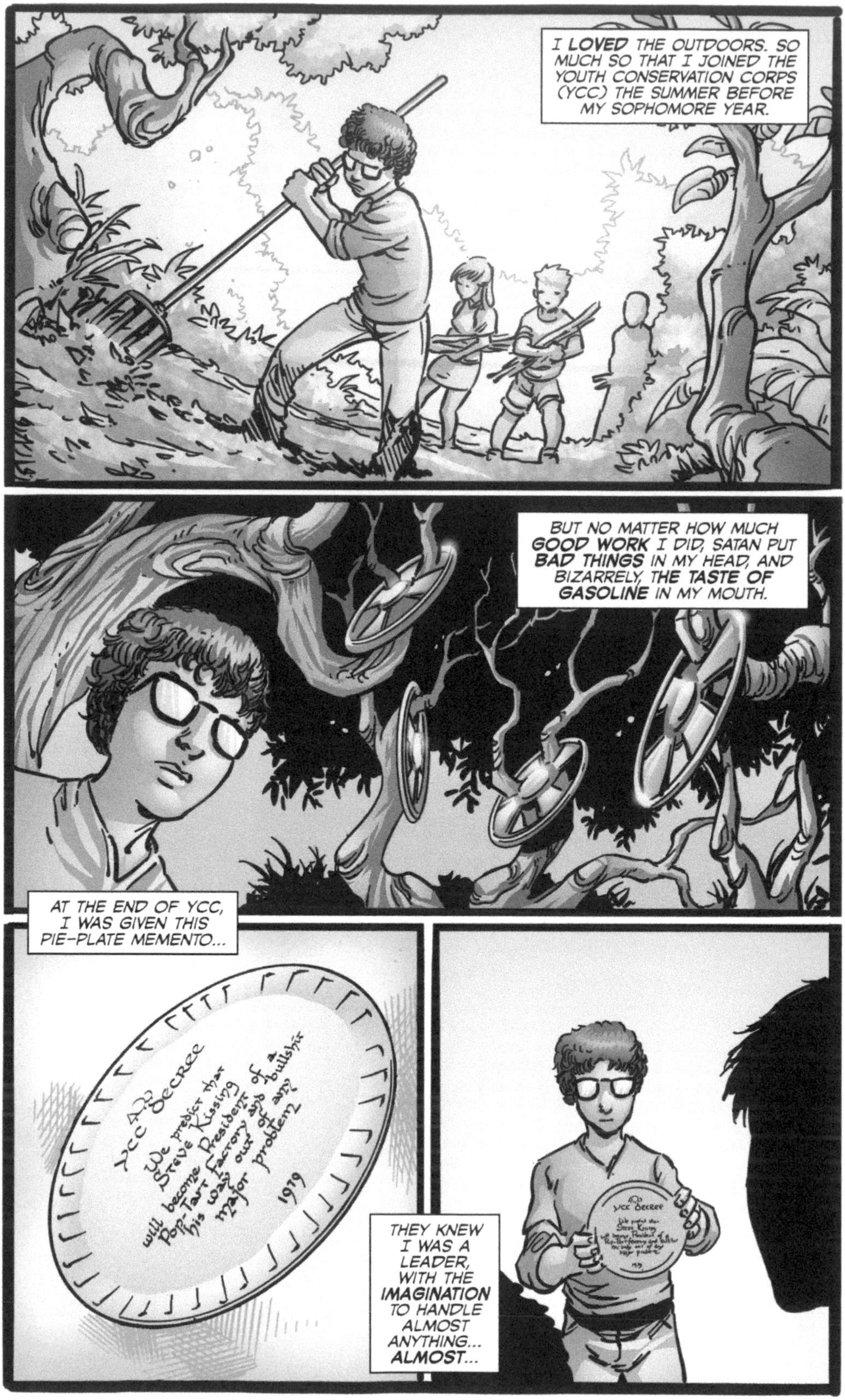

I LOVED THE OUTDOORS. SO MUCH SO THAT I JOINED THE YOUTH CONSERVATION CORPS (YCC) THE SUMMER BEFORE MY SOPHOMORE YEAR.
BUT NO MATTER HOW MUCH GOOD WORK I DID, SATAN PUT BAD THINGS IN MY HEAD, AND BIZARRELY, THE TASTE OF GASOLINE IN MY MOUTH.
AT THE END OF YCC, I WAS GIVEN THIS PIE-PLATE MEMENTO...
YCC Decree
We predict that
Steve Kissing
will become President of a
Pop-Tart Factory and bullshit
his way out of any
major problem
1979
THEY KNEW I WAS A LEADER, WITH THE IMAGINATION TO HANDLE ALMOST ANYTHING... ALMOST...

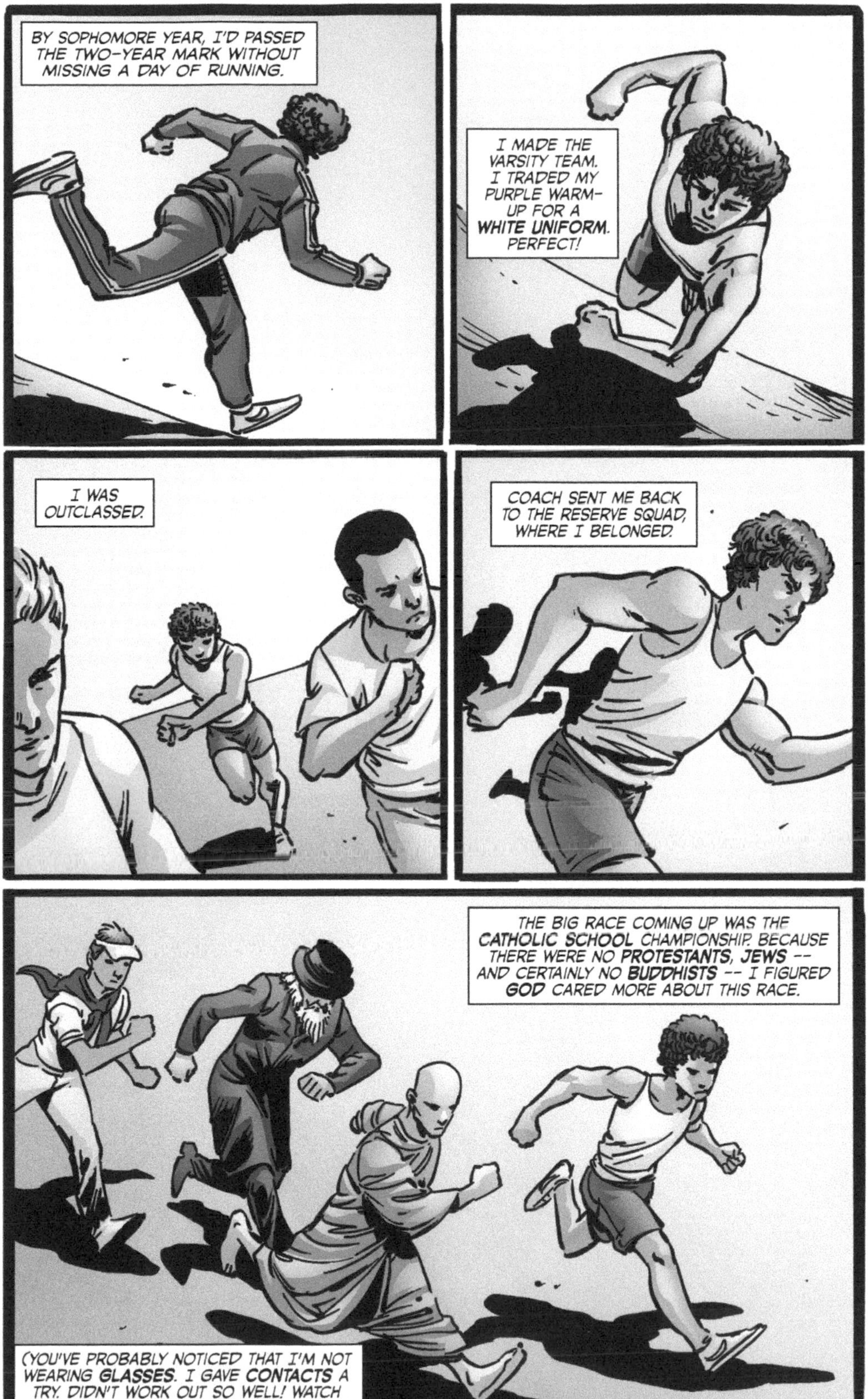
BY SOPHOMORE YEAR, I'D PASSED THE TWO-YEAR MARK WITHOUT MISSING A DAY OF RUNNING.
I MADE THE VARSITY TEAM. I TRADED MY PURPLE WARM-UP FOR A **WHITE UNIFORM**. PERFECT!
I WAS OUTCLASSED.
COACH SENT ME BACK TO THE RESERVE SQUAD, WHERE I BELONGED.
THE BIG RACE COMING UP WAS THE **CATHOLIC SCHOOL** CHAMPIONSHIP. BECAUSE THERE WERE NO **PROTESTANTS**, **JEWS** -- AND CERTAINLY NO **BUDDHISTS** -- I FIGURED **GOD** CARED MORE ABOUT THIS RACE.
(YOU'VE PROBABLY NOTICED THAT I'M NOT WEARING **GLASSES**. I GAVE **CONTACTS** A TRY. DIDN'T WORK OUT SO WELL! WATCH FOR MY GLASSES TO RE-APPEAR LATER...)

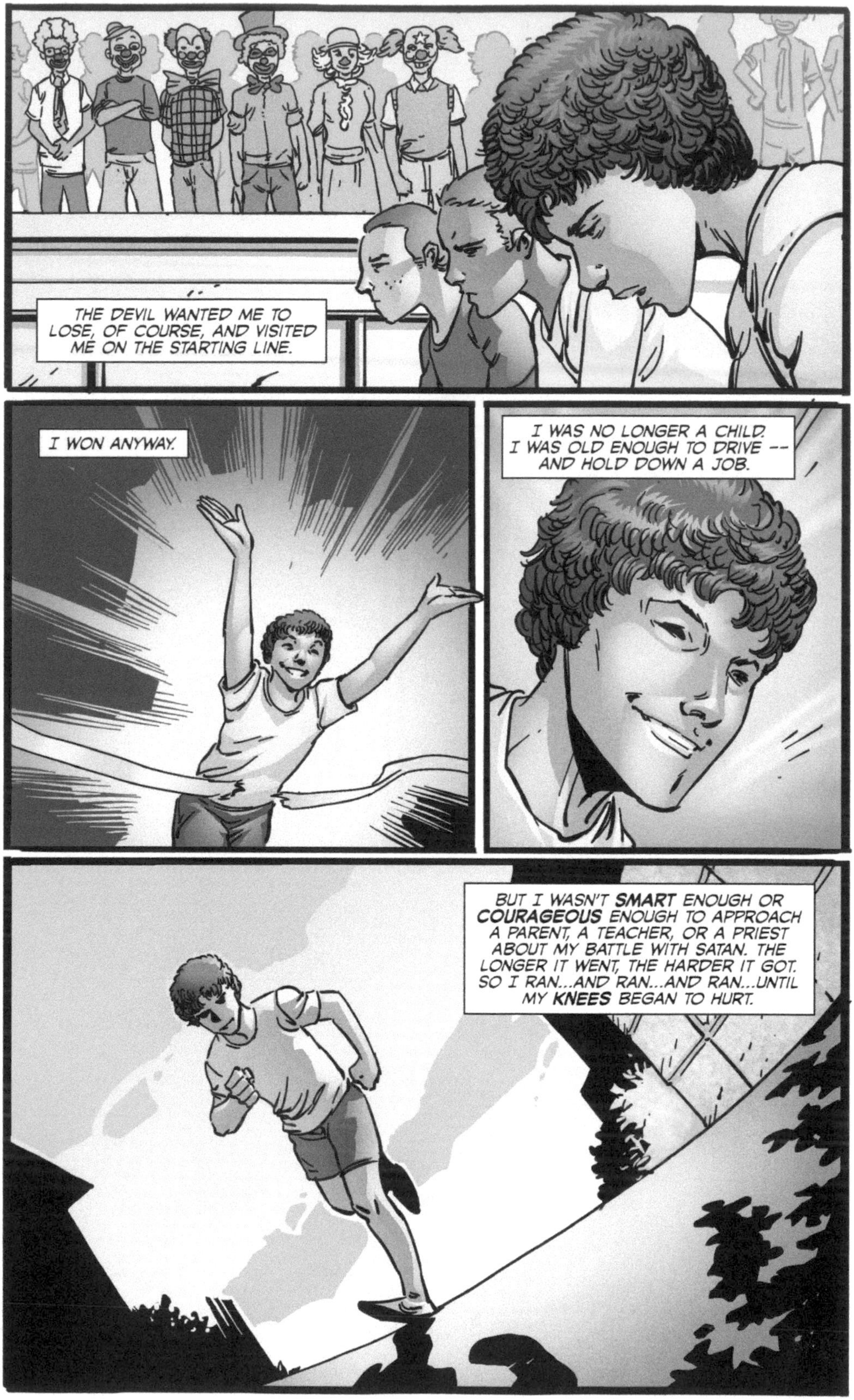
THE DEVIL WANTED ME TO LOSE, OF COURSE, AND VISITED ME ON THE STARTING LINE.
I WON ANYWAY.
I WAS NO LONGER A CHILD. I WAS OLD ENOUGH TO DRIVE -- AND HOLD DOWN A JOB.
BUT I WASN'T **SMART** ENOUGH OR **COURAGEOUS** ENOUGH TO APPROACH A PARENT, A TEACHER, OR A PRIEST ABOUT MY BATTLE WITH SATAN. THE LONGER IT WENT, THE HARDER IT GOT. SO I RAN...AND RAN...AND RAN...UNTIL MY **KNEES** BEGAN TO HURT.

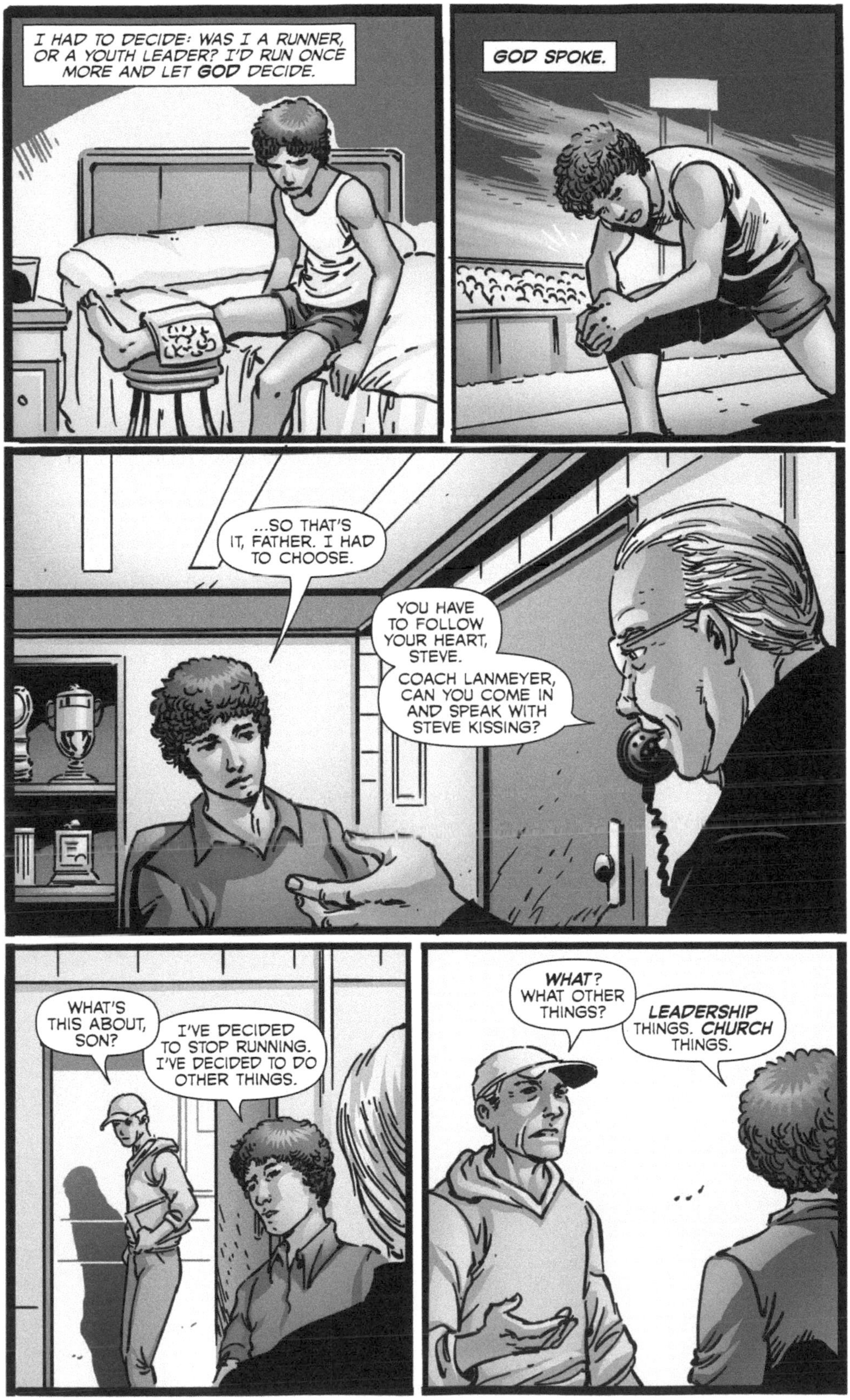
I HAD TO DECIDE: WAS I A RUNNER, OR A YOUTH LEADER? I'D RUN ONCE MORE AND LET GOD DECIDE.
GOD SPOKE.
...SO THAT'S IT, FATHER. I HAD TO CHOOSE.
YOU HAVE TO FOLLOW YOUR HEART, STEVE.
COACH LANMEYER, CAN YOU COME IN AND SPEAK WITH STEVE KISSING?
WHAT'S THIS ABOUT, SON?
I'VE DECIDED TO STOP RUNNING. I'VE DECIDED TO DO OTHER THINGS.
WHAT? WHAT OTHER THINGS?
LEADERSHIP THINGS. CHURCH THINGS.

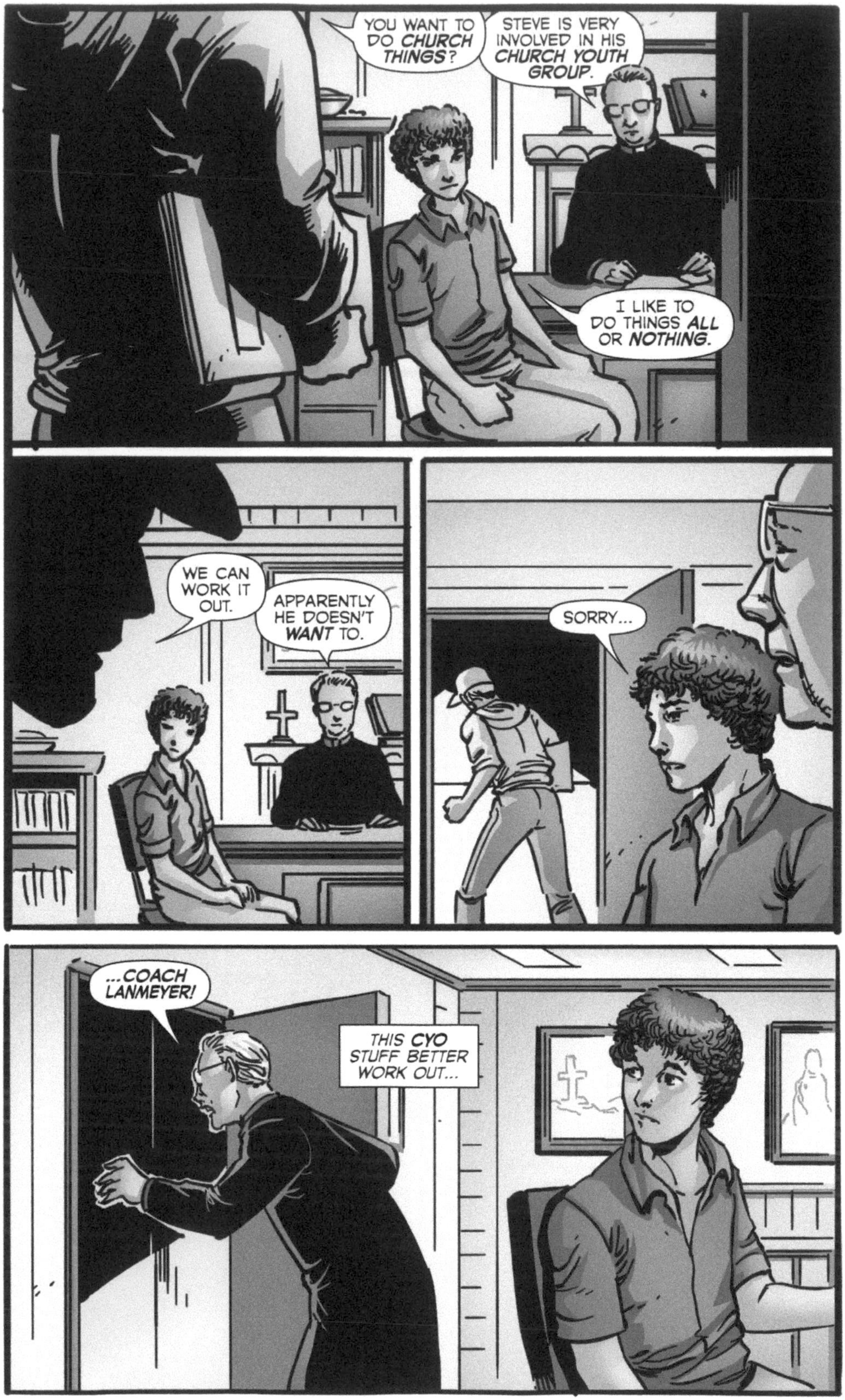
YOU WANT TO DO **CHURCH THINGS**?
STEVE IS VERY INVOLVED IN HIS **CHURCH YOUTH GROUP**.
I LIKE TO DO THINGS **ALL** OR **NOTHING**.
WE CAN WORK IT OUT.
APPARENTLY HE DOESN'T **WANT** TO.
SORRY...
...COACH LANMEYER!
THIS **CYO** STUFF BETTER WORK OUT...

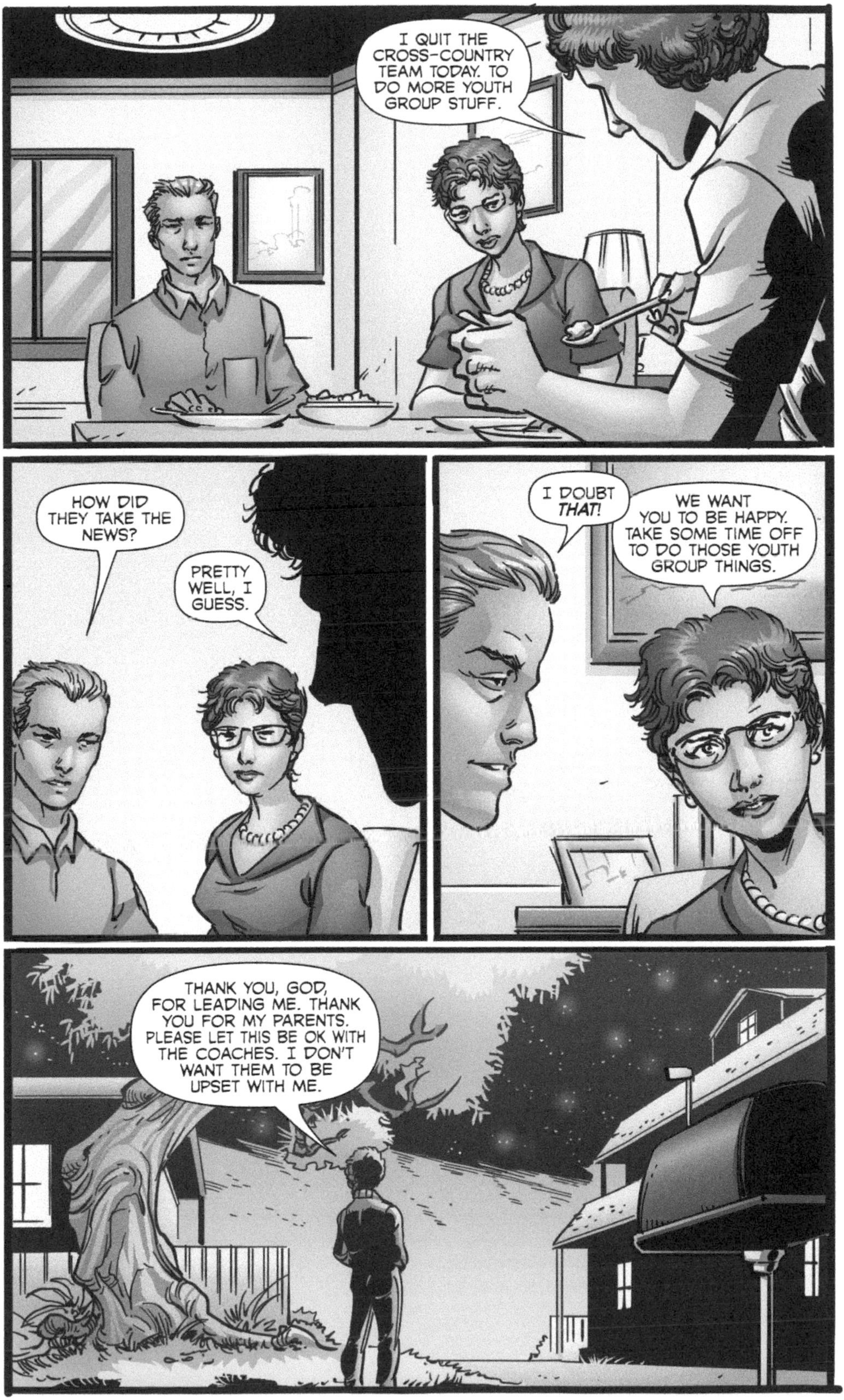
I QUIT THE CROSS-COUNTRY TEAM TODAY. TO DO MORE YOUTH GROUP STUFF.
HOW DID THEY TAKE THE NEWS?
PRETTY WELL, I GUESS.
I DOUBT *THAT*!
WE WANT YOU TO BE HAPPY. TAKE SOME TIME OFF TO DO THOSE YOUTH GROUP THINGS.
THANK YOU, GOD, FOR LEADING ME. THANK YOU FOR MY PARENTS. PLEASE LET THIS BE OK WITH THE COACHES. I DON'T WANT THEM TO BE UPSET WITH ME.

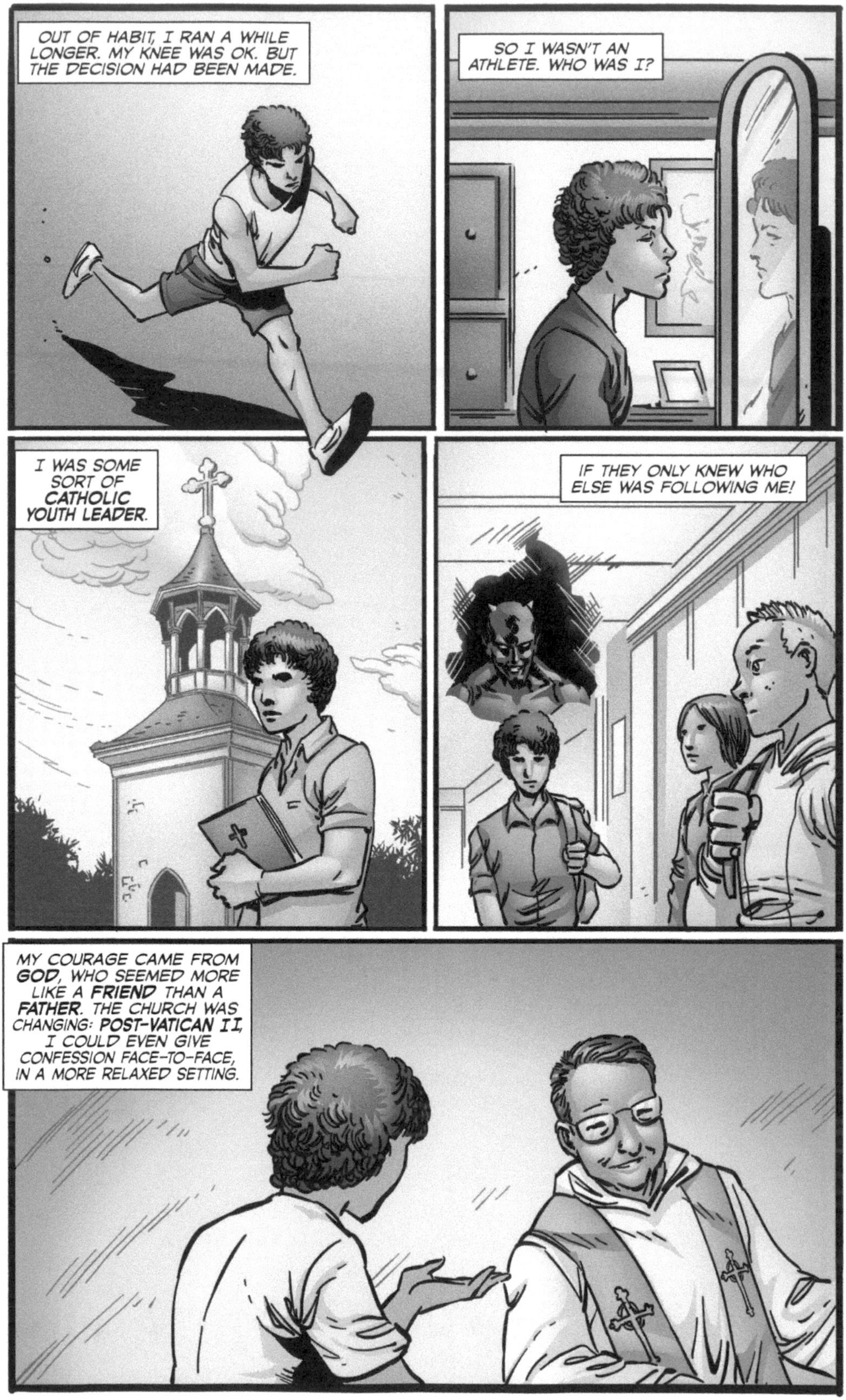
OUT OF HABIT, I RAN A WHILE LONGER. MY KNEE WAS OK. BUT THE DECISION HAD BEEN MADE.
SO I WASN'T AN ATHLETE. WHO WAS I?
I WAS SOME SORT OF CATHOLIC YOUTH LEADER.
IF THEY ONLY KNEW WHO ELSE WAS FOLLOWING ME!
MY COURAGE CAME FROM GOD, WHO SEEMED MORE LIKE A FRIEND THAN A FATHER. THE CHURCH WAS CHANGING: POST-VATICAN II, I COULD EVEN GIVE CONFESSION FACE-TO-FACE, IN A MORE RELAXED SETTING.

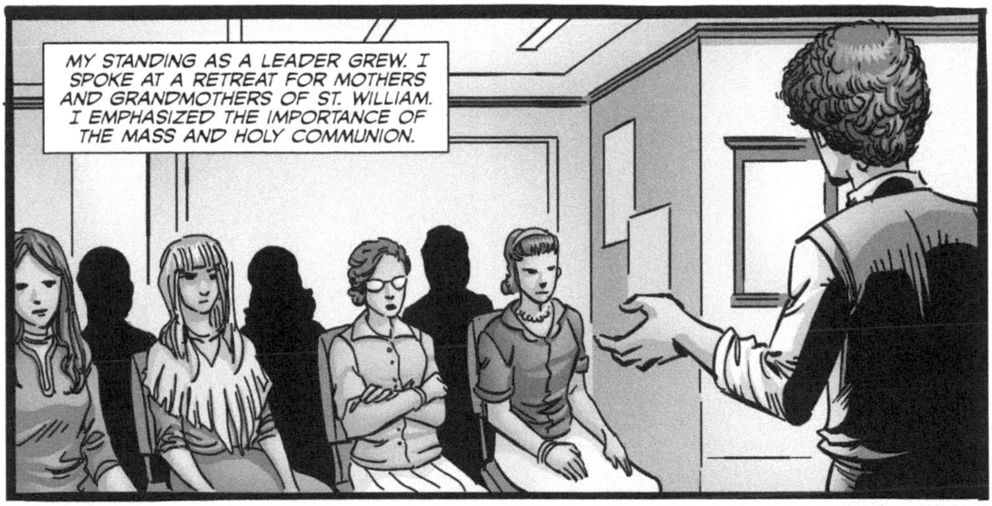
MY STANDING AS A LEADER GREW. I SPOKE AT A RETREAT FOR MOTHERS AND GRANDMOTHERS OF ST. WILLIAM. I EMPHASIZED THE IMPORTANCE OF THE MASS AND HOLY COMMUNION.

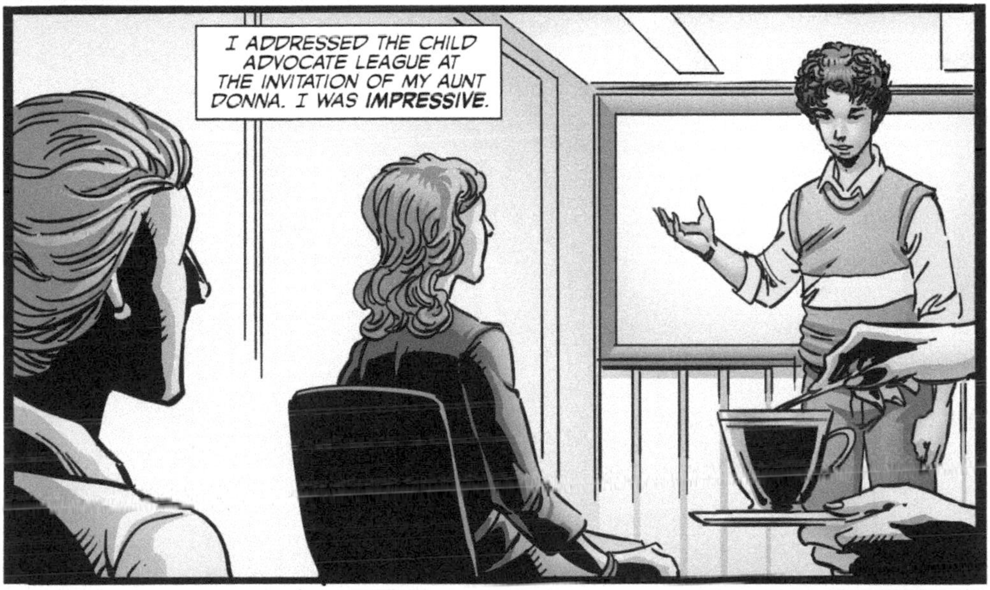
I ADDRESSED THE CHILD ADVOCATE LEAGUE AT THE INVITATION OF MY AUNT DONNA. I WAS IMPRESSIVE.

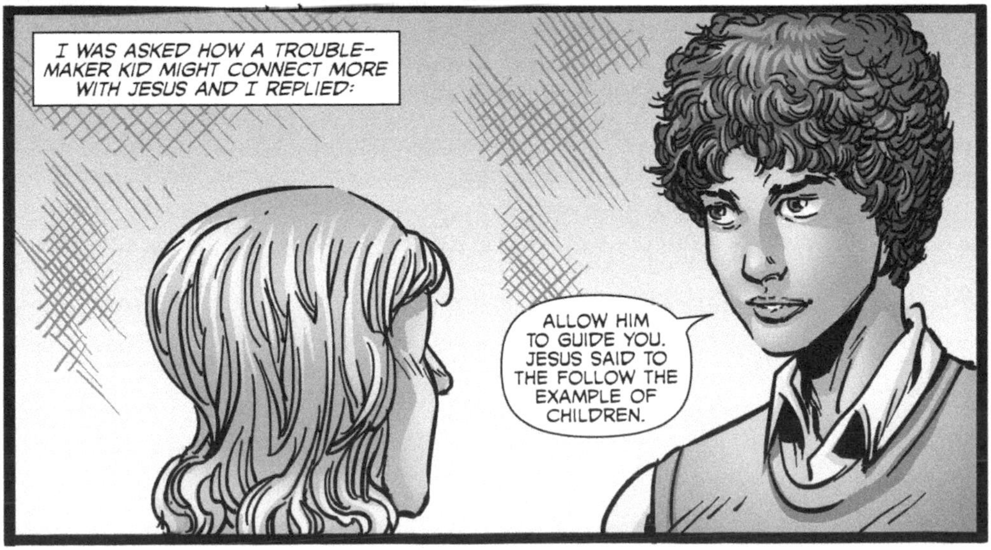
I WAS ASKED HOW A TROUBLE-MAKER KID MIGHT CONNECT MORE WITH JESUS AND I REPLIED:
ALLOW HIM TO GUIDE YOU. JESUS SAID TO THE FOLLOW THE EXAMPLE OF CHILDREN.

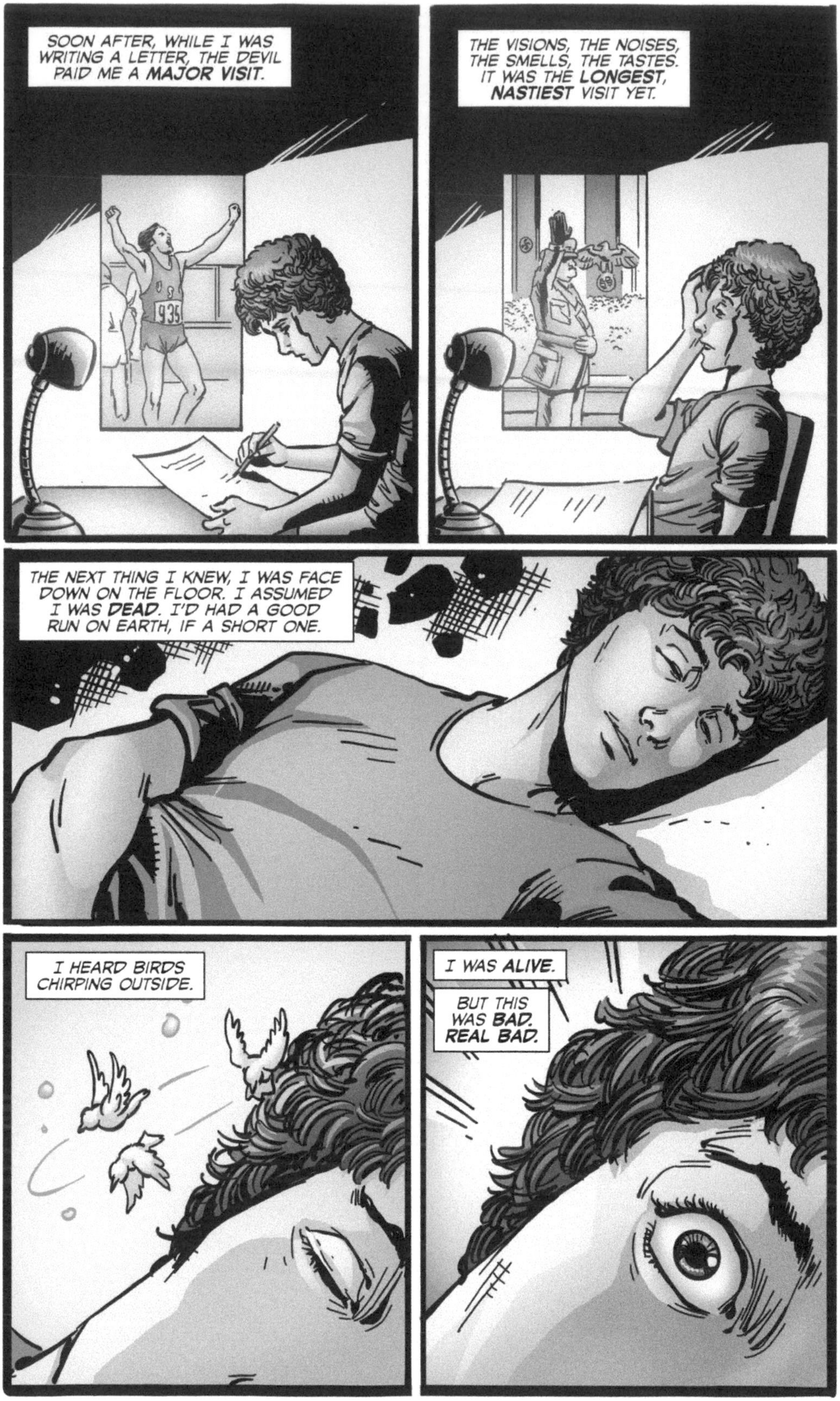
SOON AFTER, WHILE I WAS WRITING A LETTER, THE DEVIL PAID ME A **MAJOR VISIT**.
935
THE VISIONS, THE NOISES, THE SMELLS, THE TASTES. IT WAS THE **LONGEST**, **NASTIEST** VISIT YET.
THE NEXT THING I KNEW, I WAS FACE DOWN ON THE FLOOR. I ASSUMED I WAS **DEAD**. I'D HAD A GOOD RUN ON EARTH, IF A SHORT ONE.
I HEARD BIRDS CHIRPING OUTSIDE.
I WAS **ALIVE**.
BUT THIS WAS **BAD**. **REAL BAD**.

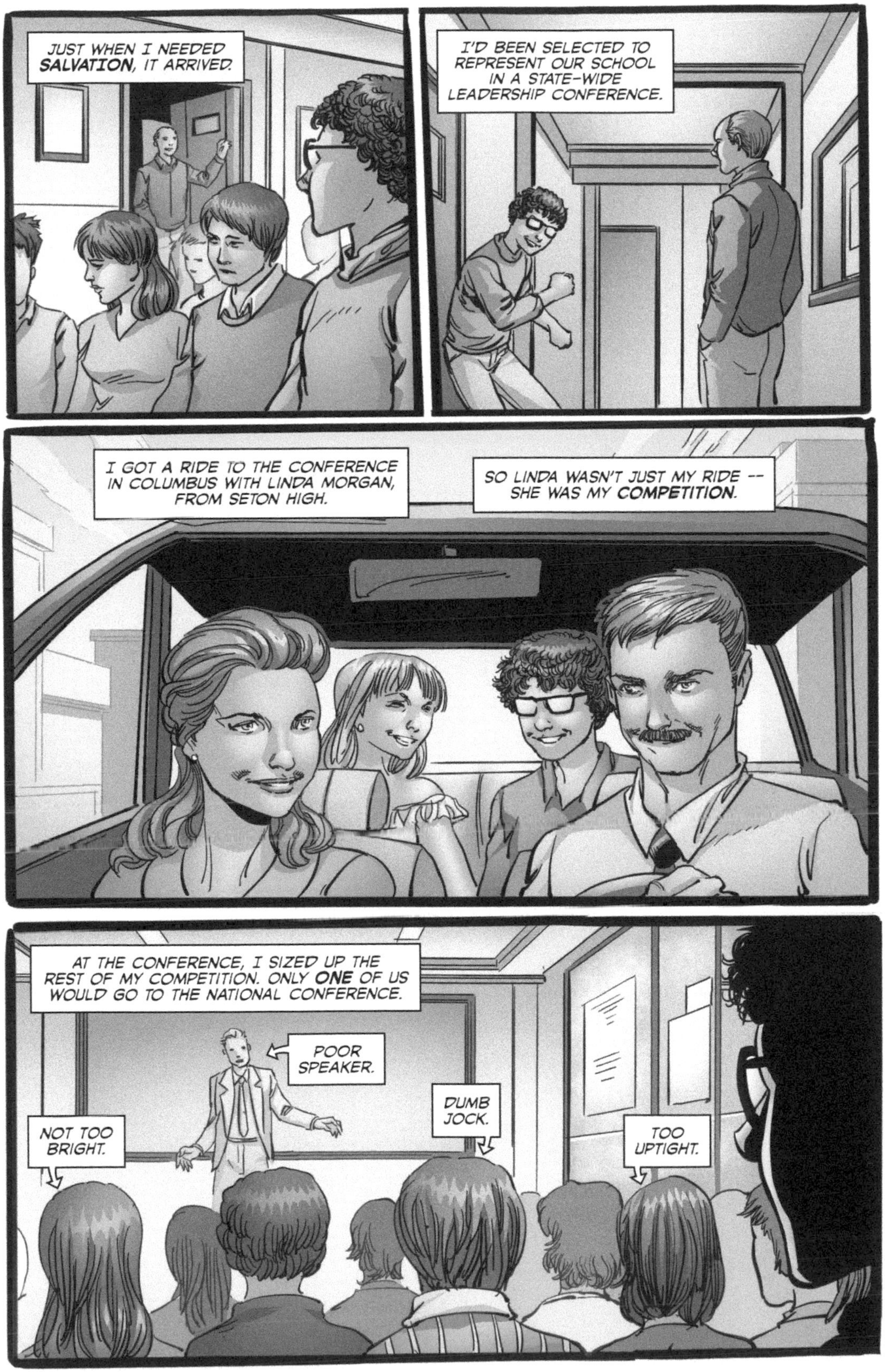
JUST WHEN I NEEDED **SALVATION**, IT ARRIVED.
I'D BEEN SELECTED TO REPRESENT OUR SCHOOL IN A STATE-WIDE LEADERSHIP CONFERENCE.
I GOT A RIDE TO THE CONFERENCE IN COLUMBUS WITH LINDA MORGAN, FROM SETON HIGH.
SO LINDA WASN'T JUST MY RIDE -- SHE WAS MY **COMPETITION**.
AT THE CONFERENCE, I SIZED UP THE REST OF MY COMPETITION. ONLY **ONE** OF US WOULD GO TO THE NATIONAL CONFERENCE.
POOR SPEAKER.
NOT TOO BRIGHT.
DUMB JOCK.
TOO UPTIGHT.

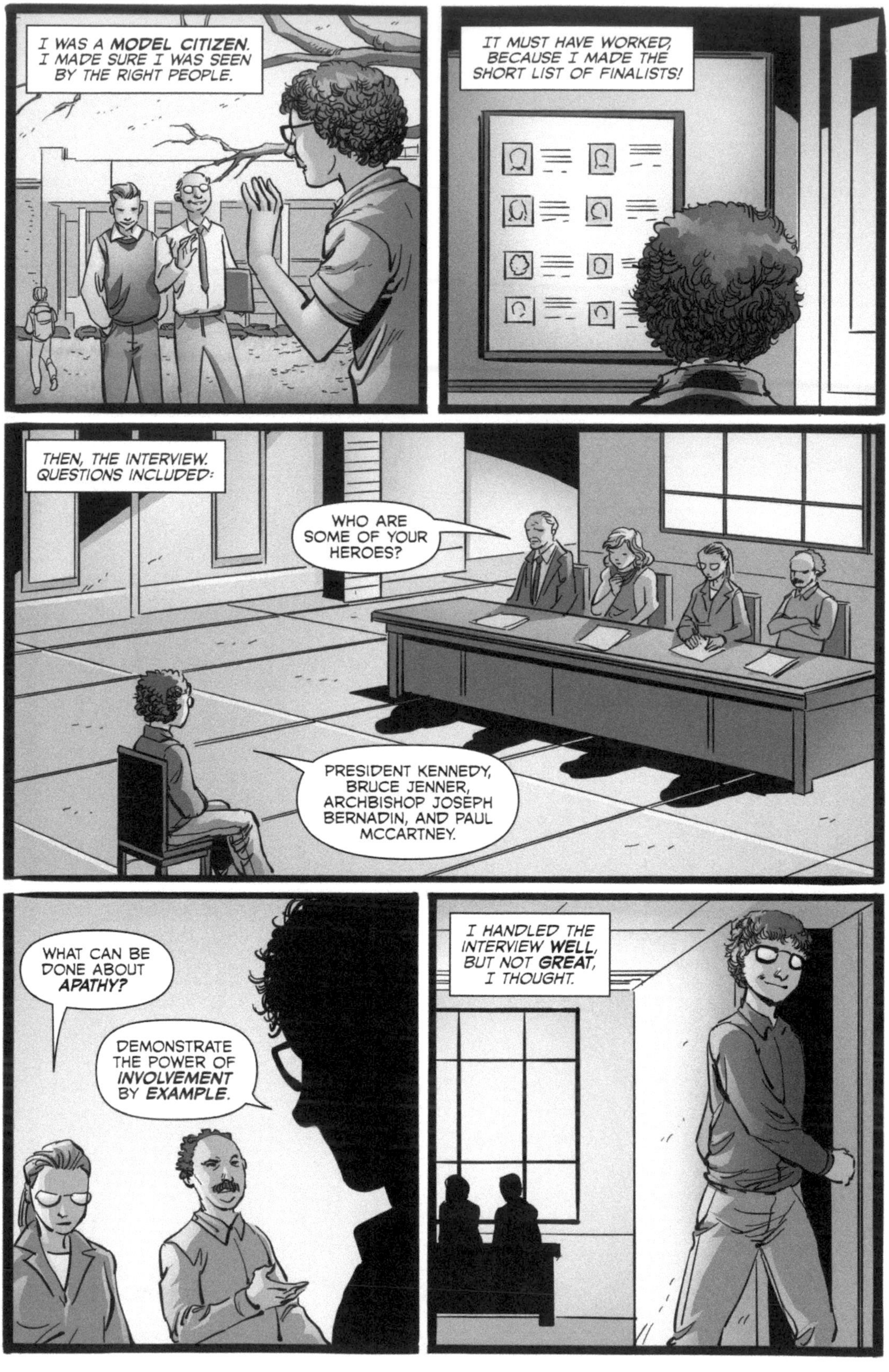
I WAS A **MODEL CITIZEN**. I MADE SURE I WAS SEEN BY THE RIGHT PEOPLE.
IT MUST HAVE WORKED, BECAUSE I MADE THE SHORT LIST OF FINALISTS!
THEN, THE INTERVIEW. QUESTIONS INCLUDED:
WHO ARE SOME OF YOUR HEROES?
PRESIDENT KENNEDY, BRUCE JENNER, ARCHBISHOP JOSEPH BERNADIN, AND PAUL McCARTNEY.
WHAT CAN BE DONE ABOUT ***APATHY?***
DEMONSTRATE THE POWER OF ***INVOLVEMENT*** BY ***EXAMPLE***.
I HANDLED THE INTERVIEW **WELL**, BUT NOT **GREAT**, I THOUGHT.

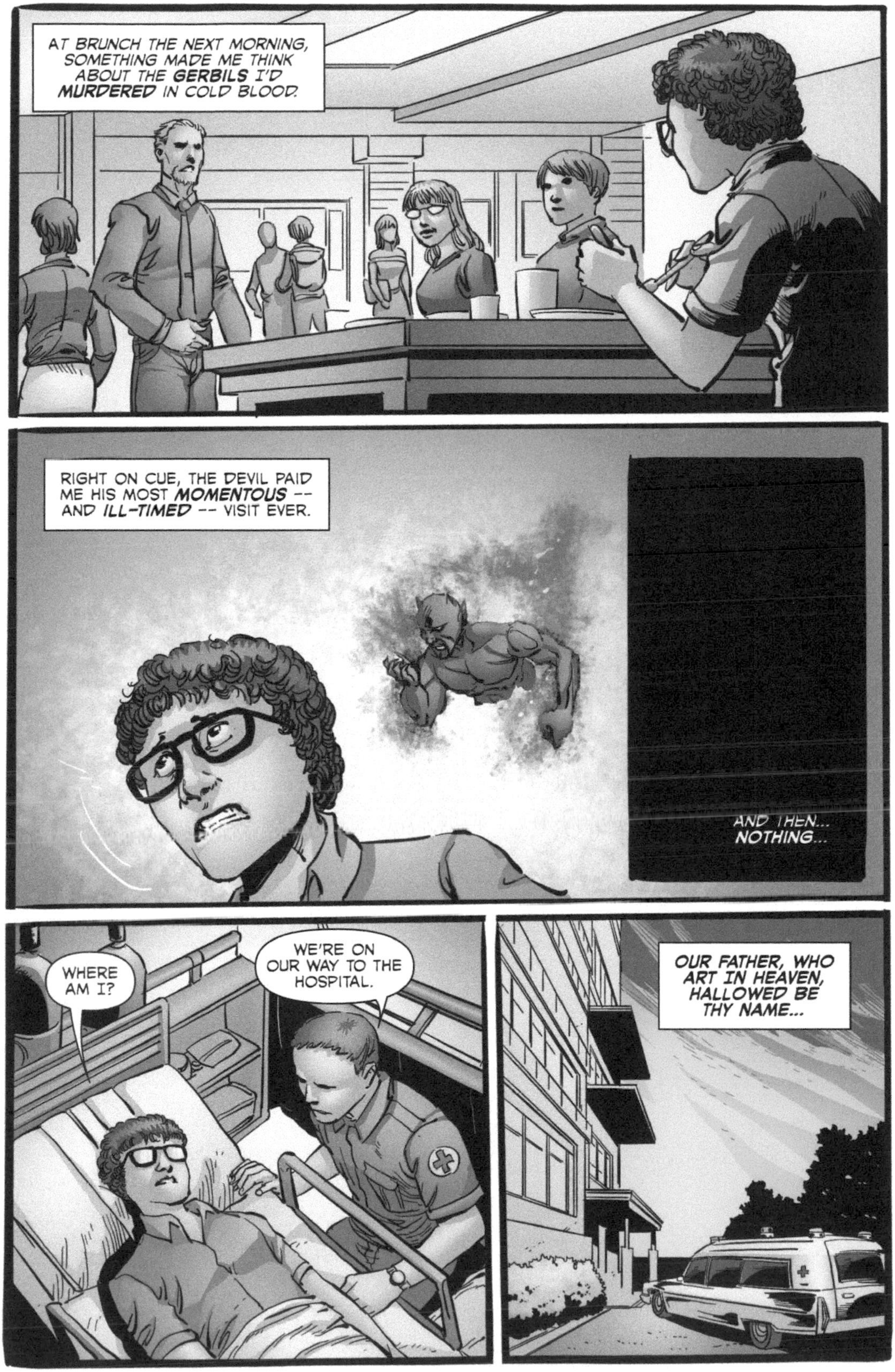
AT BRUNCH THE NEXT MORNING, SOMETHING MADE ME THINK ABOUT THE GERBILS I'D MURDERED IN COLD BLOOD.
RIGHT ON CUE, THE DEVIL PAID ME HIS MOST MOMENTOUS -- AND ILL-TIMED -- VISIT EVER.
AND THEN... NOTHING...
WHERE AM I?
WE'RE ON OUR WAY TO THE HOSPITAL.
OUR FATHER, WHO ART IN HEAVEN, HALLOWED BE THY NAME...

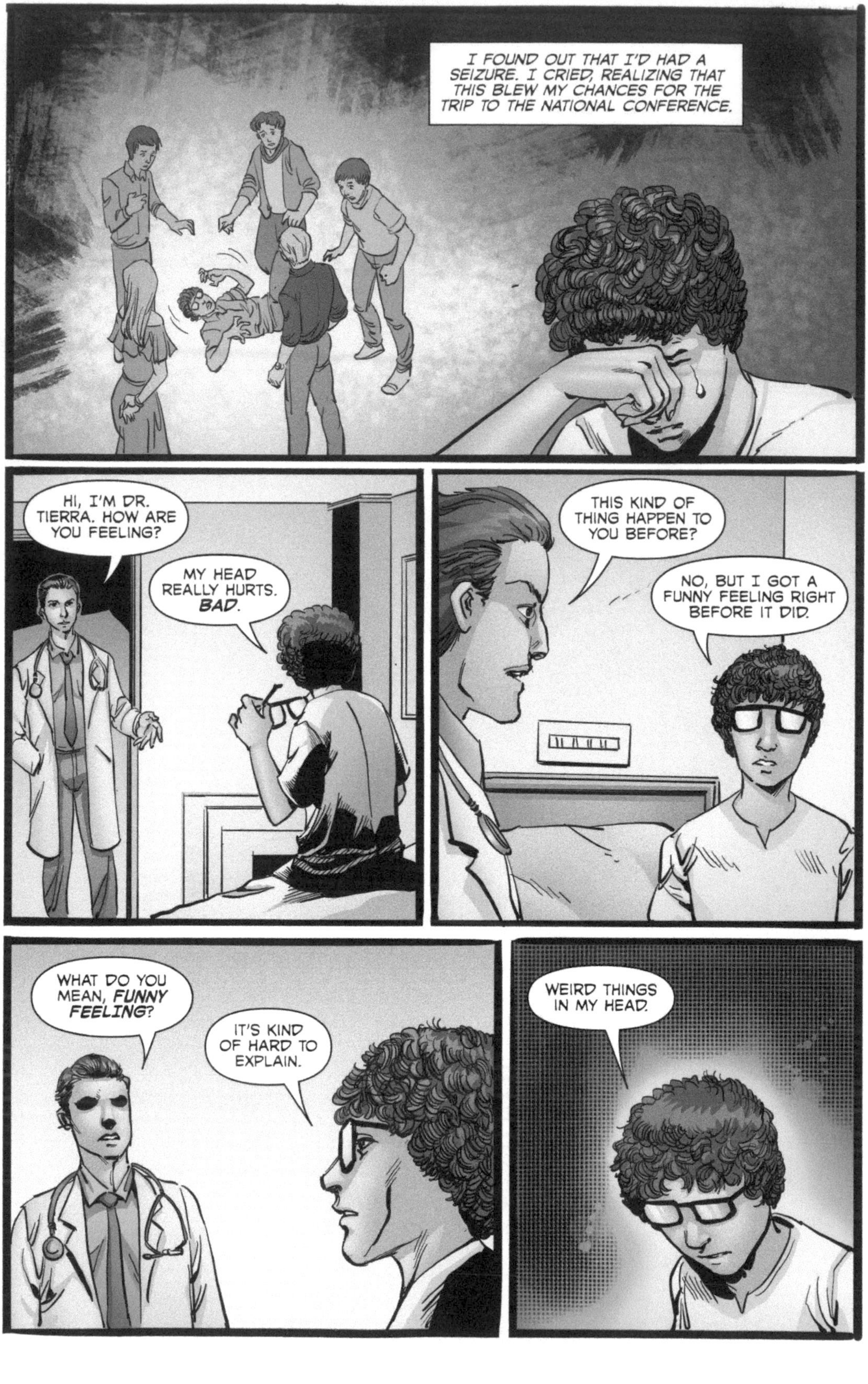
I FOUND OUT THAT I'D HAD A SEIZURE. I CRIED, REALIZING THAT THIS BLEW MY CHANCES FOR THE TRIP TO THE NATIONAL CONFERENCE.
HI, I'M DR. TIERRA. HOW ARE YOU FEELING?
MY HEAD REALLY HURTS. BAD.
THIS KIND OF THING HAPPEN TO YOU BEFORE?
NO, BUT I GOT A FUNNY FEELING RIGHT BEFORE IT DID.
WHAT DO YOU MEAN, FUNNY FEELING?
IT'S KIND OF HARD TO EXPLAIN.
WEIRD THINGS IN MY HEAD.

EXPLAIN *WEIRD* THINGS IN YOUR *HEAD*.

I DECIDED TO COME CLEAN.

EXORCISM AND A MENTAL INSTITUTION WERE IN MY FUTURE AND AT THAT POINT *I DIDN'T GIVE A DAMN*. I TOLD THE DOCTOR *EVERYTHING*.

...AND YOU HAVEN'T TOLD *ANYONE*. *HOW LONG* HAS THIS BEEN GOING ON?

YEARS. AND YEARS.

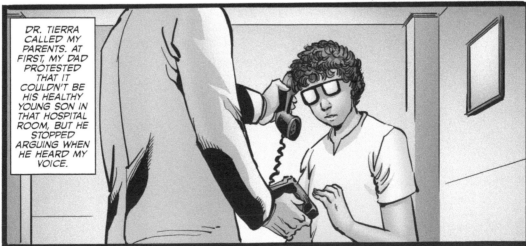

DR. TIERRA CALLED MY PARENTS. AT FIRST, MY DAD PROTESTED THAT IT COULDN'T BE HIS HEALTHY YOUNG SON IN THAT HOSPITAL ROOM, BUT HE STOPPED ARGUING WHEN HE HEARD MY VOICE.

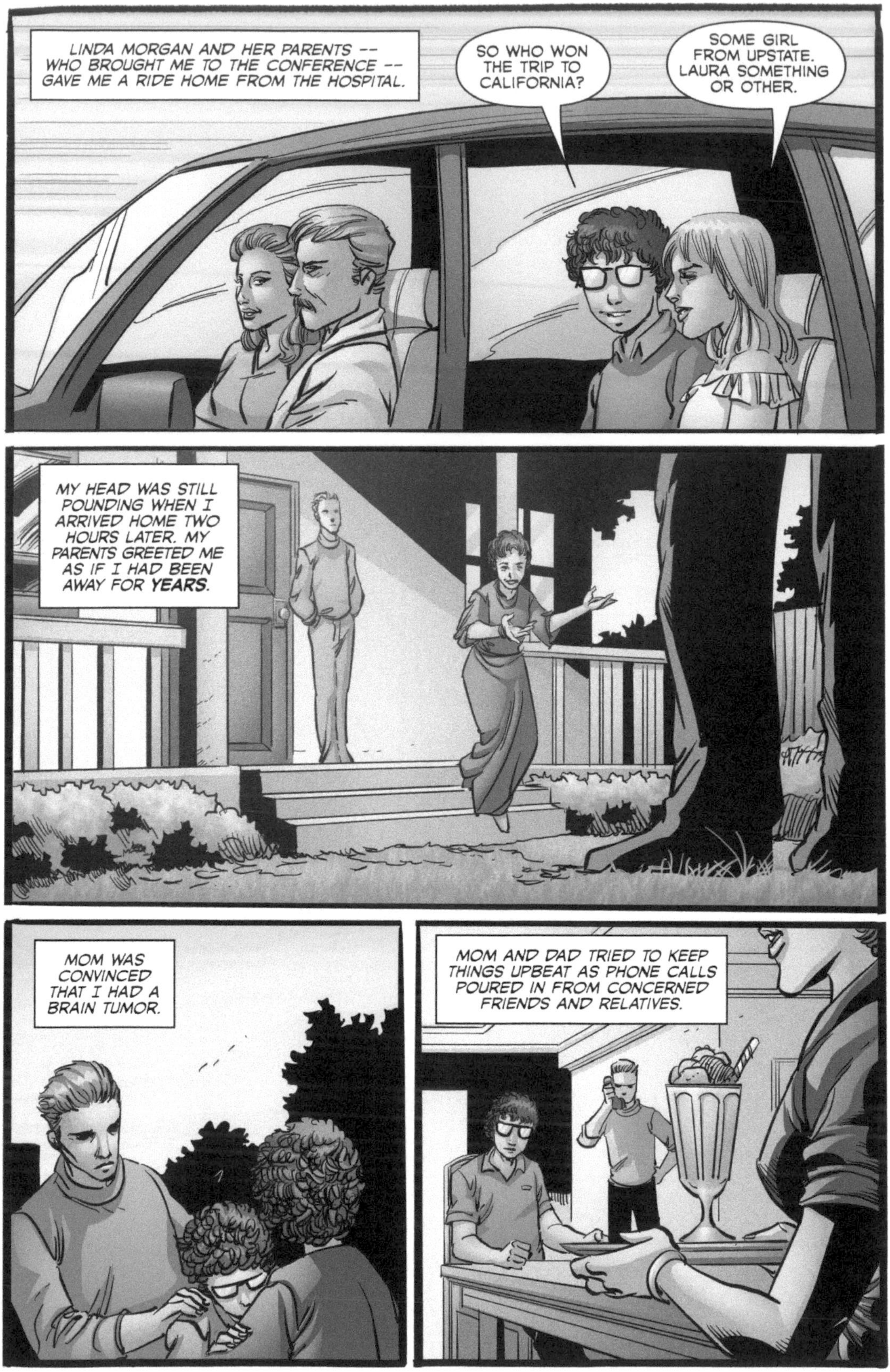
LINDA MORGAN AND HER PARENTS -- WHO BROUGHT ME TO THE CONFERENCE -- GAVE ME A RIDE HOME FROM THE HOSPITAL.
SO WHO WON THE TRIP TO CALIFORNIA?
SOME GIRL FROM UPSTATE. LAURA SOMETHING OR OTHER.
MY HEAD WAS STILL POUNDING WHEN I ARRIVED HOME TWO HOURS LATER. MY PARENTS GREETED ME AS IF I HAD BEEN AWAY FOR **YEARS**.
MOM WAS CONVINCED THAT I HAD A BRAIN TUMOR.
MOM AND DAD TRIED TO KEEP THINGS UPBEAT AS PHONE CALLS POURED IN FROM CONCERNED FRIENDS AND RELATIVES.

THEY TOOK ME TO A HOSPITAL FOR TESTS BUT WHAT I REALLY NEEDED WAS A PRIEST WITH ANOINTING OILS.

WE DIDN'T KNOW ABOUT HIS EPISODES.

HE DIDN'T TELL US. OR *ANYONE.*

YOU KNOW, SOME VERY FAMOUS PEOPLE HAD SEIZURES.

LIKE WHO?

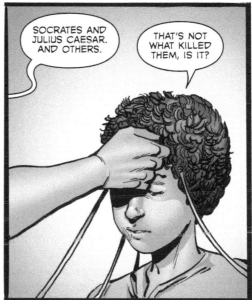

SOCRATES AND JULIUS CAESAR. AND OTHERS.

THAT'S NOT WHAT KILLED THEM, IS IT?

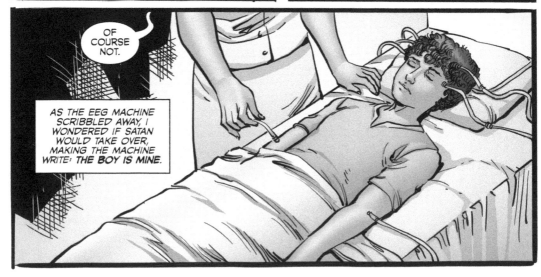

OF COURSE NOT.

AS THE EEG MACHINE SCRIBBLED AWAY, I WONDERED IF SATAN WOULD TAKE OVER, MAKING THE MACHINE WRITE: *THE BOY IS MINE.*

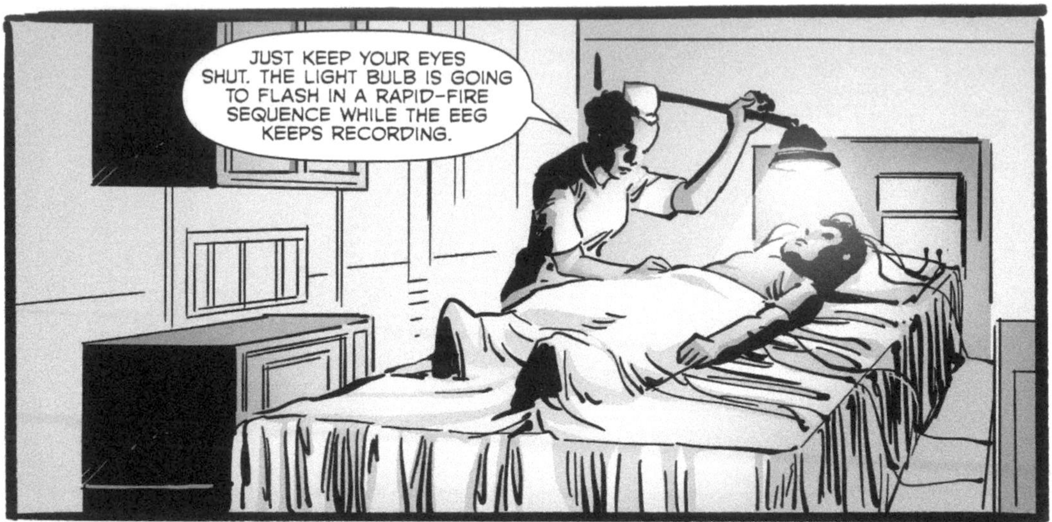
JUST KEEP YOUR EYES SHUT. THE LIGHT BULB IS GOING TO FLASH IN A RAPID-FIRE SEQUENCE WHILE THE EEG KEEPS RECORDING.

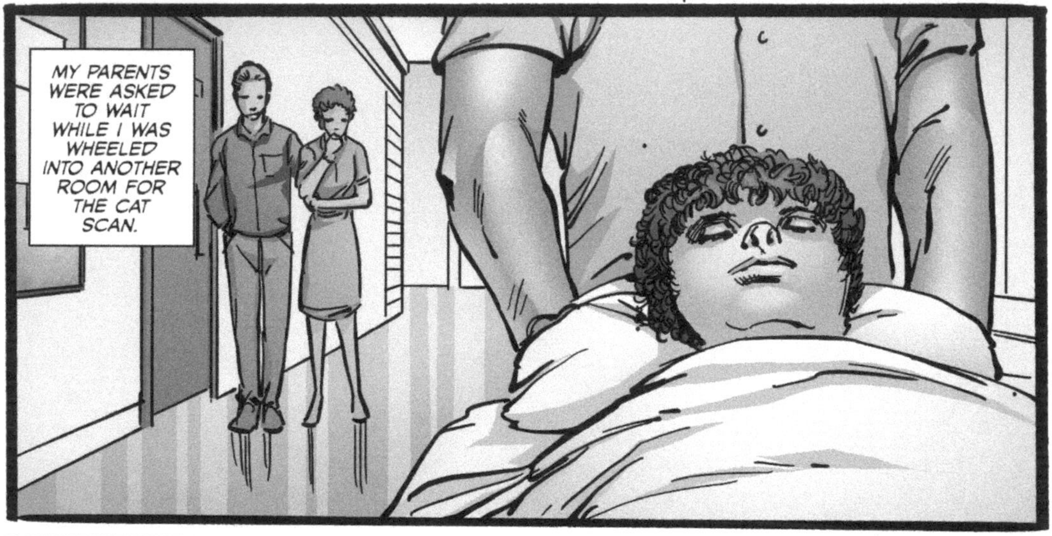
MY PARENTS WERE ASKED TO WAIT WHILE I WAS WHEELED INTO ANOTHER ROOM FOR THE CAT SCAN.

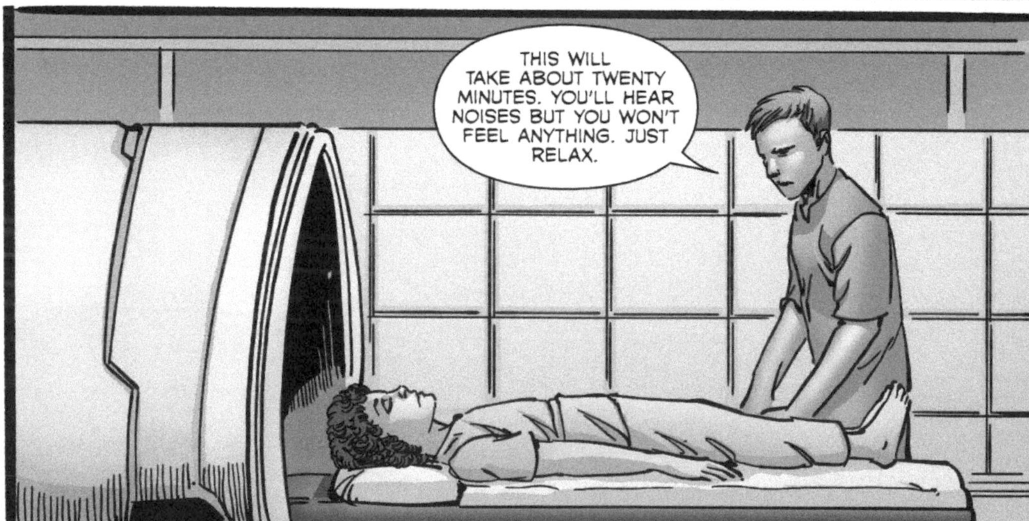
THIS WILL TAKE ABOUT TWENTY MINUTES. YOU'LL HEAR NOISES BUT YOU WON'T FEEL ANYTHING. JUST RELAX.

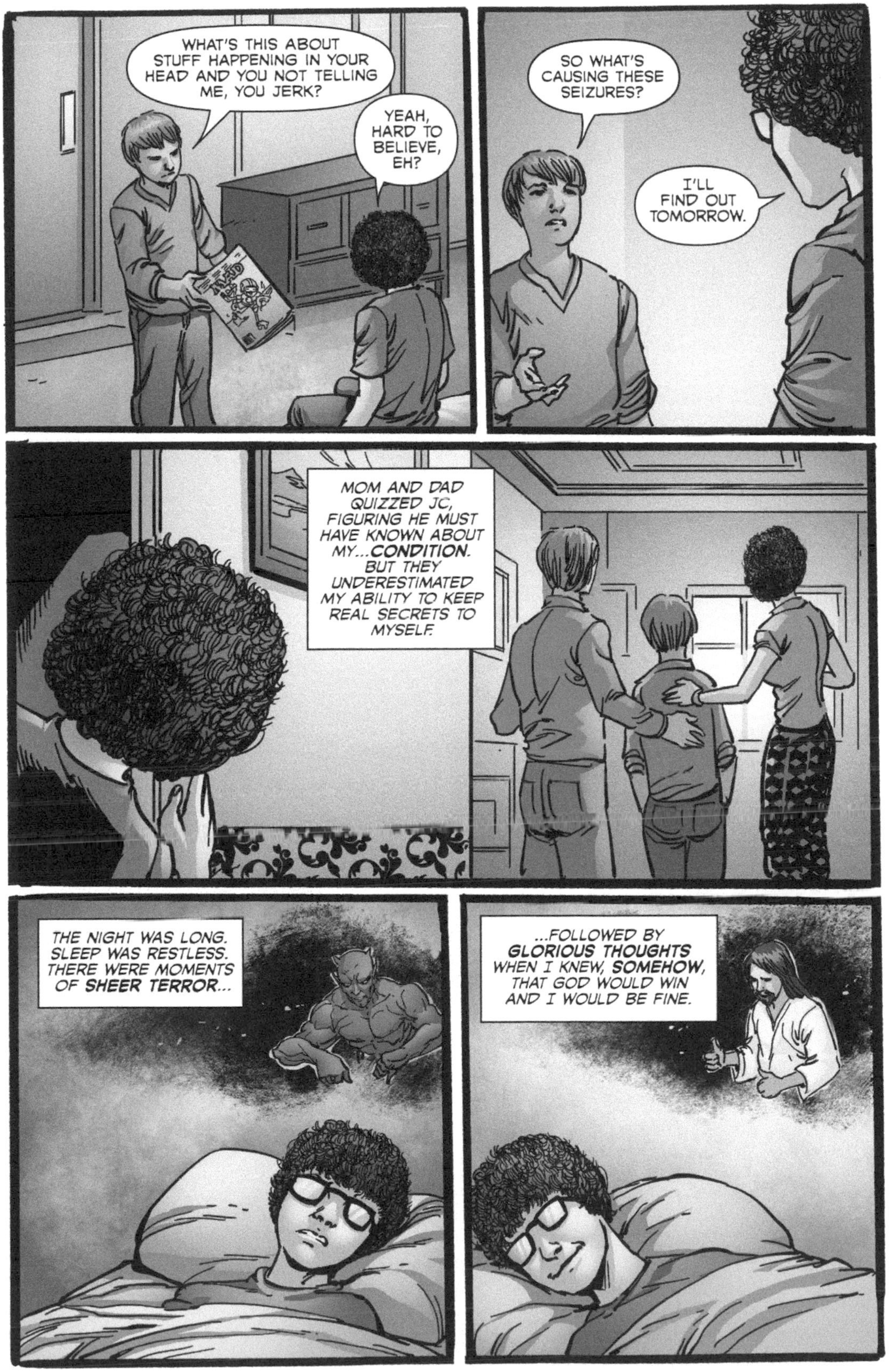
WHAT'S THIS ABOUT STUFF HAPPENING IN YOUR HEAD AND YOU NOT TELLING ME, YOU JERK?
YEAH, HARD TO BELIEVE, EH?
SO WHAT'S CAUSING THESE SEIZURES?
I'LL FIND OUT TOMORROW.
MOM AND DAD QUIZZED JC, FIGURING HE MUST HAVE KNOWN ABOUT MY... CONDITION. BUT THEY UNDERESTIMATED MY ABILITY TO KEEP REAL SECRETS TO MYSELF.
THE NIGHT WAS LONG. SLEEP WAS RESTLESS. THERE WERE MOMENTS OF SHEER TERROR...
...FOLLOWED BY GLORIOUS THOUGHTS WHEN I KNEW, SOMEHOW, THAT GOD WOULD WIN AND I WOULD BE FINE.

WE CONSULTED WITH MANY SPECIALISTS, INCLUDING A YOUNG *DR. KAPLAN*. HE KEPT SAYING *"INTERESTING"* AS HE LISTENED TO ME TELL MY TALE ONCE AGAIN...

WE BELIEVE YOU'VE BEEN EXPERIENCING A KIND OF SEIZURE ALL THOSE YEARS. IN COLUMBUS, YOU A HAD A *GRAND MAL* SEIZURE.

THAT'S FINE. BUT WHAT'S THE CAUSE?

HARD TO SAY. THERE'S NO SIGNIFICANT ABNORMALITY.

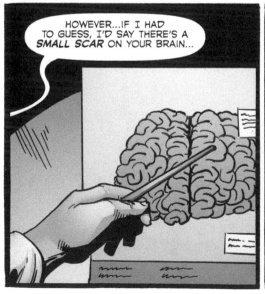

HOWEVER...IF I HAD TO GUESS, I'D SAY THERE'S A *SMALL SCAR* ON YOUR BRAIN...

...IT WAS PROBABLY CAUSED AT BIRTH.

MUST HAVE BEEN MY *BIG HEAD!*

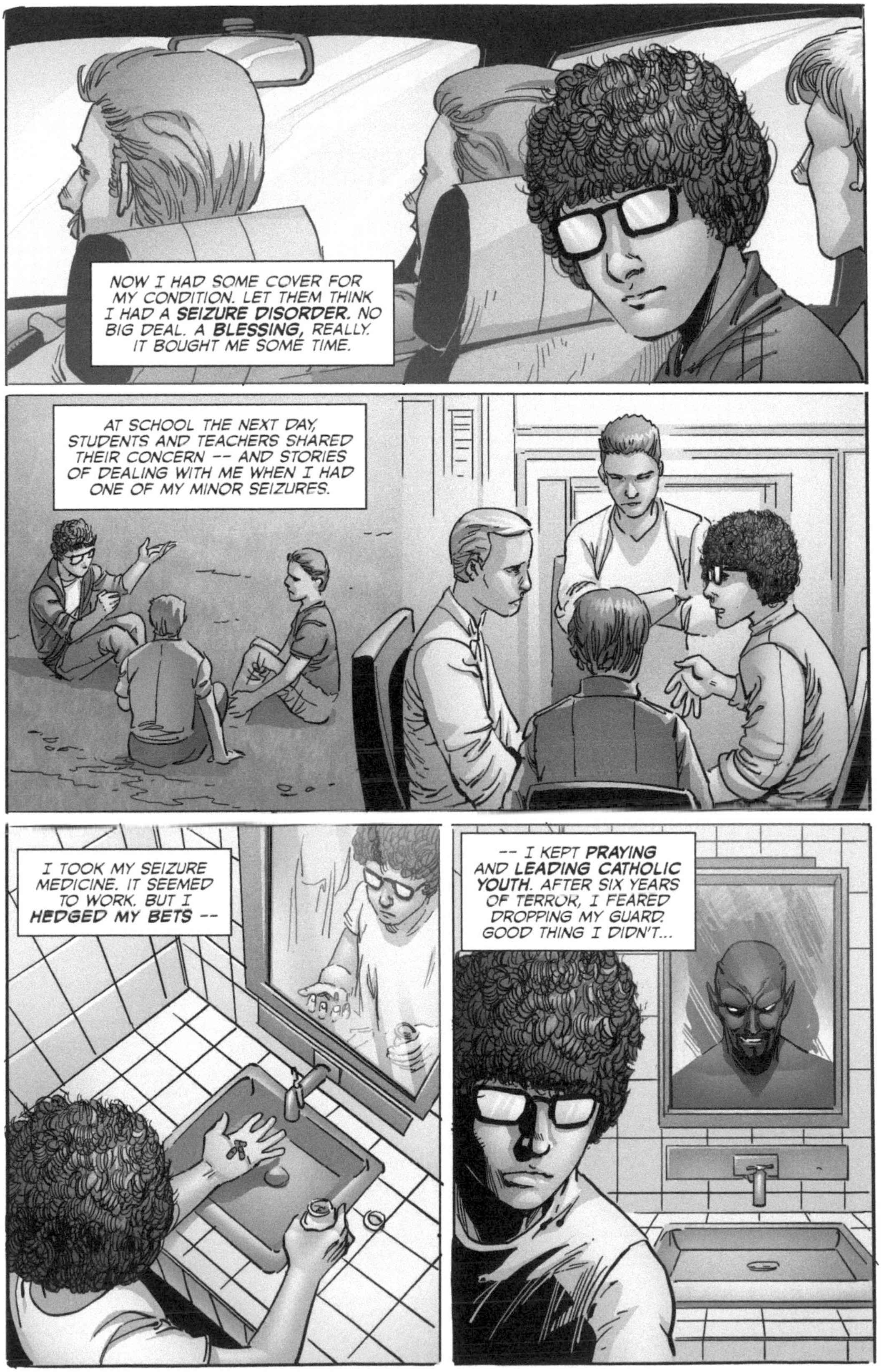
NOW I HAD SOME COVER FOR MY CONDITION. LET THEM THINK I HAD A **SEIZURE DISORDER.** NO BIG DEAL. A **BLESSING,** REALLY. IT BOUGHT ME SOME TIME.
AT SCHOOL THE NEXT DAY, STUDENTS AND TEACHERS SHARED THEIR CONCERN -- AND STORIES OF DEALING WITH ME WHEN I HAD ONE OF MY MINOR SEIZURES.
I TOOK MY SEIZURE MEDICINE. IT SEEMED TO WORK. BUT I **HEDGED MY BETS** --
-- I KEPT **PRAYING** AND **LEADING CATHOLIC YOUTH.** AFTER SIX YEARS OF TERROR, I FEARED DROPPING MY GUARD. GOOD THING I DIDN'T...

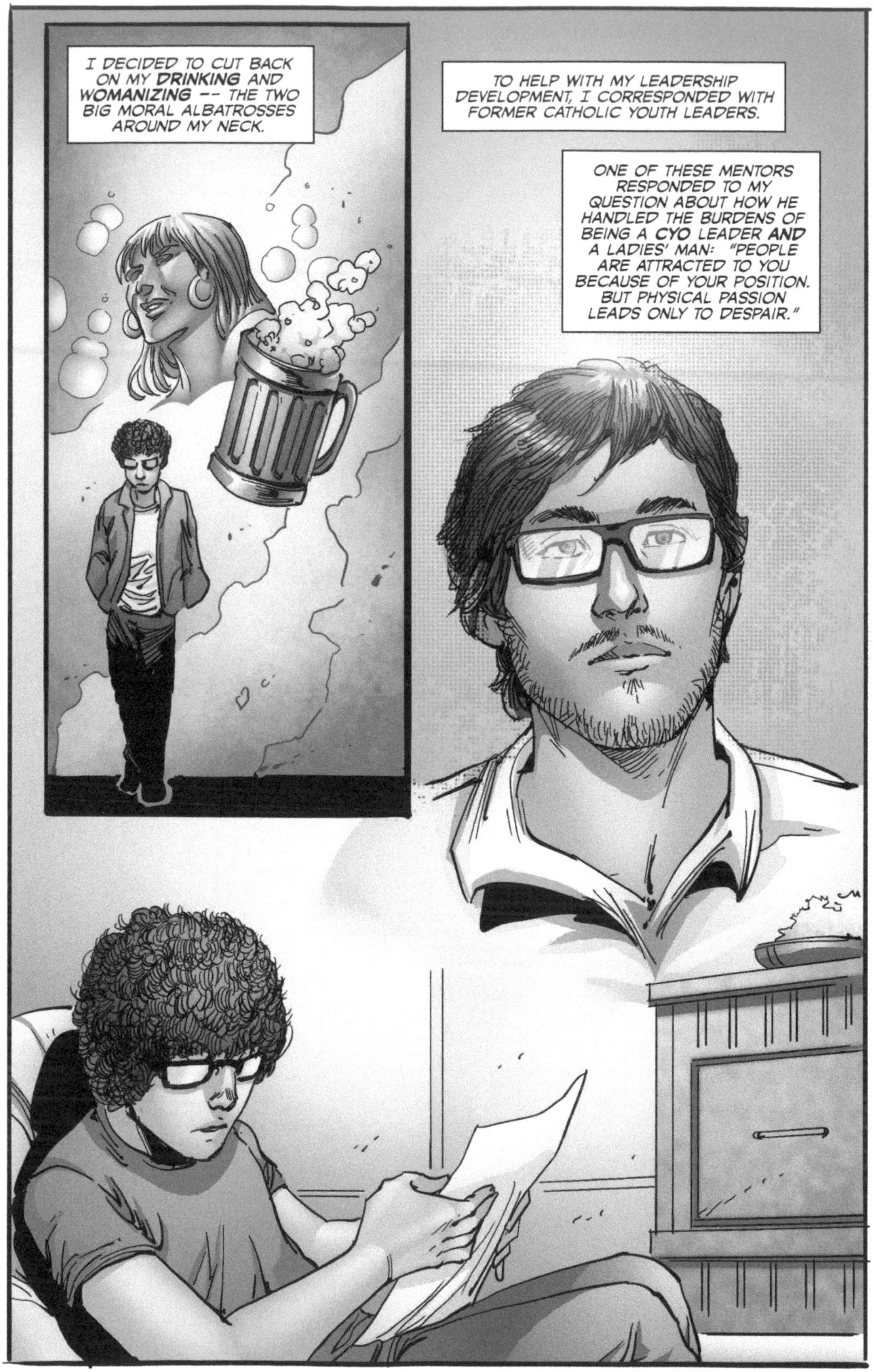
I DECIDED TO CUT BACK ON MY **DRINKING** AND **WOMANIZING** -- THE TWO BIG MORAL ALBATROSSES AROUND MY NECK.
TO HELP WITH MY LEADERSHIP DEVELOPMENT, I CORRESPONDED WITH FORMER CATHOLIC YOUTH LEADERS.
ONE OF THESE MENTORS RESPONDED TO MY QUESTION ABOUT HOW HE HANDLED THE BURDENS OF BEING A **CYO** LEADER **AND** A LADIES' MAN: "PEOPLE ARE ATTRACTED TO YOU BECAUSE OF YOUR POSITION. BUT PHYSICAL PASSION LEADS ONLY TO DESPAIR."

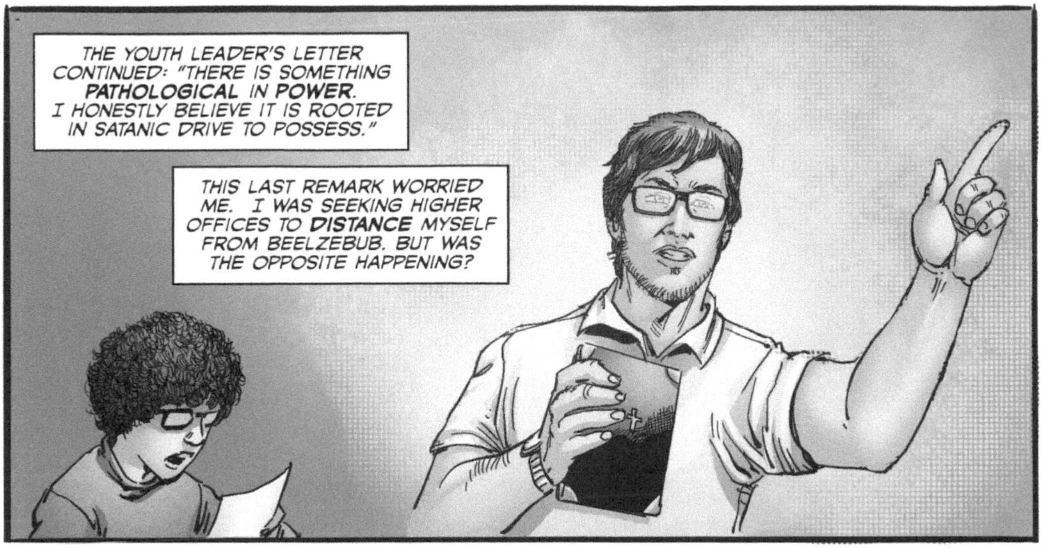
THE YOUTH LEADER'S LETTER CONTINUED: "THERE IS SOMETHING PATHOLOGICAL IN POWER. I HONESTLY BELIEVE IT IS ROOTED IN SATANIC DRIVE TO POSSESS."
THIS LAST REMARK WORRIED ME. I WAS SEEKING HIGHER OFFICES TO DISTANCE MYSELF FROM BEELZEBUB. BUT WAS THE OPPOSITE HAPPENING?

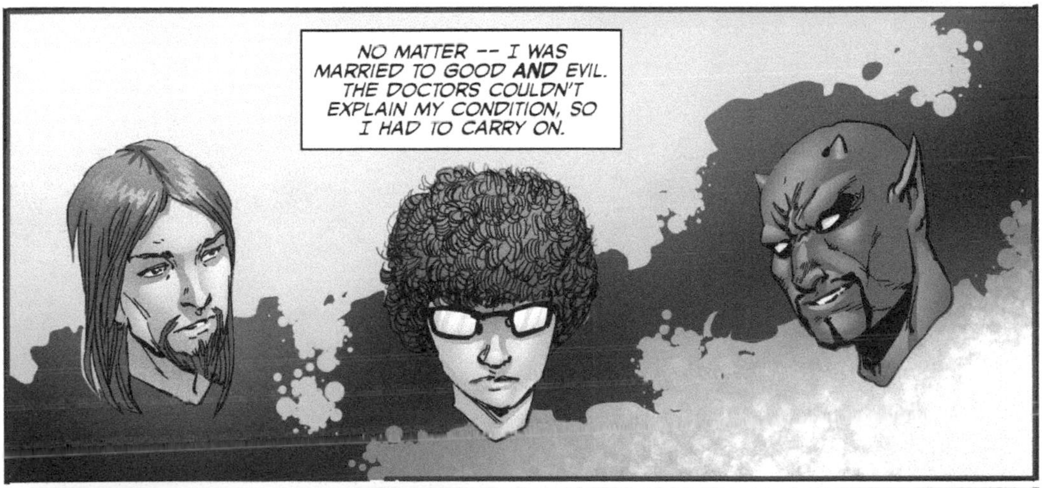
NO MATTER -- I WAS MARRIED TO GOOD AND EVIL. THE DOCTORS COULDN'T EXPLAIN MY CONDITION, SO I HAD TO CARRY ON.

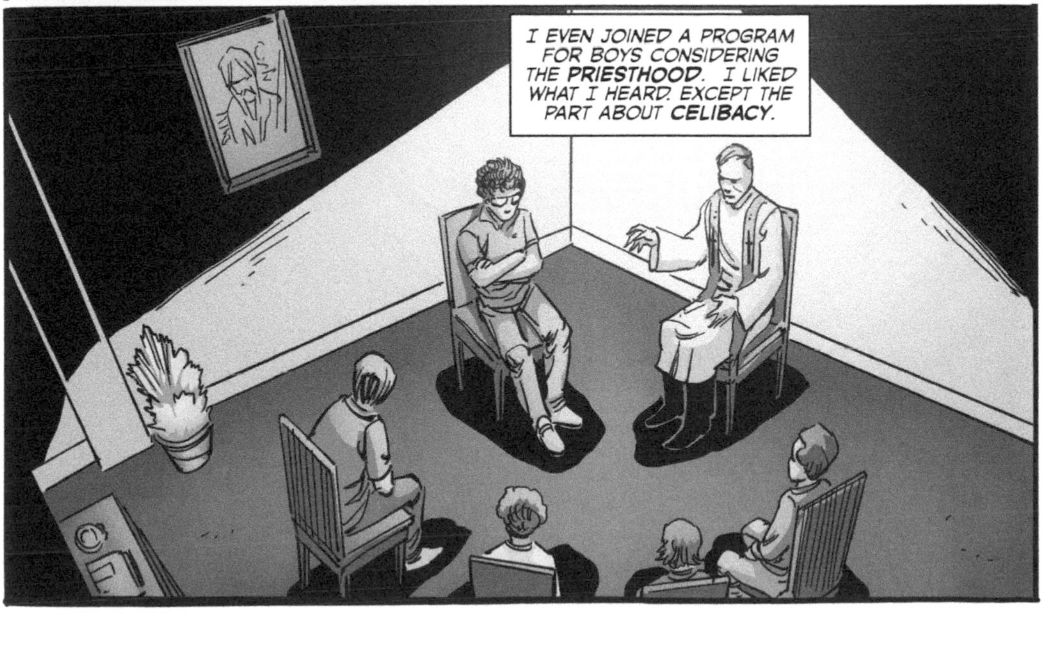
I EVEN JOINED A PROGRAM FOR BOYS CONSIDERING THE PRIESTHOOD. I LIKED WHAT I HEARD. EXCEPT THE PART ABOUT CELIBACY.

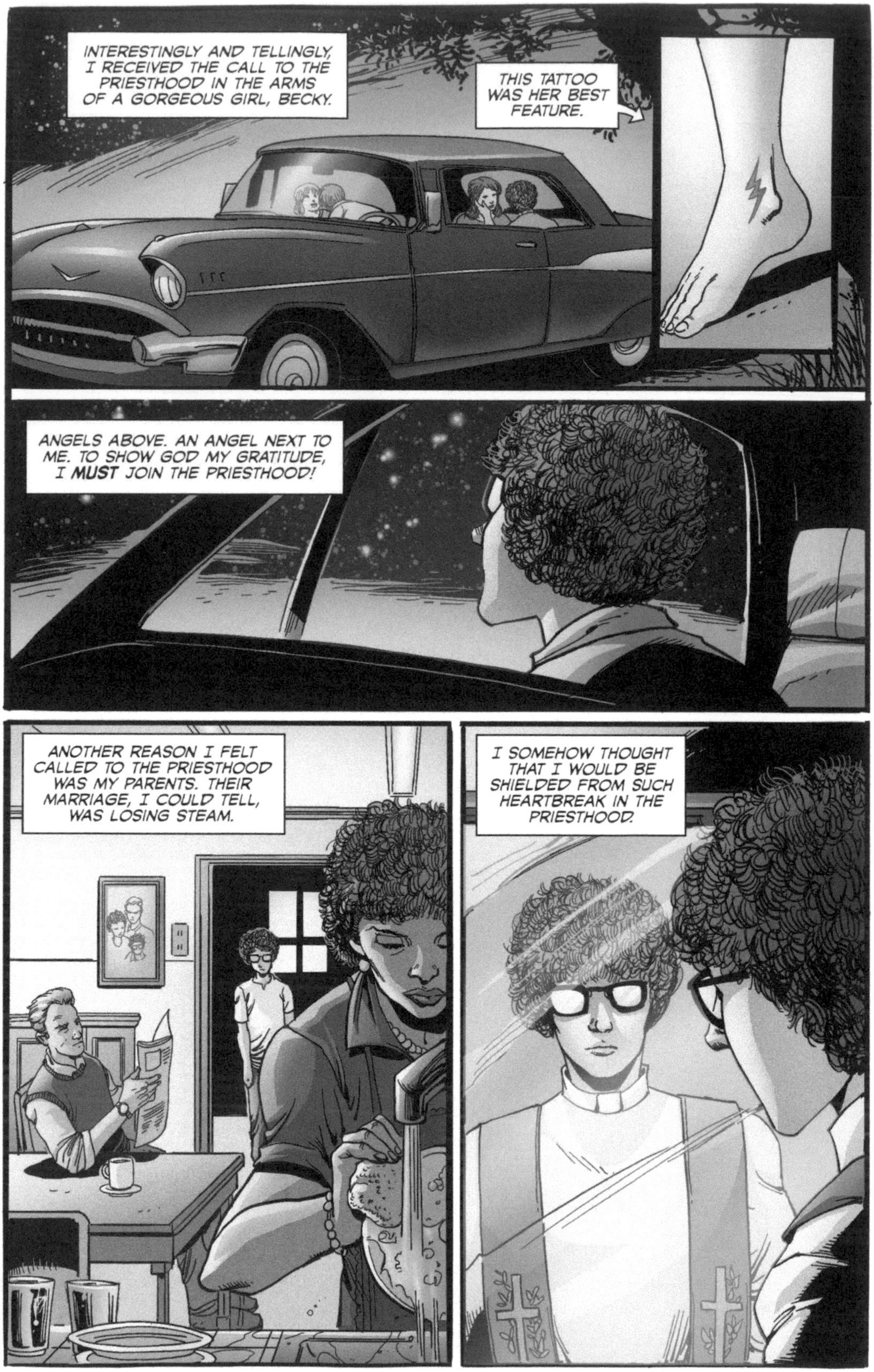
INTERESTINGLY AND TELLINGLY, I RECEIVED THE CALL TO THE PRIESTHOOD IN THE ARMS OF A GORGEOUS GIRL, BECKY.
THIS TATTOO WAS HER BEST FEATURE.
ANGELS ABOVE. AN ANGEL NEXT TO ME. TO SHOW GOD MY GRATITUDE, I **MUST** JOIN THE PRIESTHOOD!
ANOTHER REASON I FELT CALLED TO THE PRIESTHOOD WAS MY PARENTS. THEIR MARRIAGE, I COULD TELL, WAS LOSING STEAM.
I SOMEHOW THOUGHT THAT I WOULD BE SHIELDED FROM SUCH HEARTBREAK IN THE PRIESTHOOD.

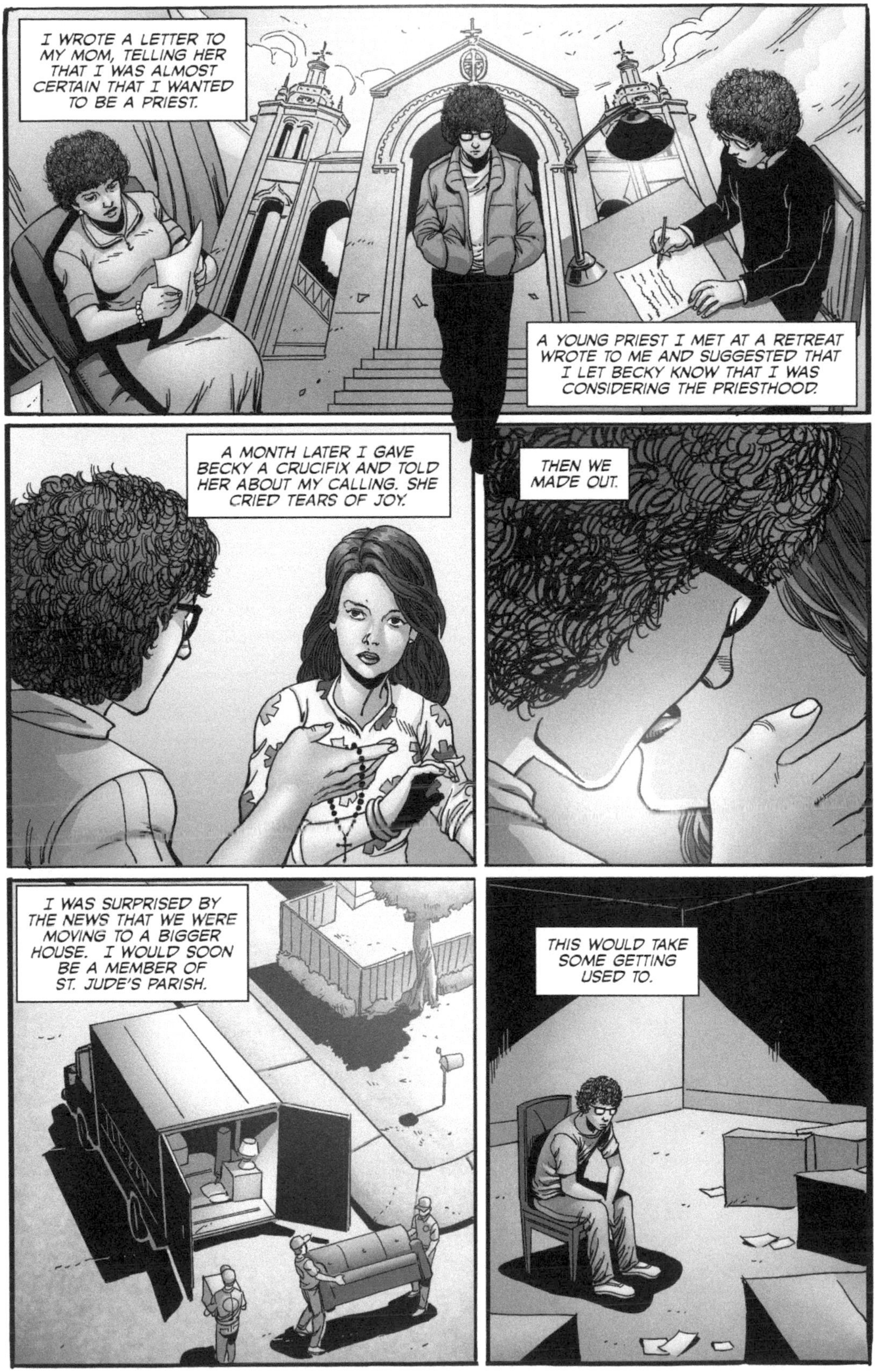
I WROTE A LETTER TO MY MOM, TELLING HER THAT I WAS ALMOST CERTAIN THAT I WANTED TO BE A PRIEST.
A YOUNG PRIEST I MET AT A RETREAT WROTE TO ME AND SUGGESTED THAT I LET BECKY KNOW THAT I WAS CONSIDERING THE PRIESTHOOD.
A MONTH LATER I GAVE BECKY A CRUCIFIX AND TOLD HER ABOUT MY CALLING. SHE CRIED TEARS OF JOY.
THEN WE MADE OUT.
I WAS SURPRISED BY THE NEWS THAT WE WERE MOVING TO A BIGGER HOUSE. I WOULD SOON BE A MEMBER OF ST. JUDE'S PARISH.
THIS WOULD TAKE SOME GETTING USED TO.

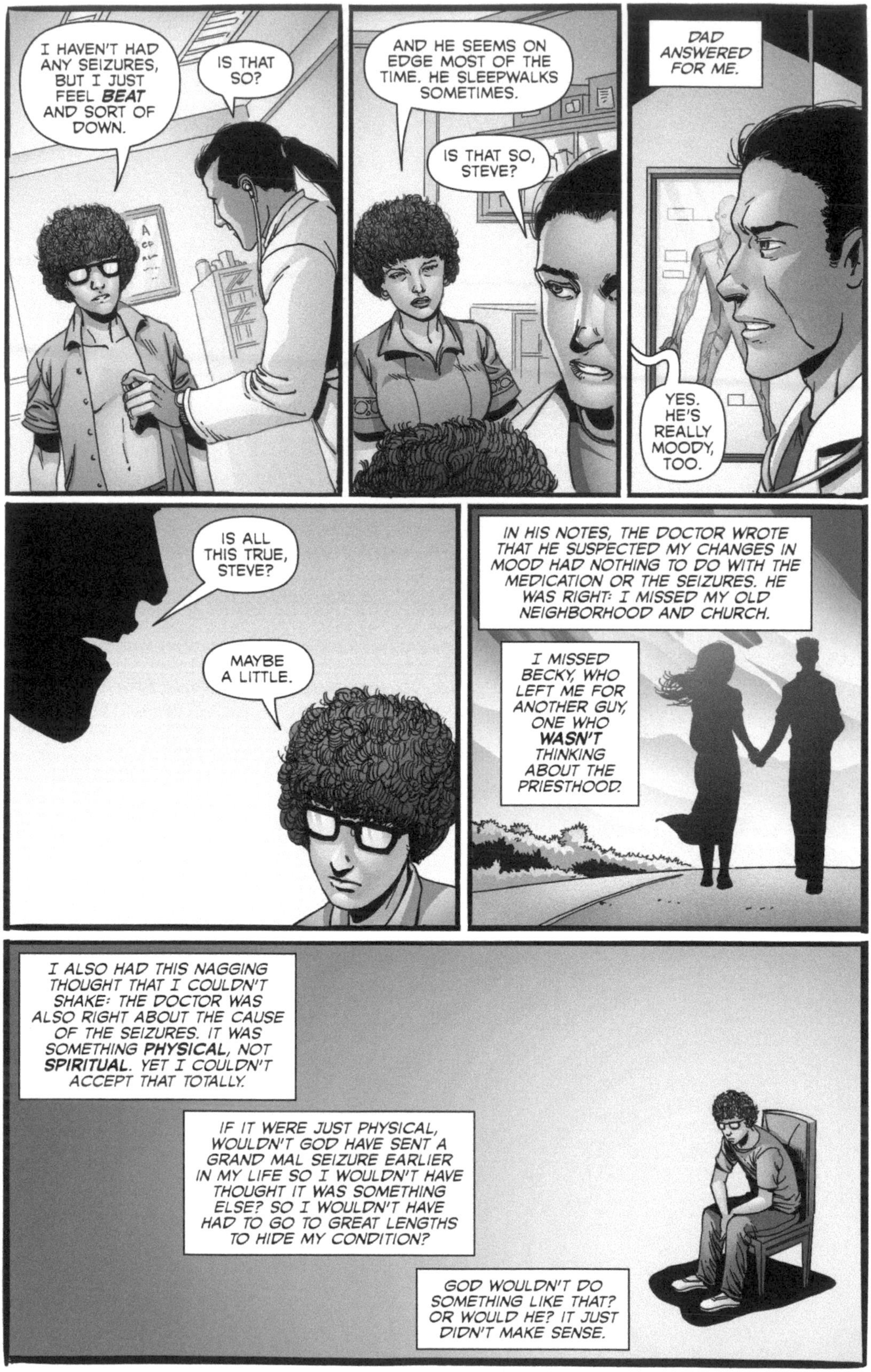
I HAVEN'T HAD ANY SEIZURES, BUT I JUST FEEL **BEAT** AND SORT OF DOWN.
IS THAT SO?
AND HE SEEMS ON EDGE MOST OF THE TIME. HE SLEEPWALKS SOMETIMES.
IS THAT SO, STEVE?
DAD ANSWERED FOR ME.
YES. HE'S REALLY MOODY, TOO.
IS ALL THIS TRUE, STEVE?
MAYBE A LITTLE.
IN HIS NOTES, THE DOCTOR WROTE THAT HE SUSPECTED MY CHANGES IN MOOD HAD NOTHING TO DO WITH THE MEDICATION OR THE SEIZURES. HE WAS RIGHT: I MISSED MY OLD NEIGHBORHOOD AND CHURCH.
I MISSED BECKY, WHO LEFT ME FOR ANOTHER GUY, ONE WHO **WASN'T** THINKING ABOUT THE PRIESTHOOD.
I ALSO HAD THIS NAGGING THOUGHT THAT I COULDN'T SHAKE: THE DOCTOR WAS ALSO RIGHT ABOUT THE CAUSE OF THE SEIZURES. IT WAS SOMETHING **PHYSICAL**, NOT **SPIRITUAL**. YET I COULDN'T ACCEPT THAT TOTALLY.
IF IT WERE JUST PHYSICAL, WOULDN'T GOD HAVE SENT A GRAND MAL SEIZURE EARLIER IN MY LIFE SO I WOULDN'T HAVE THOUGHT IT WAS SOMETHING ELSE? SO I WOULDN'T HAVE HAD TO GO TO GREAT LENGTHS TO HIDE MY CONDITION?
GOD WOULDN'T DO SOMETHING LIKE THAT? OR WOULD HE? IT JUST DIDN'T MAKE SENSE.

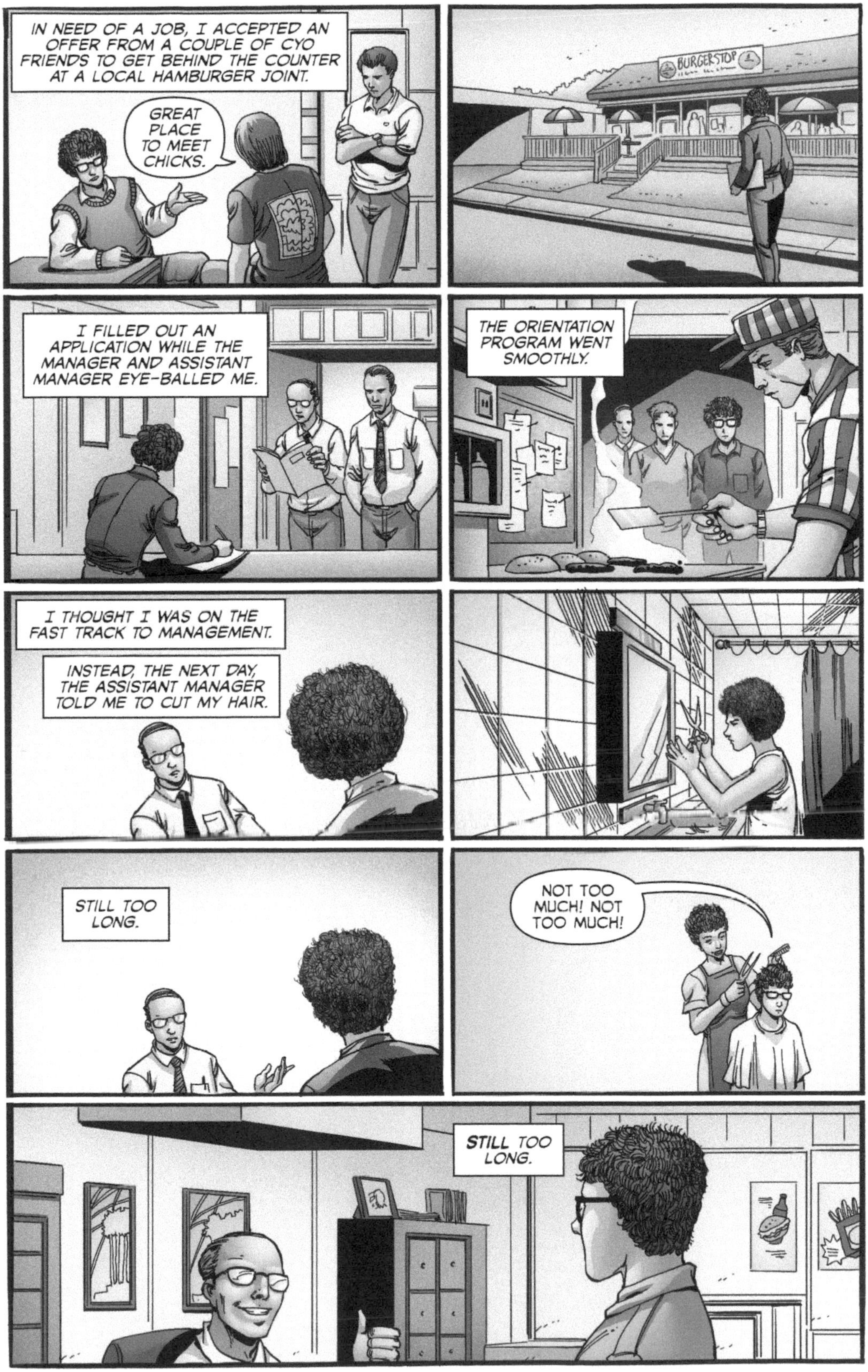
IN NEED OF A JOB, I ACCEPTED AN OFFER FROM A COUPLE OF CYO FRIENDS TO GET BEHIND THE COUNTER AT A LOCAL HAMBURGER JOINT.
GREAT PLACE TO MEET CHICKS.
BURGERSTOP
I FILLED OUT AN APPLICATION WHILE THE MANAGER AND ASSISTANT MANAGER EYE-BALLED ME.
THE ORIENTATION PROGRAM WENT SMOOTHLY.
I THOUGHT I WAS ON THE FAST TRACK TO MANAGEMENT.
INSTEAD, THE NEXT DAY, THE ASSISTANT MANAGER TOLD ME TO CUT MY HAIR.
STILL TOO LONG.
NOT TOO MUCH! NOT TOO MUCH!
STILL TOO LONG.

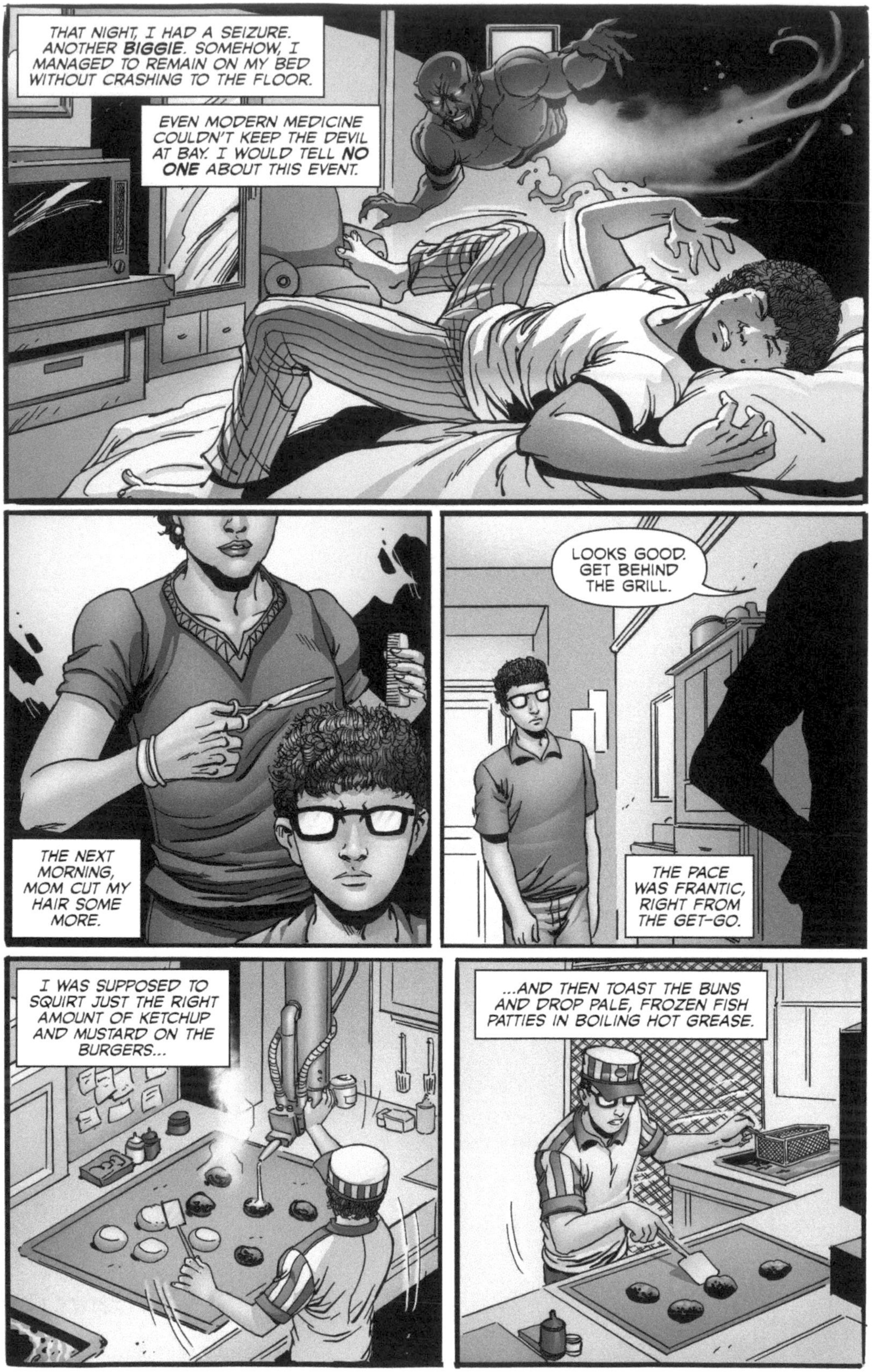
THAT NIGHT, I HAD A SEIZURE. ANOTHER **BIGGIE**. SOMEHOW, I MANAGED TO REMAIN ON MY BED WITHOUT CRASHING TO THE FLOOR.
EVEN MODERN MEDICINE COULDN'T KEEP THE DEVIL AT BAY. I WOULD TELL **NO ONE** ABOUT THIS EVENT.
THE NEXT MORNING, MOM CUT MY HAIR SOME MORE.
LOOKS GOOD. GET BEHIND THE GRILL.
THE PACE WAS FRANTIC, RIGHT FROM THE GET-GO.
I WAS SUPPOSED TO SQUIRT JUST THE RIGHT AMOUNT OF KETCHUP AND MUSTARD ON THE BURGERS...
...AND THEN TOAST THE BUNS AND DROP PALE, FROZEN FISH PATTIES IN BOILING HOT GREASE.

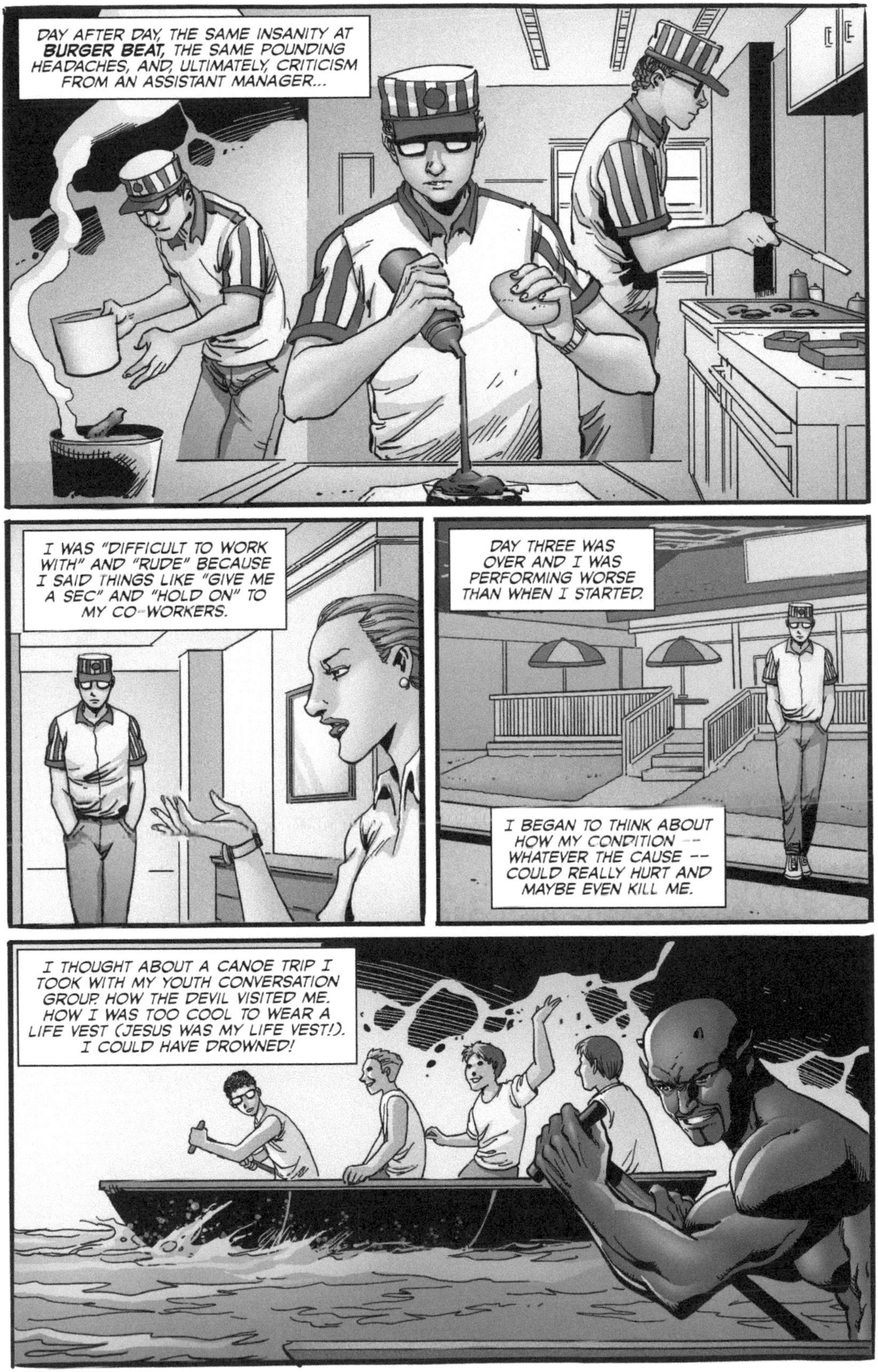
DAY AFTER DAY, THE SAME INSANITY AT **BURGER BEAT,** THE SAME POUNDING HEADACHES, AND, ULTIMATELY, CRITICISM FROM AN ASSISTANT MANAGER...
I WAS "DIFFICULT TO WORK WITH" AND "RUDE" BECAUSE I SAID THINGS LIKE "GIVE ME A SEC" AND "HOLD ON" TO MY CO-WORKERS.
DAY THREE WAS OVER AND I WAS PERFORMING WORSE THAN WHEN I STARTED.
I BEGAN TO THINK ABOUT HOW MY CONDITION -- WHATEVER THE CAUSE -- COULD REALLY HURT AND MAYBE EVEN KILL ME.
I THOUGHT ABOUT A CANOE TRIP I TOOK WITH MY YOUTH CONVERSATION GROUP. HOW THE DEVIL VISITED ME. HOW I WAS TOO COOL TO WEAR A LIFE VEST (JESUS WAS MY LIFE VEST!). I COULD HAVE DROWNED!

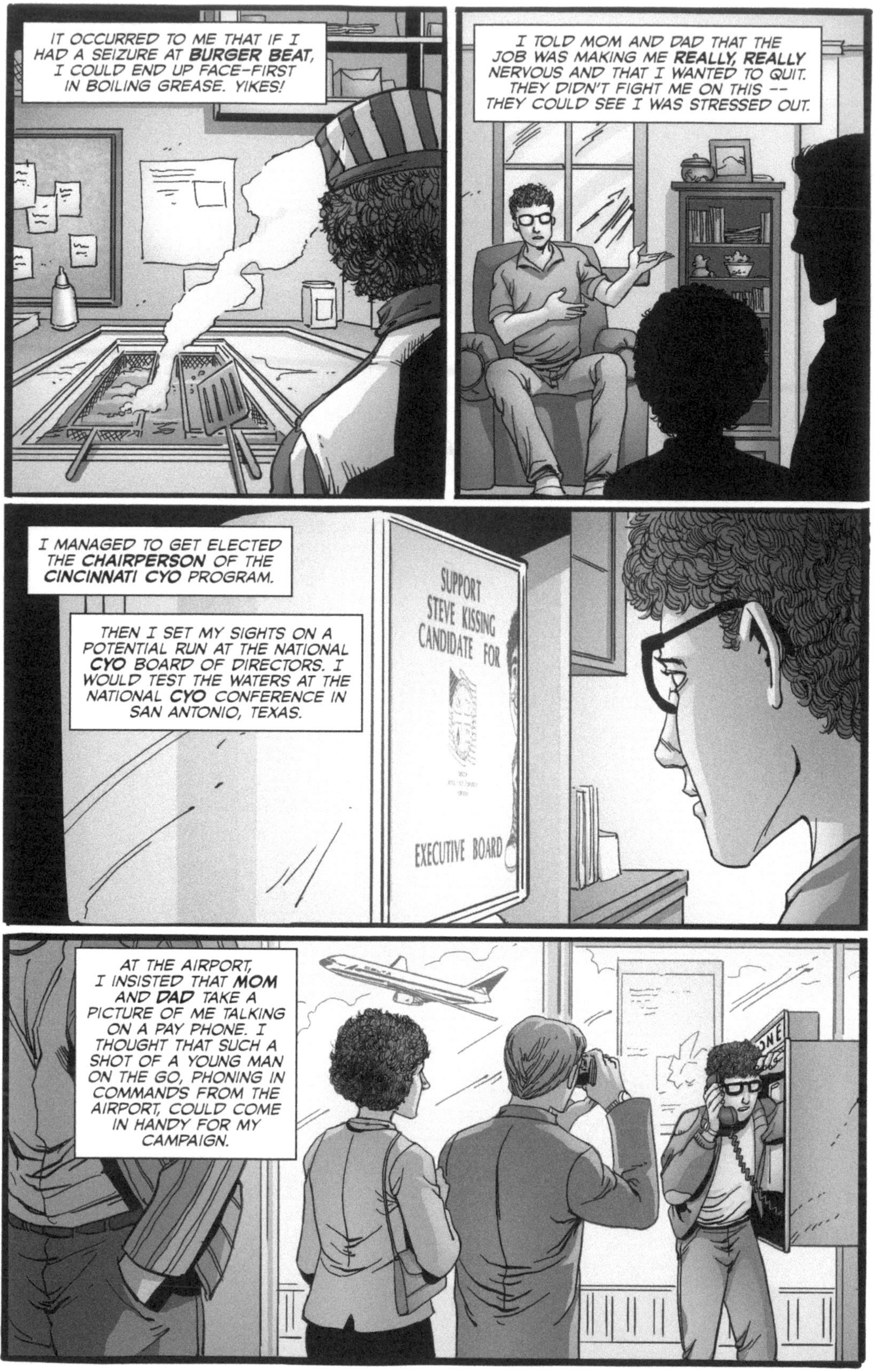
IT OCCURRED TO ME THAT IF I HAD A SEIZURE AT **BURGER BEAT**, I COULD END UP FACE-FIRST IN BOILING GREASE. YIKES!
I TOLD MOM AND DAD THAT THE JOB WAS MAKING ME **REALLY, REALLY** NERVOUS AND THAT I WANTED TO QUIT. THEY DIDN'T FIGHT ME ON THIS -- THEY COULD SEE I WAS STRESSED OUT.
I MANAGED TO GET ELECTED THE **CHAIRPERSON** OF THE **CINCINNATI CYO** PROGRAM.
THEN I SET MY SIGHTS ON A POTENTIAL RUN AT THE NATIONAL **CYO** BOARD OF DIRECTORS. I WOULD TEST THE WATERS AT THE NATIONAL **CYO** CONFERENCE IN SAN ANTONIO, TEXAS.
SUPPORT STEVE KISSING CANDIDATE FOR
EXECUTIVE BOARD
AT THE AIRPORT, I INSISTED THAT **MOM** AND **DAD** TAKE A PICTURE OF ME TALKING ON A PAY PHONE. I THOUGHT THAT SUCH A SHOT OF A YOUNG MAN ON THE GO, PHONING IN COMMANDS FROM THE AIRPORT, COULD COME IN HANDY FOR MY CAMPAIGN.

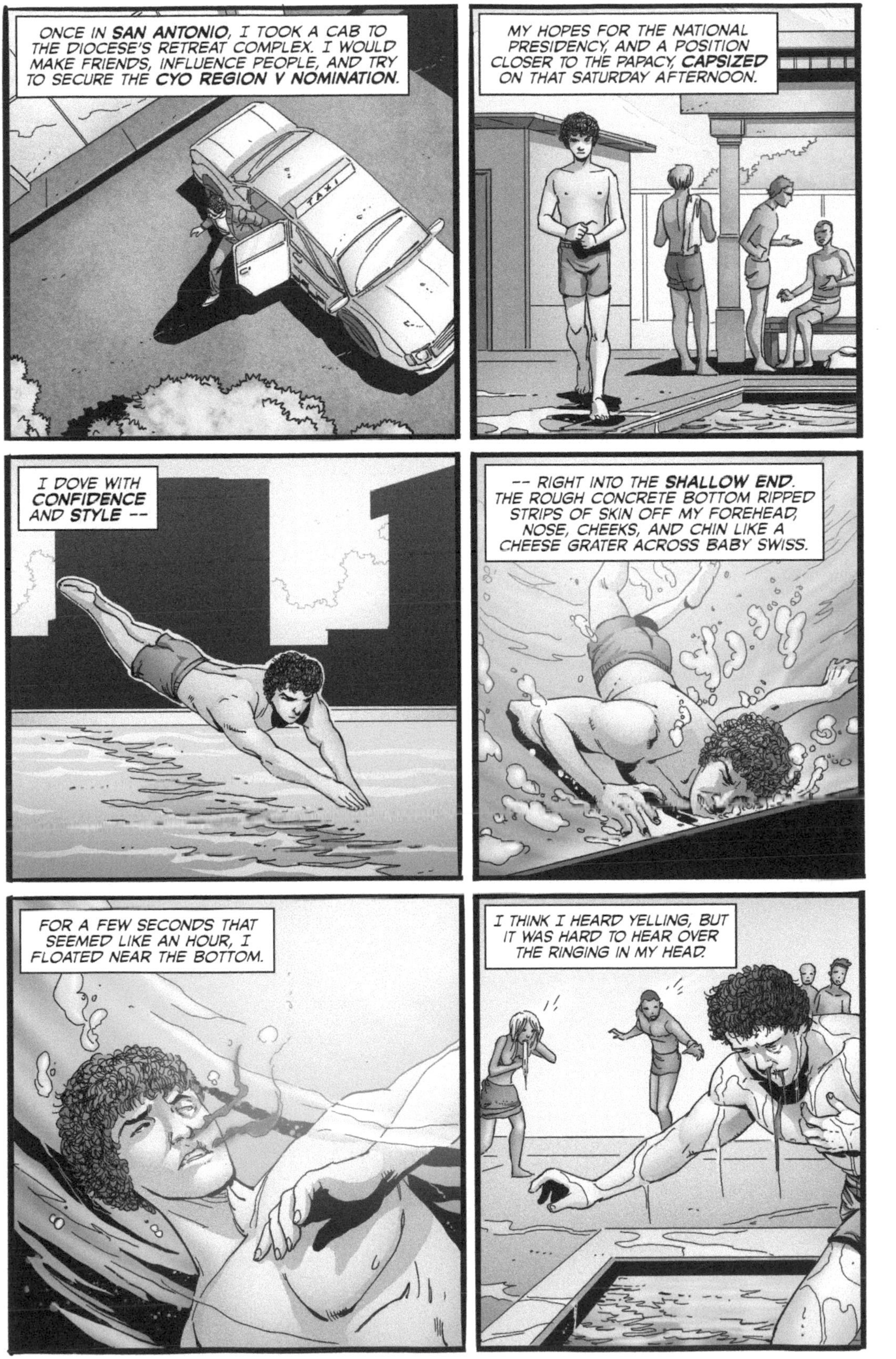
ONCE IN **SAN ANTONIO**, I TOOK A CAB TO THE DIOCESE'S RETREAT COMPLEX. I WOULD MAKE FRIENDS, INFLUENCE PEOPLE, AND TRY TO SECURE THE **CYO REGION V NOMINATION**.
TAXI
MY HOPES FOR THE NATIONAL PRESIDENCY, AND A POSITION CLOSER TO THE PAPACY, **CAPSIZED** ON THAT SATURDAY AFTERNOON.
I DOVE WITH **CONFIDENCE** AND **STYLE** --
-- RIGHT INTO THE **SHALLOW END**. THE ROUGH CONCRETE BOTTOM RIPPED STRIPS OF SKIN OFF MY FOREHEAD, NOSE, CHEEKS, AND CHIN LIKE A CHEESE GRATER ACROSS BABY SWISS.
FOR A FEW SECONDS THAT SEEMED LIKE AN HOUR, I FLOATED NEAR THE BOTTOM.
I THINK I HEARD YELLING, BUT IT WAS HARD TO HEAR OVER THE RINGING IN MY HEAD.

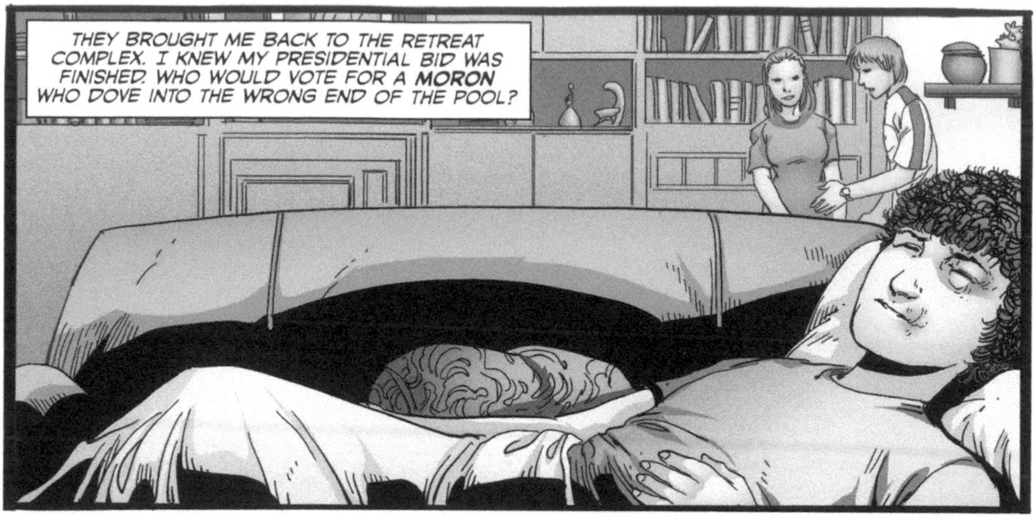
THEY BROUGHT ME BACK TO THE RETREAT COMPLEX. I KNEW MY PRESIDENTIAL BID WAS FINISHED. WHO WOULD VOTE FOR A MORON WHO DOVE INTO THE WRONG END OF THE POOL?

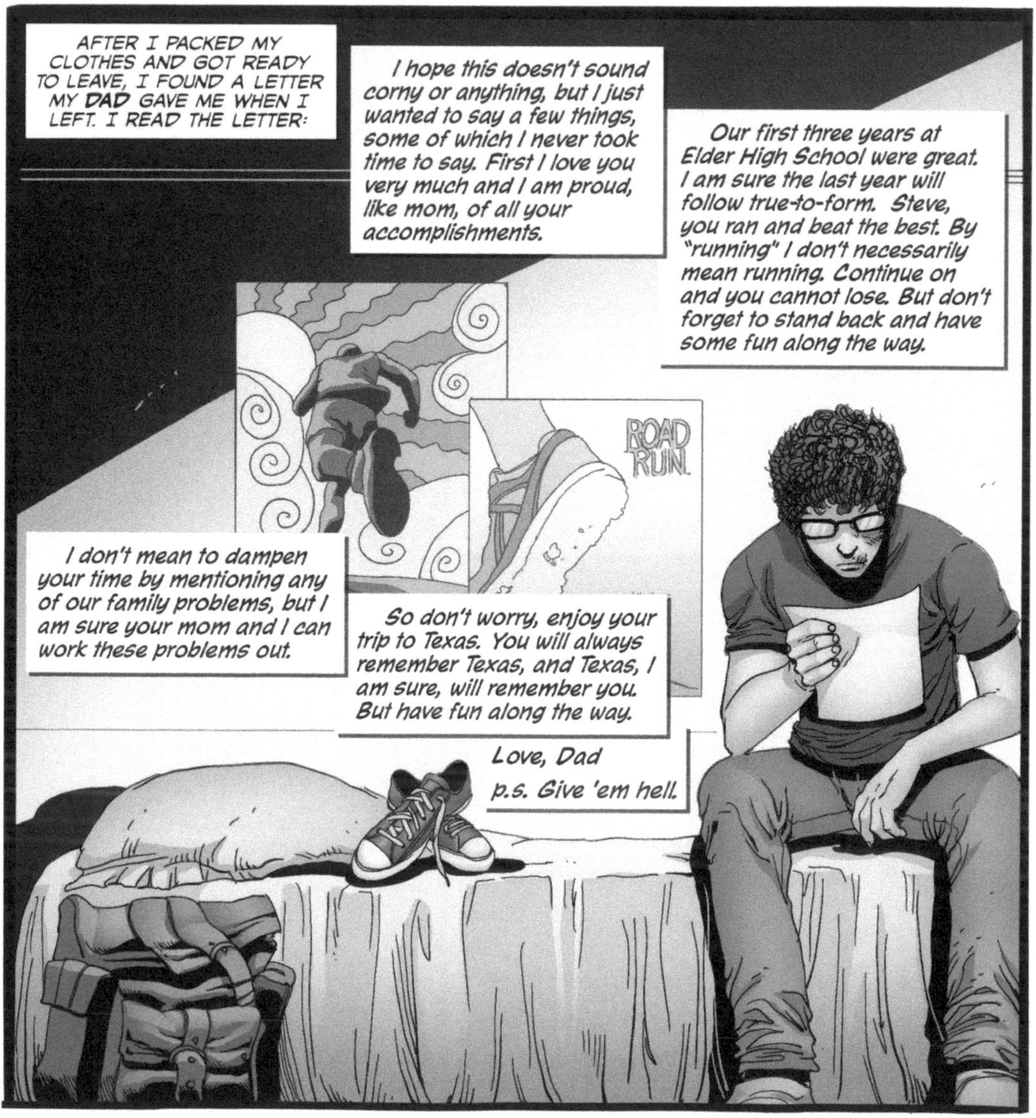
AFTER I PACKED MY CLOTHES AND GOT READY TO LEAVE, I FOUND A LETTER MY DAD GAVE ME WHEN I LEFT. I READ THE LETTER:
I hope this doesn't sound corny or anything, but I just wanted to say a few things, some of which I never took time to say. First I love you very much and I am proud, like mom, of all your accomplishments.
Our first three years at Elder High School were great. I am sure the last year will follow true-to-form. Steve, you ran and beat the best. By "running" I don't necessarily mean running. Continue on and you cannot lose. But don't forget to stand back and have some fun along the way.
ROAD RUN.
I don't mean to dampen your time by mentioning any of our family problems, but I am sure your mom and I can work these problems out.
So don't worry, enjoy your trip to Texas. You will always remember Texas, and Texas, I am sure, will remember you. But have fun along the way.
Love, Dad
p.s. Give 'em hell.

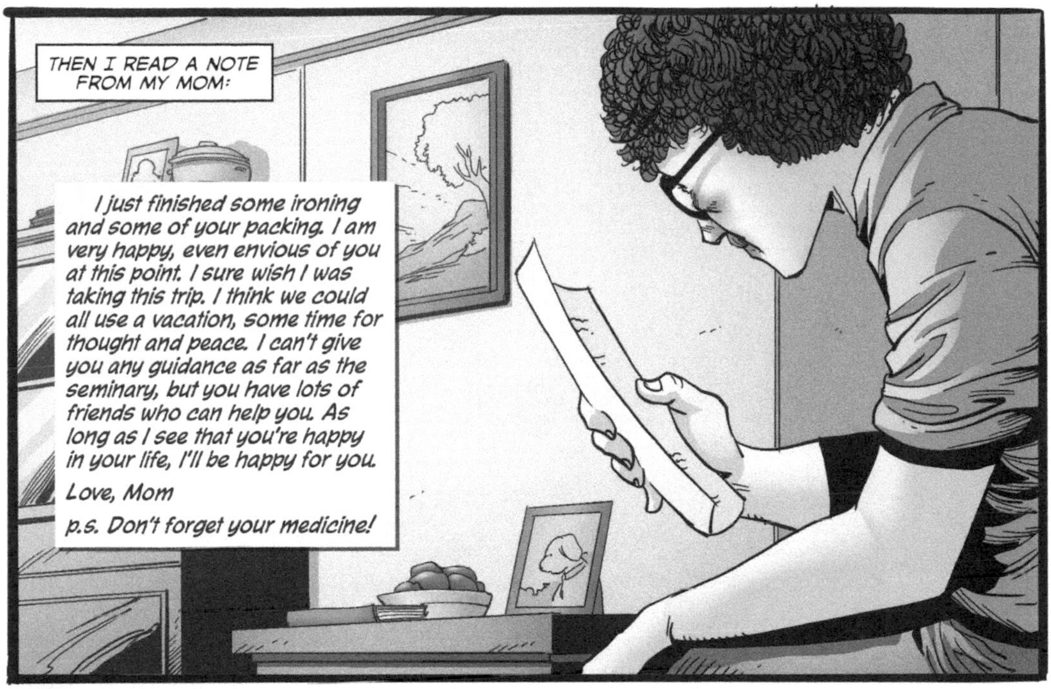
THEN I READ A NOTE FROM MY MOM:
I just finished some ironing and some of your packing. I am very happy, even envious of you at this point. I sure wish I was taking this trip. I think we could all use a vacation, some time for thought and peace. I can't give you any guidance as far as the seminary, but you have lots of friends who can help you. As long as I see that you're happy in your life, I'll be happy for you.
Love, Mom
p.s. Don't forget your medicine!

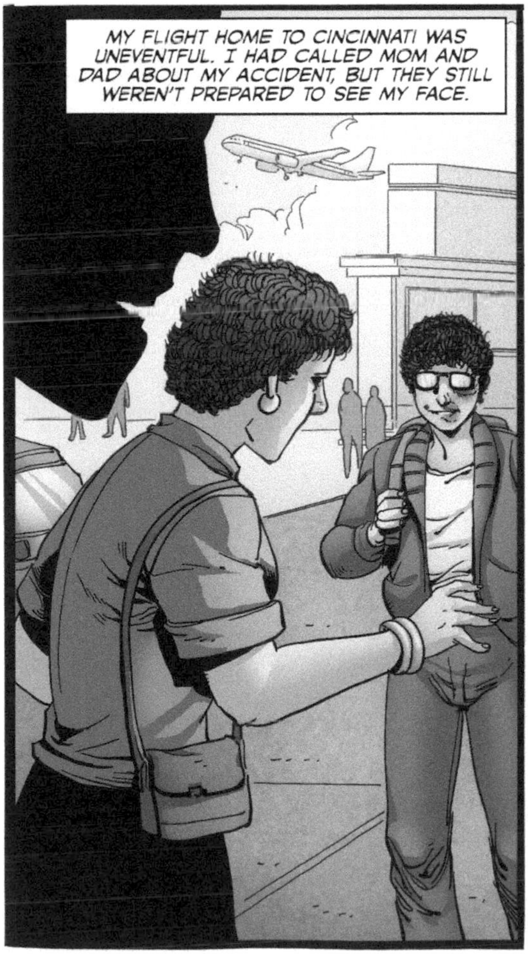
MY FLIGHT HOME TO CINCINNATI WAS UNEVENTFUL. I HAD CALLED MOM AND DAD ABOUT MY ACCIDENT, BUT THEY STILL WEREN'T PREPARED TO SEE MY FACE.

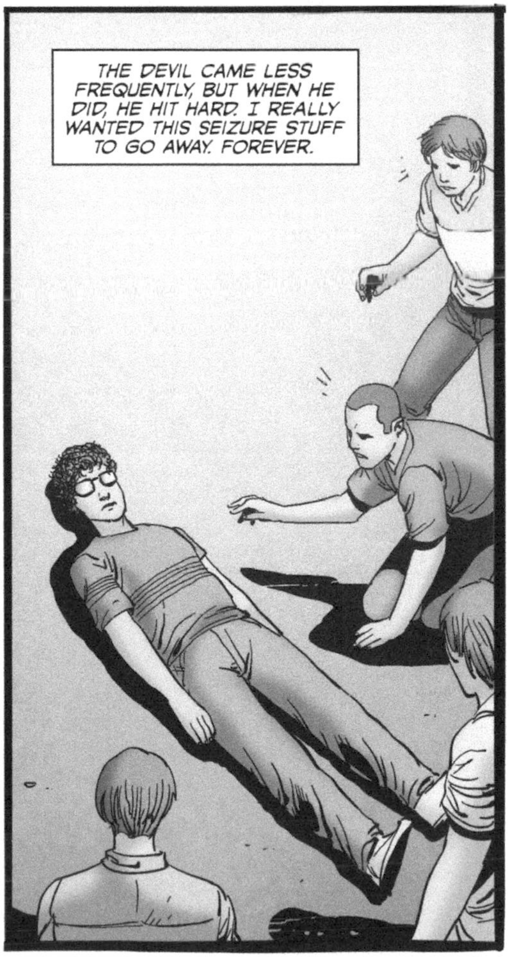
THE DEVIL CAME LESS FREQUENTLY, BUT WHEN HE DID, HE HIT HARD. I REALLY WANTED THIS SEIZURE STUFF TO GO AWAY. FOREVER.

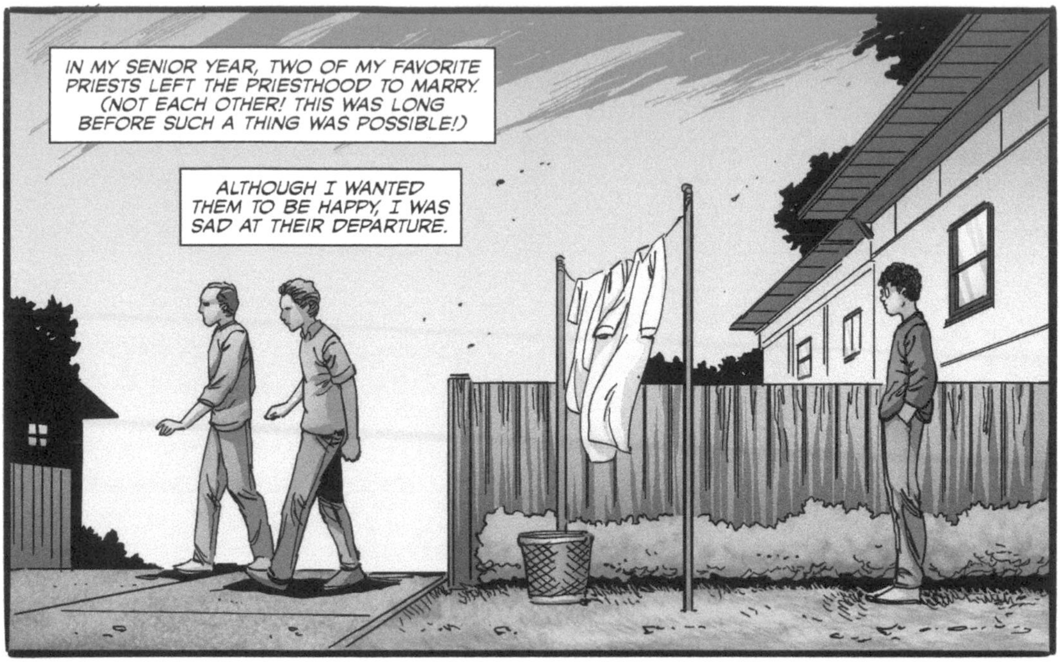
IN MY SENIOR YEAR, TWO OF MY FAVORITE PRIESTS LEFT THE PRIESTHOOD TO MARRY. (NOT EACH OTHER! THIS WAS LONG BEFORE SUCH A THING WAS POSSIBLE!)
ALTHOUGH I WANTED THEM TO BE HAPPY, I WAS SAD AT THEIR DEPARTURE.

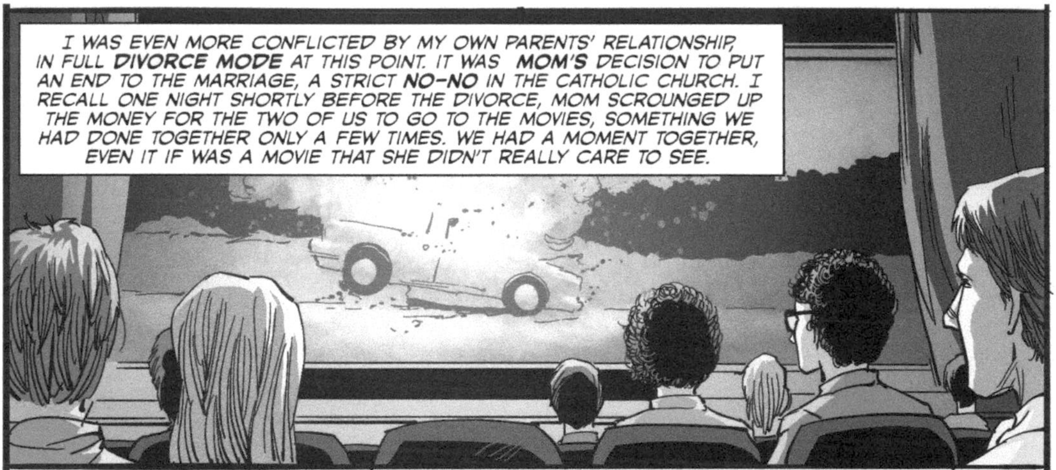
I WAS EVEN MORE CONFLICTED BY MY OWN PARENTS' RELATIONSHIP, IN FULL DIVORCE MODE AT THIS POINT. IT WAS MOM'S DECISION TO PUT AN END TO THE MARRIAGE, A STRICT NO-NO IN THE CATHOLIC CHURCH. I RECALL ONE NIGHT SHORTLY BEFORE THE DIVORCE, MOM SCROUNGED UP THE MONEY FOR THE TWO OF US TO GO TO THE MOVIES, SOMETHING WE HAD DONE TOGETHER ONLY A FEW TIMES. WE HAD A MOMENT TOGETHER, EVEN IT IF WAS A MOVIE THAT SHE DIDN'T REALLY CARE TO SEE.

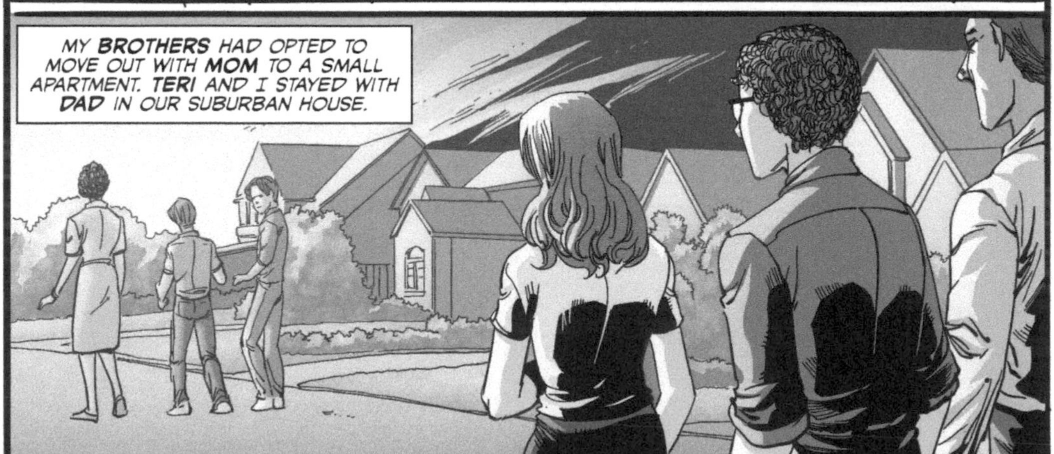
MY BROTHERS HAD OPTED TO MOVE OUT WITH MOM TO A SMALL APARTMENT. TERI AND I STAYED WITH DAD IN OUR SUBURBAN HOUSE.

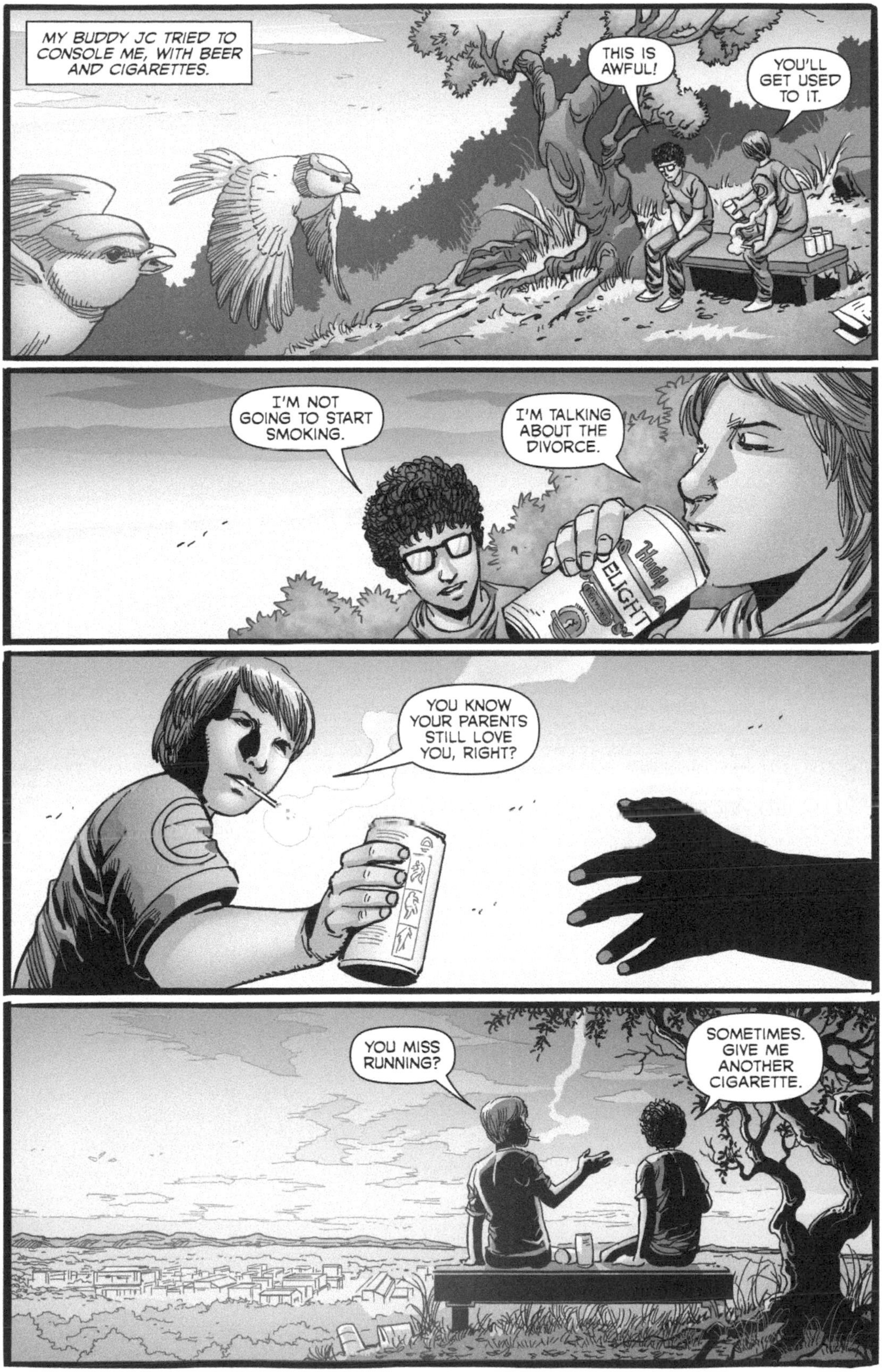
MY BUDDY JC TRIED TO CONSOLE ME, WITH BEER AND CIGARETTES.
THIS IS AWFUL!
YOU'LL GET USED TO IT.
I'M NOT GOING TO START SMOKING.
I'M TALKING ABOUT THE DIVORCE.
YOU KNOW YOUR PARENTS STILL LOVE YOU, RIGHT?
YOU MISS RUNNING?
SOMETIMES. GIVE ME ANOTHER CIGARETTE.

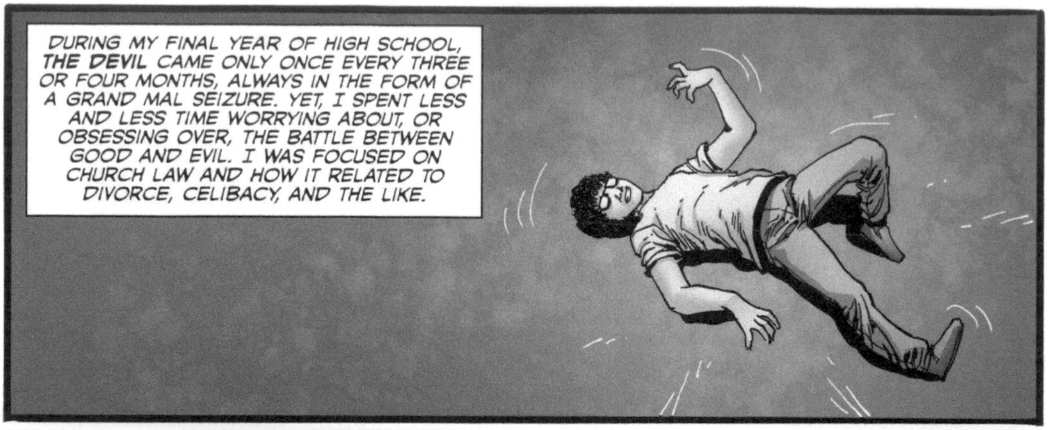
DURING MY FINAL YEAR OF HIGH SCHOOL, **THE DEVIL** CAME ONLY ONCE EVERY THREE OR FOUR MONTHS, ALWAYS IN THE FORM OF A GRAND MAL SEIZURE. YET, I SPENT LESS AND LESS TIME WORRYING ABOUT, OR OBSESSING OVER, THE BATTLE BETWEEN GOOD AND EVIL. I WAS FOCUSED ON CHURCH LAW AND HOW IT RELATED TO DIVORCE, CELIBACY, AND THE LIKE.

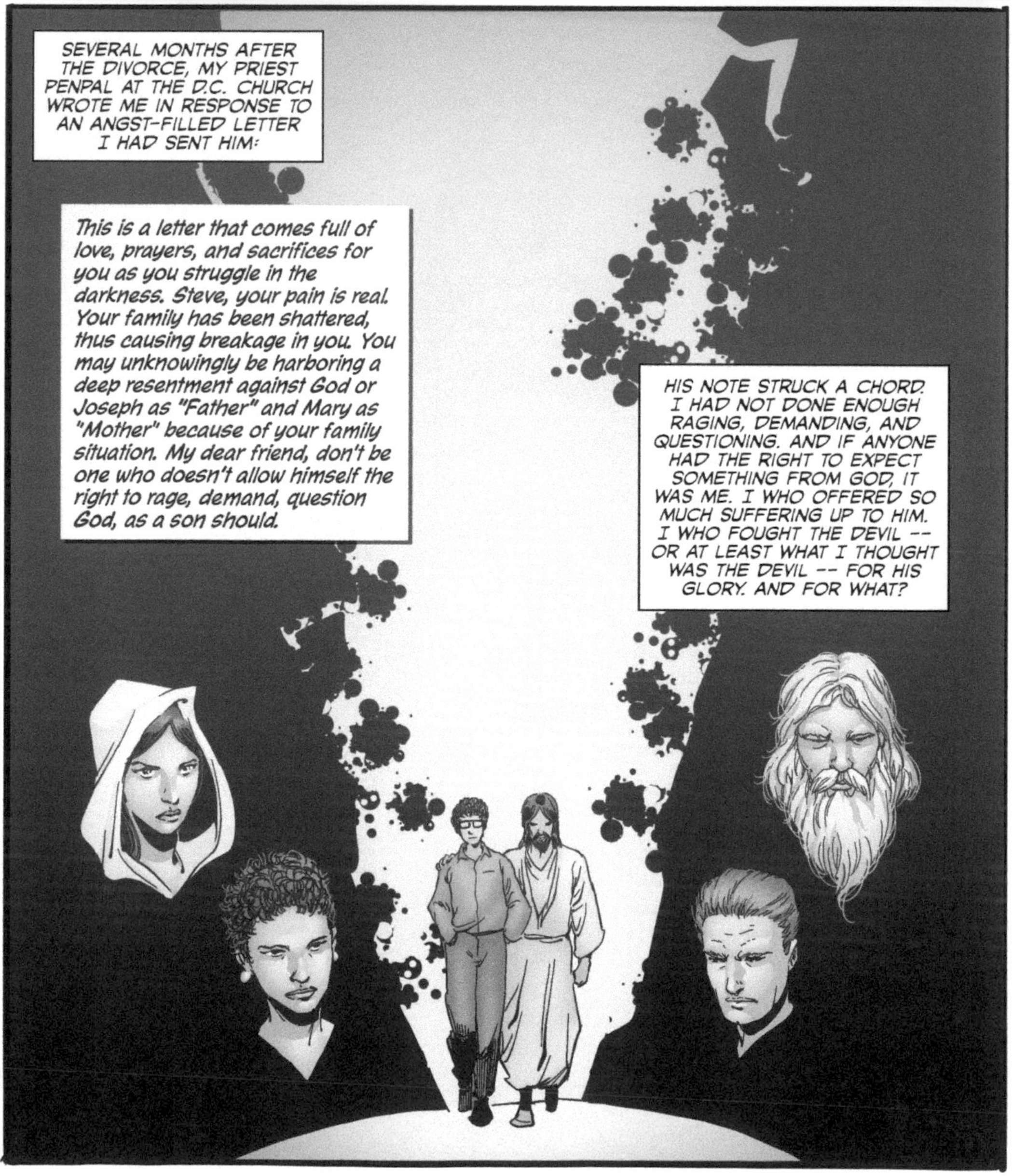
SEVERAL MONTHS AFTER THE DIVORCE, MY PRIEST PENPAL AT THE D.C. CHURCH WROTE ME IN RESPONSE TO AN ANGST-FILLED LETTER I HAD SENT HIM:
This is a letter that comes full of love, prayers, and sacrifices for you as you struggle in the darkness. Steve, your pain is real. Your family has been shattered, thus causing breakage in you. You may unknowingly be harboring a deep resentment against God or Joseph as "Father" and Mary as "Mother" because of your family situation. My dear friend, don't be one who doesn't allow himself the right to rage, demand, question God, as a son should.
HIS NOTE STRUCK A CHORD. I HAD NOT DONE ENOUGH RAGING, DEMANDING, AND QUESTIONING. AND IF ANYONE HAD THE RIGHT TO EXPECT SOMETHING FROM GOD, IT WAS ME. I WHO OFFERED SO MUCH SUFFERING UP TO HIM. I WHO FOUGHT THE DEVIL -- OR AT LEAST WHAT I THOUGHT WAS THE DEVIL -- FOR HIS GLORY. AND FOR WHAT?

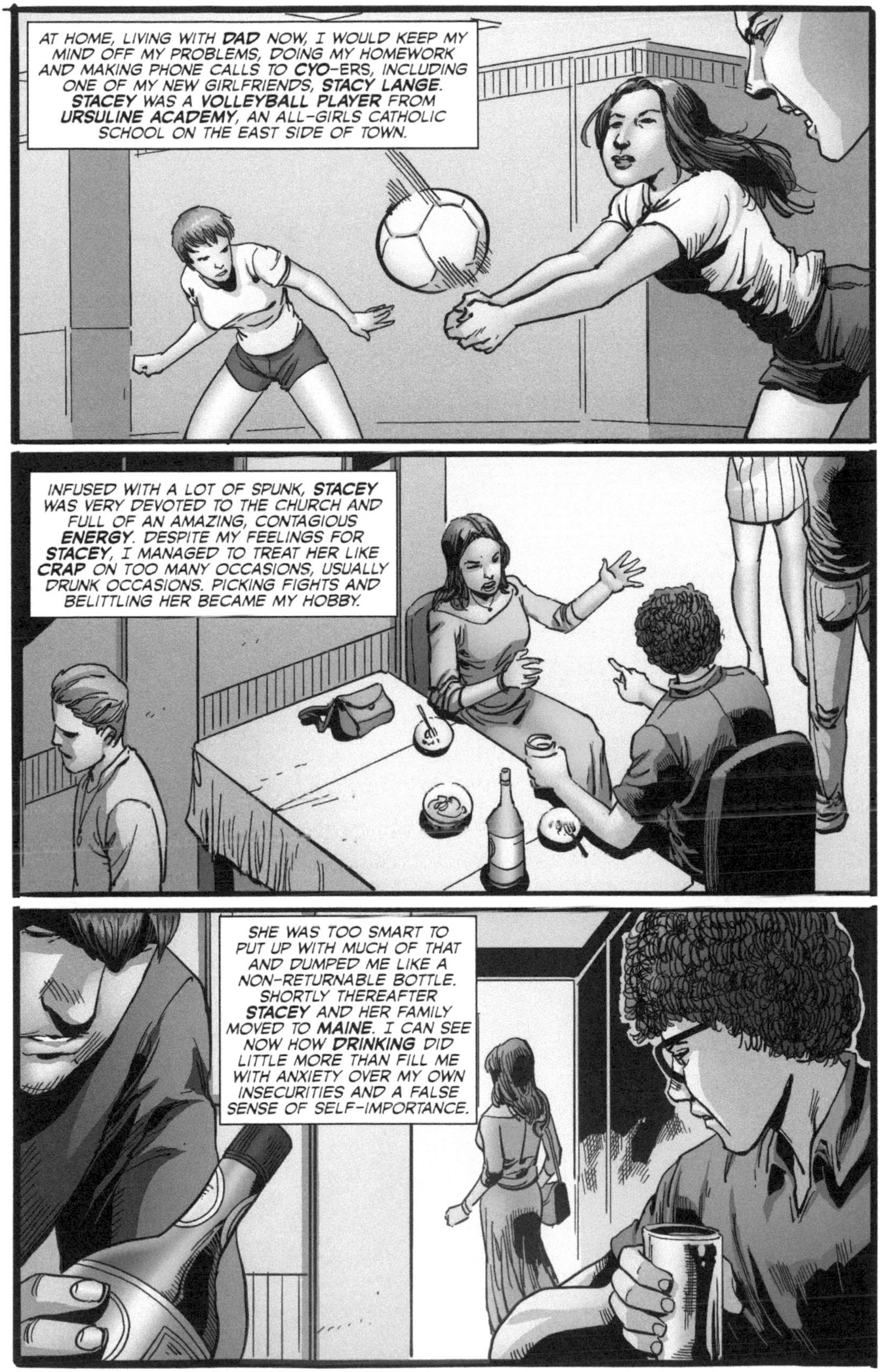
AT HOME, LIVING WITH DAD NOW, I WOULD KEEP MY MIND OFF MY PROBLEMS, DOING MY HOMEWORK AND MAKING PHONE CALLS TO CYO-ERS, INCLUDING ONE OF MY NEW GIRLFRIENDS, STACY LANGE. STACEY WAS A VOLLEYBALL PLAYER FROM URSULINE ACADEMY, AN ALL-GIRLS CATHOLIC SCHOOL ON THE EAST SIDE OF TOWN.
INFUSED WITH A LOT OF SPUNK, STACEY WAS VERY DEVOTED TO THE CHURCH AND FULL OF AN AMAZING, CONTAGIOUS ENERGY. DESPITE MY FEELINGS FOR STACEY, I MANAGED TO TREAT HER LIKE CRAP ON TOO MANY OCCASIONS, USUALLY DRUNK OCCASIONS. PICKING FIGHTS AND BELITTLING HER BECAME MY HOBBY.
SHE WAS TOO SMART TO PUT UP WITH MUCH OF THAT AND DUMPED ME LIKE A NON-RETURNABLE BOTTLE. SHORTLY THEREAFTER STACEY AND HER FAMILY MOVED TO MAINE. I CAN SEE NOW HOW DRINKING DID LITTLE MORE THAN FILL ME WITH ANXIETY OVER MY OWN INSECURITIES AND A FALSE SENSE OF SELF-IMPORTANCE.

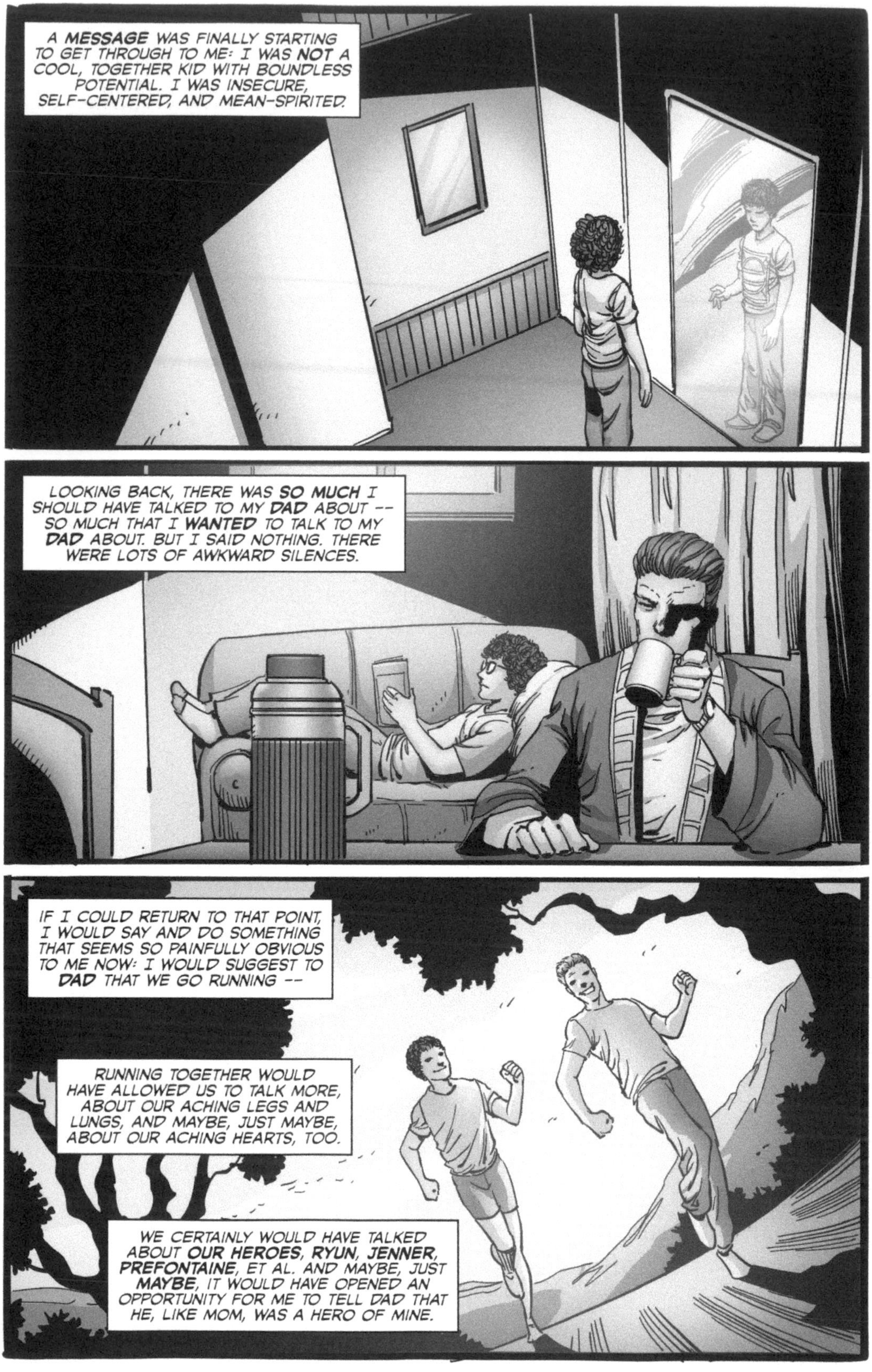
A MESSAGE WAS FINALLY STARTING TO GET THROUGH TO ME: I WAS NOT A COOL, TOGETHER KID WITH BOUNDLESS POTENTIAL. I WAS INSECURE, SELF-CENTERED, AND MEAN-SPIRITED.
LOOKING BACK, THERE WAS SO MUCH I SHOULD HAVE TALKED TO MY DAD ABOUT -- SO MUCH THAT I WANTED TO TALK TO MY DAD ABOUT. BUT I SAID NOTHING. THERE WERE LOTS OF AWKWARD SILENCES.
IF I COULD RETURN TO THAT POINT, I WOULD SAY AND DO SOMETHING THAT SEEMS SO PAINFULLY OBVIOUS TO ME NOW: I WOULD SUGGEST TO DAD THAT WE GO RUNNING --
RUNNING TOGETHER WOULD HAVE ALLOWED US TO TALK MORE, ABOUT OUR ACHING LEGS AND LUNGS, AND MAYBE, JUST MAYBE, ABOUT OUR ACHING HEARTS, TOO.
WE CERTAINLY WOULD HAVE TALKED ABOUT OUR HEROES, RYUN, JENNER, PREFONTAINE, ET AL. AND MAYBE, JUST MAYBE, IT WOULD HAVE OPENED AN OPPORTUNITY FOR ME TO TELL DAD THAT HE, LIKE MOM, WAS A HERO OF MINE.

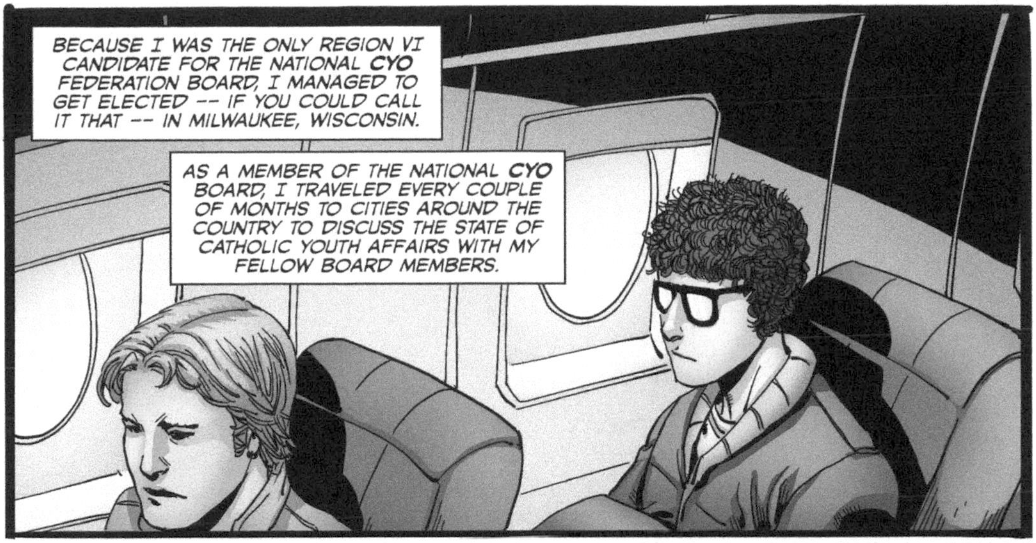
BECAUSE I WAS THE ONLY REGION VI CANDIDATE FOR THE NATIONAL **CYO** FEDERATION BOARD, I MANAGED TO GET ELECTED -- IF YOU COULD CALL IT THAT -- IN MILWAUKEE, WISCONSIN.
AS A MEMBER OF THE NATIONAL **CYO** BOARD, I TRAVELED EVERY COUPLE OF MONTHS TO CITIES AROUND THE COUNTRY TO DISCUSS THE STATE OF CATHOLIC YOUTH AFFAIRS WITH MY FELLOW BOARD MEMBERS.

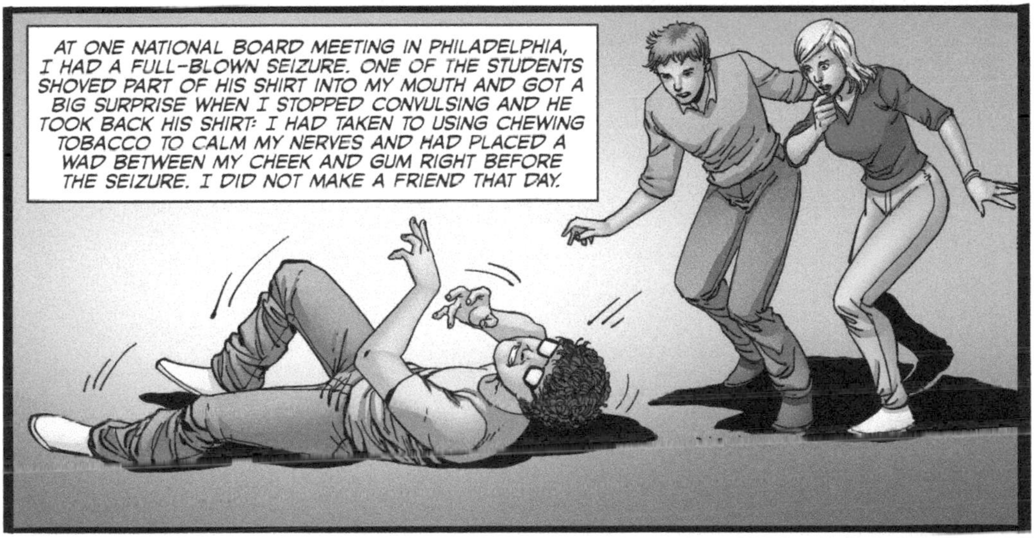
AT ONE NATIONAL BOARD MEETING IN PHILADELPHIA, I HAD A FULL-BLOWN SEIZURE. ONE OF THE STUDENTS SHOVED PART OF HIS SHIRT INTO MY MOUTH AND GOT A BIG SURPRISE WHEN I STOPPED CONVULSING AND HE TOOK BACK HIS SHIRT: I HAD TAKEN TO USING CHEWING TOBACCO TO CALM MY NERVES AND HAD PLACED A WAD BETWEEN MY CHEEK AND GUM RIGHT BEFORE THE SEIZURE. I DID NOT MAKE A FRIEND THAT DAY.

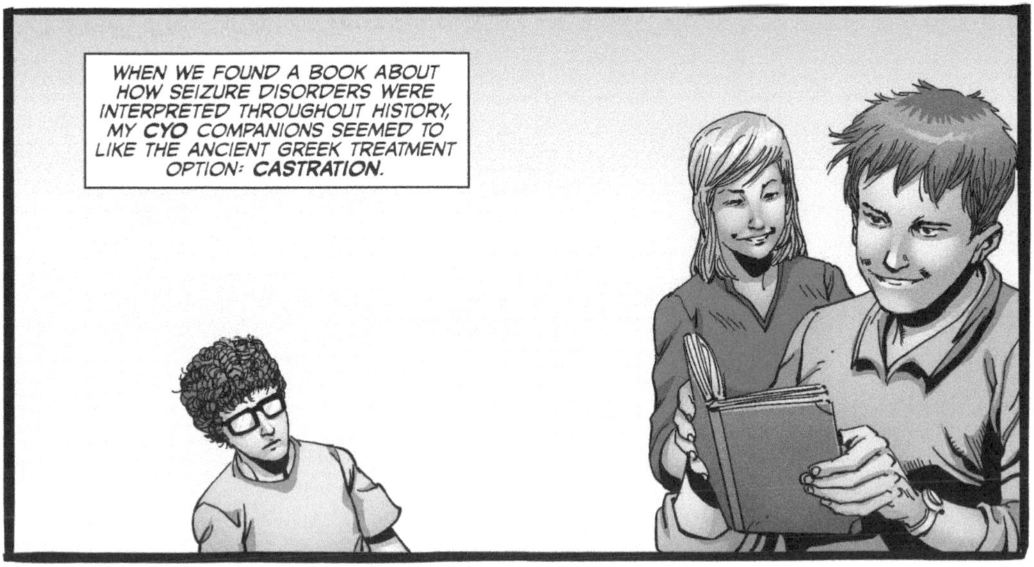
WHEN WE FOUND A BOOK ABOUT HOW SEIZURE DISORDERS WERE INTERPRETED THROUGHOUT HISTORY, MY **CYO** COMPANIONS SEEMED TO LIKE THE ANCIENT GREEK TREATMENT OPTION: **CASTRATION**.

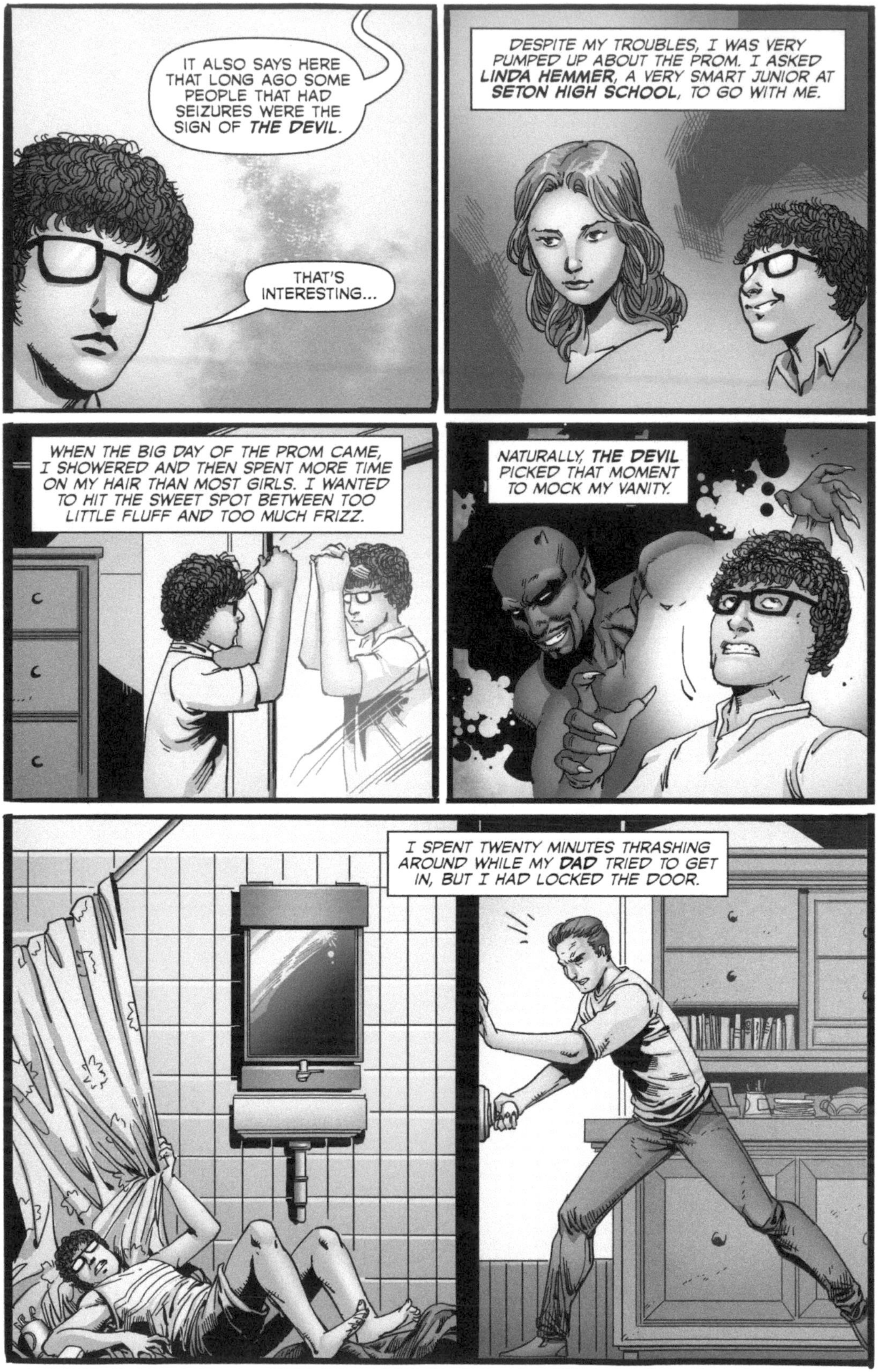
IT ALSO SAYS HERE THAT LONG AGO SOME PEOPLE THAT HAD SEIZURES WERE THE SIGN OF THE DEVIL.
THAT'S INTERESTING...
DESPITE MY TROUBLES, I WAS VERY PUMPED UP ABOUT THE PROM. I ASKED LINDA HEMMER, A VERY SMART JUNIOR AT SETON HIGH SCHOOL, TO GO WITH ME.
WHEN THE BIG DAY OF THE PROM CAME, I SHOWERED AND THEN SPENT MORE TIME ON MY HAIR THAN MOST GIRLS. I WANTED TO HIT THE SWEET SPOT BETWEEN TOO LITTLE FLUFF AND TOO MUCH FRIZZ.
NATURALLY, THE DEVIL PICKED THAT MOMENT TO MOCK MY VANITY.
I SPENT TWENTY MINUTES THRASHING AROUND WHILE MY DAD TRIED TO GET IN, BUT I HAD LOCKED THE DOOR.

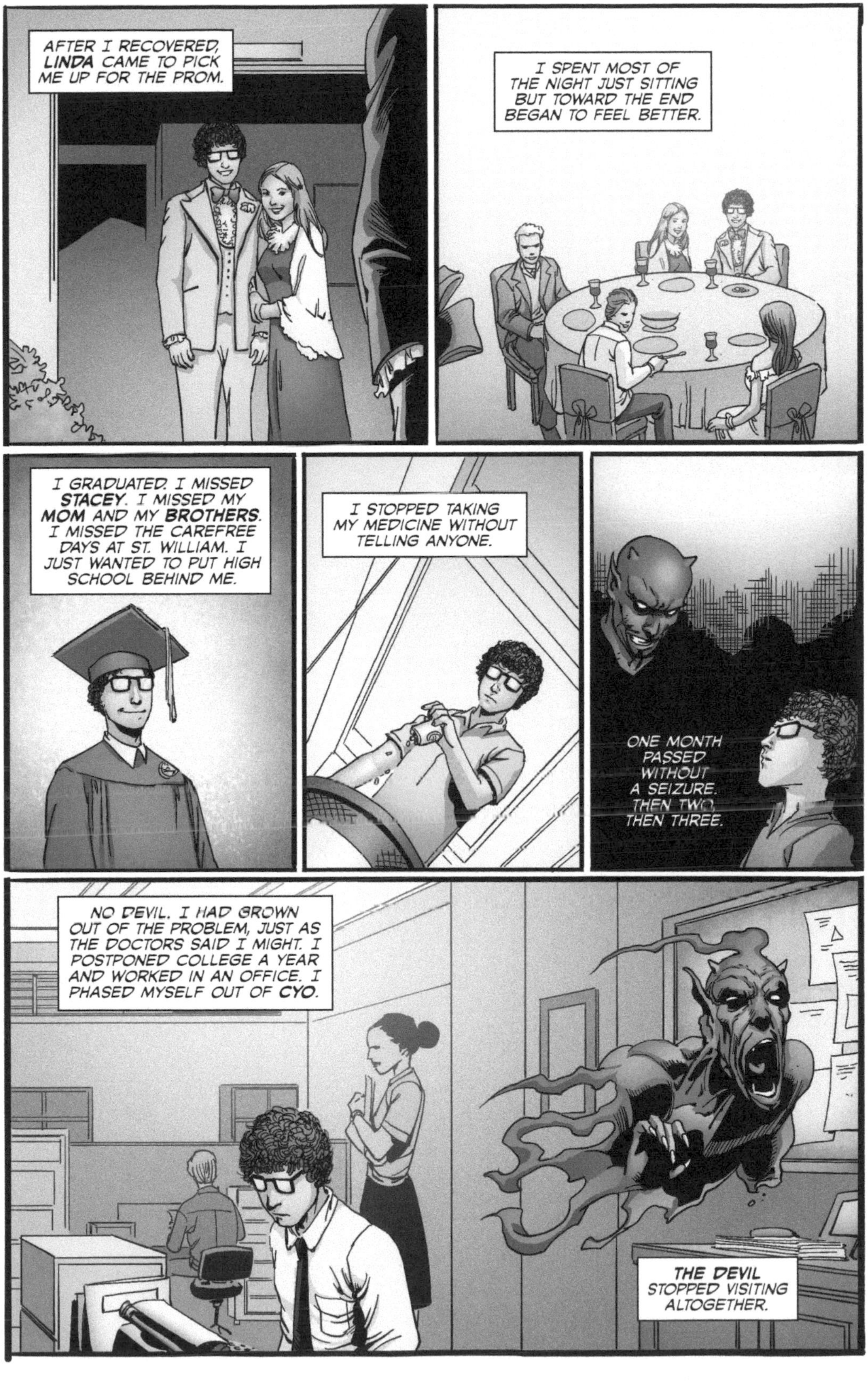
AFTER I RECOVERED, LINDA CAME TO PICK ME UP FOR THE PROM.
I SPENT MOST OF THE NIGHT JUST SITTING BUT TOWARD THE END BEGAN TO FEEL BETTER.
I GRADUATED. I MISSED STACEY. I MISSED MY MOM AND MY BROTHERS. I MISSED THE CAREFREE DAYS AT ST. WILLIAM. I JUST WANTED TO PUT HIGH SCHOOL BEHIND ME.
I STOPPED TAKING MY MEDICINE WITHOUT TELLING ANYONE.
ONE MONTH PASSED WITHOUT A SEIZURE. THEN TWO, THEN THREE.
NO DEVIL. I HAD GROWN OUT OF THE PROBLEM, JUST AS THE DOCTORS SAID I MIGHT. I POSTPONED COLLEGE A YEAR AND WORKED IN AN OFFICE. I PHASED MYSELF OUT OF CYO.
THE DEVIL STOPPED VISITING ALTOGETHER.

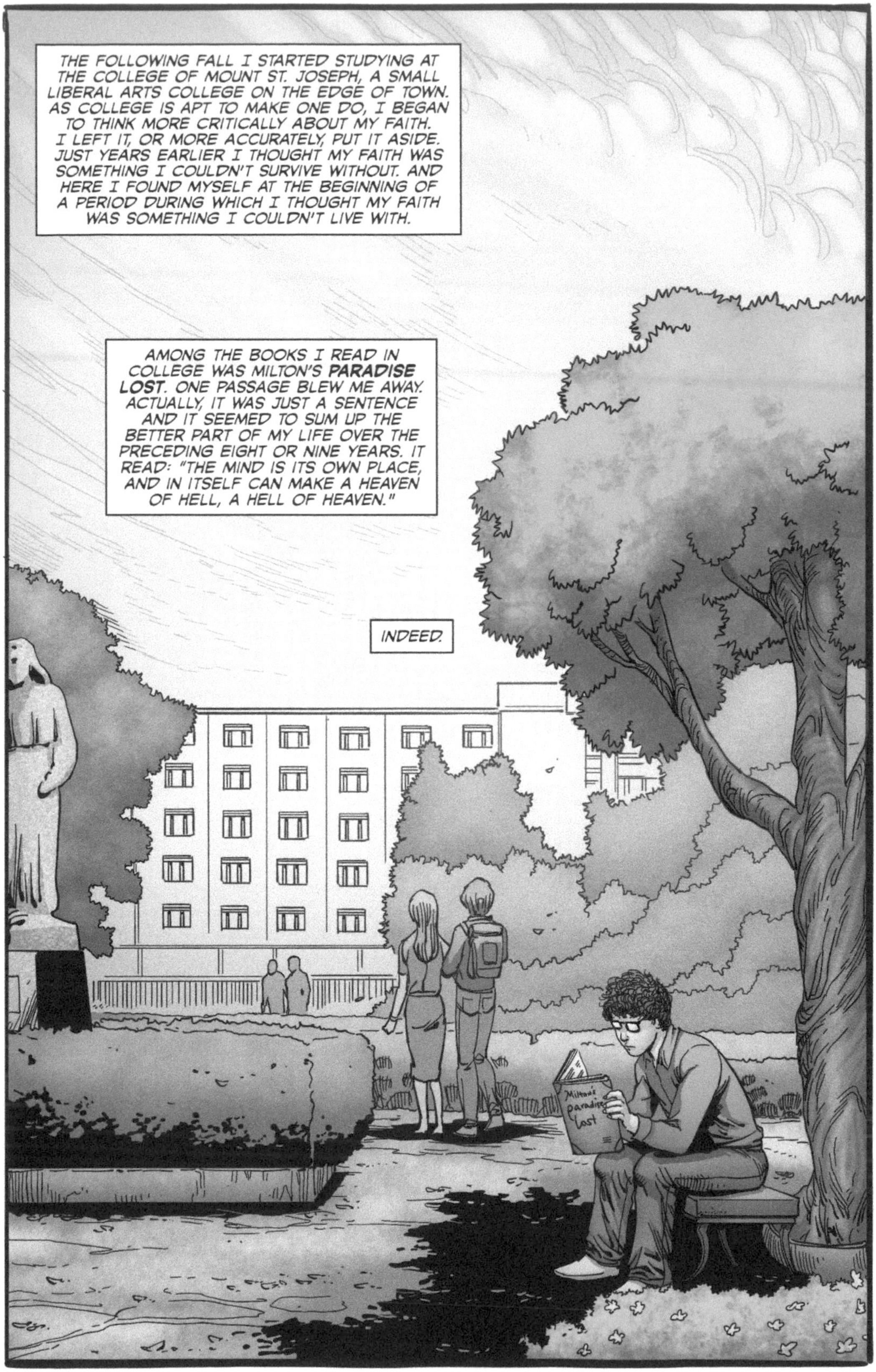
THE FOLLOWING FALL I STARTED STUDYING AT THE COLLEGE OF MOUNT ST. JOSEPH, A SMALL LIBERAL ARTS COLLEGE ON THE EDGE OF TOWN. AS COLLEGE IS APT TO MAKE ONE DO, I BEGAN TO THINK MORE CRITICALLY ABOUT MY FAITH. I LEFT IT, OR MORE ACCURATELY, PUT IT ASIDE. JUST YEARS EARLIER I THOUGHT MY FAITH WAS SOMETHING I COULDN'T SURVIVE WITHOUT. AND HERE I FOUND MYSELF AT THE BEGINNING OF A PERIOD DURING WHICH I THOUGHT MY FAITH WAS SOMETHING I COULDN'T LIVE WITH.
AMONG THE BOOKS I READ IN COLLEGE WAS MILTON'S **PARADISE LOST**. ONE PASSAGE BLEW ME AWAY. ACTUALLY, IT WAS JUST A SENTENCE AND IT SEEMED TO SUM UP THE BETTER PART OF MY LIFE OVER THE PRECEDING EIGHT OR NINE YEARS. IT READ: "THE MIND IS ITS OWN PLACE, AND IN ITSELF CAN MAKE A HEAVEN OF HELL, A HELL OF HEAVEN."
INDEED.
Milton's Paradise Lost

epilogue

I no longer get Afro perms. And I haven't had a seizure since I was about twenty. However, I still occasionally have tiny flashbacks reminiscent of the auras that used to precede my grand mal seizures. Typically, these are the result of smelling gasoline or cut grass. Or by seeing a shiny, metallic color. I've long given up on trying to figure that out.

I no longer believe that seizures — or any other medical condition — are caused by the hand of Satan. Or of God. The mere suggestion is, now, enough to make me laugh. Out loud.

Others have suggested that my hallucinations could have been glimpses into parallel universes. I don't buy that either, though it can be fun to think about alternative worlds in which I am the supreme ruler, or at least a member of a popular rock band.

Some ask if I'm angry at the Catholic Church for what they "put me through." I am not. I believe the Church, along with my family, helped hone my sense of right and wrong, so that, in the bigger picture at least, I ran away from rather than toward the darkness. That said, after several attempts to reconnect with the Church in my adult life, I have left it. I am a confirmed agnostic and, while I can still see some beauty and goodness in organized religion, I no longer see God-given, fundamental truths.

As for some key people in this tale of mine, I am happy to say that my father and mother remain good friends. And that I still hang out with my friend JC, who now prefers to be called "John," though we no longer swim in garbage cans. Part of me wishes we did.

1. The power of the imagination in children is legendary. Some kids invent imaginary friends while others become convinced that there are monsters under their beds. Did you have an imaginary friend or foe when you were a kid? What was he/she/it like? How did elements of your real world impact your imagined world as a child?

2. Steve's Catholic faith is largely what caused him to conclude that he was possessed by Satan. Has your faith ever led you to a situation, solution, or point of view that you later came to realize was misguided and wrong? What lessons did you learn from that experience?

3. Steve grew up in a "Catholic bubble" that colored virtually everything he experienced. What religious or cultural bubbles, if any, did you grow up in? What bubbles might you be living in now?

4. Did you believe in the Devil as a kid? Do you believe in him now? If you're a believer, what would you say to those who think Satan isn't real? If you're not a believer, what would you say to those who are convinced the Evil One is for real?

5. If, when you were a kid, you started experiencing weird things in your head like Steve did, do you think you would have said something to someone? Would you have assumed it was a medical condition or might you have come to a different conclusion?

6. What secrets and worries did you keep to yourself as a child? What compelled you not to tell anyone? What ramifications did you fear if your secret became known? If you're a parent, do you ever wonder or worry about what secrets your child or children may be keeping from you?

7. Who was your best childhood friend? What did the two of you enjoy doing together the most? Did you have any special or silly routines, as JC and Steve had with streaking and swimming in garbage cans?

8. Steve was fanatical about his long-distance running, going nearly three years without missing a day of training. As a child, were you that intensely dedicated to a sport or hobby of some sort? How and why did that passion come to an end? Or is that passion still alive? How did the passion shape who you are today?

9. Has anyone you know ever had a seizure in your presence? What was witnessing that like for you? If you've had a seizure yourself, what was that experience like for you?

creator bios

Steve Kissing is an award-winning writer and an accomplished public speaker. He is also managing partner of Wordsworth Communications, a highly decorated PR and marketing firm. He's currently at work on a collection of essays and a chapbook of poetry. He lives in Cincinnati with his wife and four daughters. He is no longer possessed by the devil. Or so he says. You can reach him at stevekissing@yahoo.com.

Charles Santino, the scripter for this book, is the co-creator and co-author of the upcoming Markosia comic book and graphic novel, Danny and Harry Private Detectives with artist Walter Brogan. For the Edgar Rice Burroughs website, he is adapting The Girl from Hollywood and The Girl from Farris's. Past credits include Louis L'Amour's Law of the Desert Born for Random House and Conan the Barbarian for Marvel Comics.

Jim Jimenez has been drawing professionally since high school. He's worked in animation, including Gummi Bears, Winnie the Pooh, The X-Men and The Mask. More recently. he's drawn comics such as Grand Theft Galaxy for Tokyo Pop.

RUNNING FROM THE DEVIL

runningfromthedevil.com

MARKOSIA

markosia.com

CPSIA information can be obtained
at www.ICGtesting.com
Printed in the USA
LVHW01s0145260318
571033LV00003B/3/P